ON THE WILD EDGE

ON THE WILD EDGE

In Search of a Natural Life

DAVID PETERSEN

A JOHN MACRAE/HOLT PAPERBACK
Henry Holt and Company | New York

Holt Paperbacks
Henry Holt and Company, LLC
Publishers since 1866
175 Fifth Avenue
New York, New York 10010
www.henryholt.com

A Holt Paperback® and ® are registered trademarks of
Henry Holt and Company, LLC.

Library of Congress Cataloging-in-Publication Data
Petersen, David, 1946–
    On the wild edge : in search of a natural life / David Petersen.—1st ed.
    p.   cm.
    ISBN-13: 978-0-8050-8003-2

    1. Natural history—Colorado—Durango Region.   2. Mountain life—
Colorado—Durango Region.   3. Petersen, David, 1946–   I. Title.

QH105.C6P48 2005
508.788'29—dc22   2004047539

Henry Holt books are available for special promotions and
premiums. For details contact: Director, Special Markets.

Originally published in hardcover in 2005 by John Macrae Books/Henry Holt and Company

Designed by Kelly S. Too

Printed in the United States of America

D 20 19 18 17 16 15

for Jack Macrae

But perhaps we may make our stand along the edge . . . like a person who, having lived among another tribe, can no longer wholly return to his own. He lingers half within and half outside of his community, open as well, then, to the shifting voices and flapping forms that crawl and hover beyond the mirrored walls of the city.

—DAVID ABRAM,
The Spell of the Sensuous

contents

A MEMORY IN NATURE

David Petersen is a careful man in the forest. He moves unobtrusively and lusts to be alone. There is a tract of mountain land near his home that he knows as intimately as anyone has ever known family, lover, or their own true self. When he moves through this place, he does not put his scent on bark or branches or make any noise. He goes in and out of places with care and respect, leaving the area utterly undisturbed. He is familiar with every path taken in the forest by elk and deer. At all times he understands everything around him—odors, casual noises, birdcalls, impending weather. When a dead twig snaps somewhere, he knows what stepped on it, how much the creature weighs, and what its intentions likely are.

A true hunter, Petersen rarely kills, and then only for the meat. But he spends countless days observing the natural scene around him. He calls himself a neo-animist and speaks to trees, rocks, the colorful aspen leaves of September. Bears have walked right by him unawares while he was sitting motionless in the woods. Elk have approached so close he could have reached out and touched their muzzles or antlers, but chose not to out of respect for the animals and himself.

As he grows older, Dave Petersen feels less affinity for "civilization" and more at one with the natural world. His compassion for wild territory is close to unique and, in this chaotic age of global development, that compassion is priceless. The fact that he can write so intimately and convincingly about wild country and animals makes him one of our more interesting literary figures as well as a valuable environmentalist. His observations are scientific, lyrical, from the heart. His clear, direct, and often humorous prose is imbued with much knowledge, many marvels, and occasional outrage. His writing is also rich with mystery and soul.

Over the years, Petersen's body of work, steeped in a personal natural history and conservation ethic, has helped explain the American West. As we have listened in the past to our Thoreaus, Rachel Carsons, and Aldo Leopolds, we must listen now to the David Petersens among us. His work transcends science and even literature: it is polemic for survival.

On the day last October that we hiked together to one of his cherished spots, Dave showed me several "marker trees," his term for landmarks. In another spot he pointed out bear-claw scars on aspen bark and recognized an immature nuthatch from its call alone. Each step of the way had a personal history and a story. A flake of gray paper among the leaves was all that remained of a wasp's nest he'd been watching decay for months. He remembered a spotted mule deer fawn that had bolted "from right here" many years ago, ravens once feeding on a winter-killed doe carcass over there, a drumming blue grouse in a particular tree. His history in this place is rich with changing seasons and breathtaking moments of wildlife encounters. It's a territory made vivid in Dave's prose by his awareness of how the place counts in the macroscopic universe, from the tallest tree to the smallest bug. More than twenty years of intense observation mean that he now notices *all* the subtle changes. When a tree falls, the "hole in the sky" it leaves behind is to him a visible ghost.

"Sacred" and "holy" are words so overused by charlatans that I find them empty. Instead, for Dave, let's just say the natural landscape is *home.*

In the past fifteen years, David has written eight books (and edited four more), all of which focus to one degree or another on his home landscape. Together, these works constitute a fine collection of intensely personal nature writing and objective scientific observation. There are many philosophical details. The prose is as lyrical as anything written by Edward Abbey, Jim Harrison, or Thomas McGuane and is often better informed. What distinguishes his writing is a lack of pretense and a refreshing dearth of intellectual egotism. David Petersen the writer speaks clearly, to the point, with an abiding love not only for the natural world but for the written word.

Even so, Dave claims he could live without writing in his life, "but never without the things I write about." I wonder if this is true. Technically, his observations on paper are as harmoniously put together as the worlds they describe. Obviously, the man has spent as much time perfecting his craft and sullen art as he has treading the forest paths near his home. The ecstasy engendered by his out-of-doors experience is captured by every phrase he conjures in his articles and books.

And the author is a man on a mission, angry about the collapsing ecosystem and the economics of development destroying the world around us. Each book can make you think of *Walden, Desert Solitaire,* Joseph Wood Krutch, or John C. Van Dyke. Petersen is quick to point out that his primary mentors were A. B. Guthrie Jr., Edward Abbey, and Paul Shepard (the father of human ecology). Fair enough. But today, his own work has achieved the strength, maturity, and moral clarity that make it mentor to others.

David Petersen is six feet tall, slim as a marathon runner, and, now in his fifties, as fit as the wild beasts he so admires. He has been with his lovely wife, Caroline, for twenty-five years—they share everything. They live in a snug little cabin surrounded by aspens and evergreen trees. Dave built it himself over several years. There's a tiny barnlike office out behind the cabin with a National Park Service sign on the door proclaiming, BEAR COUNTRY: AVOID CONFRONTATION. Nearby is a thirty-foot-long woodpile of ponderosa, oak, and aspen logs. Two handsome dogs, an arthritic black Lab, Otis, and a giant aged shepherd-Akita mix, Angel, complement the family. Chipmunks and juncos frequent a feeder by the side door, and a box freezer in a storage shed is full of elk meat and New Mexico green chilies, all hand-wrapped in trim white packages. In the cabin, there are a couple of tattered but comfortable easy chairs in the living room, a woodstove, antlers and paintings on the wood-plank walls. Everything is tight, shipshape, clean, and easy.

Same deal in Dave's half-pint office, which has a few pictures on the walls, a desk made of plywood, a couple of bookcases, a little heater. Dave keeps it simple and unobtrusive, and he keeps it neat. He moves through the world lightly. "It's a pretty streamlined operation," he says of his life. His prose has the same qualities of organization and belief. It's clean, honest, organized, and unaffected. No bullshit.

Petersen began his journey to what he calls "the edge" in 1975, when, after being honorably discharged from six years in the Marines as a helicopter pilot, he took a "bottom-end" job as a typesetter for a motorcycle magazine published in the artist and hippie enclave of Laguna Beach, California. While manually typesetting articles (computers were not yet common), he soon developed a previously unrecognized interest in how prose is written and edited, began making suggestions to his bosses, and before he knew it, he was the managing editor. The rest of his tenure there he spent biking around America, Mexico, and Canada with Caroline (whom he had "hired away from the lawyers next door to be my editorial assistant") and writing articles about their junkets on the powerful machines. That led to a job at *Mother Earth News*, where his first article, he recalls with a chuckle, was "How to Build a Solar-Powered Composting Toilet." In 1983 he was assigned to interview Edward Abbey; the ensuing friendship lasted until Abbey's death six years later. Ed was a strong influence on Dave's writing as well as his worldview.

So was A. B. Guthrie Jr., whom Petersen met and befriended in Montana in 1983. David's father had given him a copy of *The Big Sky* when he was ten, and the boy had loved the book and the wild, free life it portrayed. Guthrie taught him a lot about writing, and Dave returned the favor by compiling and editing the anthology *Big Sky, Fair Land: The Environmental Essays of A. B. Guthrie, Jr.* and by writing a memorable afterword to Guthrie's autobiography, *The Blue Hen's Chick*.

After moving from Laguna Beach to Durango, Colorado, Dave taught composition, magazine writing, and nature writing at "the local ski college." At the same time he wrote freelance magazine articles and *Among the Elk*, his first book (1988).

Today, Petersen labors hard at his craft during the winter and summer months, so that he can spend spring and autumn in the shining mountains. He's up at daylight, "writes like crazy until noon," then breaks for lunch. He often tackles three projects at once. In the afternoon he'll edit what he wrote that morning, then answer e-mail and make phone calls. By five or six P.M., it's time for a drink, a long walk with the dogs, dinner with Caroline, and a couple of hours of reading before bed. He reads *a lot*, mostly nonfiction. His own books, though very personal and informed by his own experiences, are extensively researched as well.

The writing life is a struggle, but it's what he wants to do.

"My die is cast and there's no going back at this point. I live my life the way I want to. The most important things to me are nature, love, freedom, independence, and dignity. Beyond paying doctors' bills, money really doesn't figure in."

The Petersens do not suffer intrusions, or intruders, lightly. Their simplicity thrives on anonymity. They have been debt-free for years. Dave calls himself a "minimalist" and declares, "Right from the start, what was most valuable to me was having as much control as possible of the hours and days in my life." He likes being his own boss, but he admits in private that as he and Caroline grow older, they would rest somewhat easier if they had "a bit more financial security. Even so," he adds, "I'd make all the same choices again. We all must age and weaken and die. What we are, and are not, is largely a product of the choices we make. We only live once, and most of us don't even do that."

The day David Petersen and I spent hiking together in October was intermittently sunny and warm, then cool and overcast— one of those gently volatile times when you'd really have to be misanthropic not to exult at being alive. The scrub oak was turning russet, the aspen leaves were bright shiny yellow, and thick layers of pine and fir needles softened the ground beneath our boots. As we walked, I asked Dave, "What's this?" and "What's that?" and "What's this other thing?" He replied, "Snowberry bushes" and "Grape holly" and "A deer antler rub" on that aspen sapling ("too low and fresh to have been made by an elk, since they're so much bigger and rut a month earlier"). Farther along he pointed out some fawn pellets and knew exactly what kind of animal had made that nest in the grass and how long ago. And when a tree creaked in the wind, startling us both, he likened it to a certain "mood" of elk call. At another point he sniffed the air and smiled, having caught the faint scent of a cow elk. How did he know it was a cow?

"Because it has a slight licorice flavor."

Of course.

"There's no place in the world I'm more at peace or happier," he said of that wild region after we'd returned to his cabin. "The natural world is the only reality, thus the only valid base for spirituality there is."

Walking that talk, Dave truly considers each familiar rock and tree to be a friend. "While I have trouble remembering anything material in the human-made world for more than minutes, out here in the woods I remember in photographic detail every place I've ever laid eyes on and everything that ever happened—every smell, every sound, every feeling and mood—no matter how long ago. My memory lives in nature. I feel like a secret sharer."

Autumn is his favored season, and Dave goes hiking every day through glades of fern and fallen aspen leaves, where his fellow creatures have recently wandered. Walking down a grassy gully together, we paused at several small springs where elk had recently wallowed—trampled up the mud, peed in it, and rolled around. Dave studied all the signs and related their stories. Some surrounding aspen trunks were plastered with mud from being rubbed against by excited bulls.

At one seep, my guide sat on a log and detailed for me how he had shot an elk "right here," with his simple bow and hickory arrow the month before. For hours an evening, several evenings in a row, he had sat quietly, blending in, listening to the forest, to the flutter of birds' wings, to the wind rustling through pine needles. "I hunt mostly with my ears," he says, "listening for a step, a snapped twig. It gets so quiet out here sometimes that you can hear a mouse fart." In fact, often while out there alone he hears voles or other tiny mammals foraging among the grass and leaves. When finally one evening he heard an elk coming, he made ready. It was a mature bull weighing some six hundred pounds, predictably nervous as it approached the water hole, where instinct told it predators might lurk. At one point the wary beast stared right at Dave, but it failed to recognize his camouflaged form, sitting motionless in the shadows with a tree to his back. When the animal finally lowered its head to drink, Dave killed it, instantly, with a single arrow shot from just fourteen yards away. And there was his meat for the winter.

More than any other author I have read, David Petersen can explain a hunter's heart and the need for a renewed acceptance of this heart if humanity, which requires healthy ecosystems, is to survive. All life consumes other lives in order to live. Our damaged planet *needs* the exquisite balance implied by the ethical hunter's law of mutual respect. The human world has largely abandoned that natural balance, leading to global warming, holes in the ozone, the extinction of countless species, expanding misery, and, increasingly, worldwide catastrophe. By their work, and by the way they lead their lives, people like David Petersen are trying to reassert the basic principles of ecocentric living crucial to a healthy world and personified by a simple love of life—*all* life.

On the Wild Edge: In Search of a Natural Life is a deeply affecting and passionate declaration of these principles, as well as a beautiful portrait of David and Caroline's adventures with the natural world. It is a capstone to Dave's work and life so far, and the most hopeful vision I've come across in ages. As a love story of two people bonded together through nature, the book is a radiant prose poem that speaks eloquently to the major issue of our time. Joy bubbles up through the pages like aspen leaves tossed skyward on a whirlwind.

John Nichols
Taos, New Mexico

New Year's Eve already, again. Stepping out through boot-deep snow.

Here on Spring Mountain it's traditional to celebrate the final evening of each calendar year with a good stiff hike, accompanied by whatever hounds are currently at hand and up to the effort. This year, I'm down to Mr. Otis, since Angel dog is thirteen and on her last leg and that last leg is lame. While Otis is nine, which in big-dog years makes him a borderline senior like me, he, also like me, still thinks he's a stud. In fact, old Oats frequently wins compliments as a supremely handsome example of the Labrador breed, even in his muzzled grayness. He's been blessed with glossy black hair (recently, a visiting Alaskan trapper friend made Caroline nervous when he stroked Otis appraisingly and remarked on what a "fine pelt" he has), long sturdy legs (Dr. Woody, Otis's personal physician, calls them "mountain legs"), clean white teeth, and a broad intelligent head (as opposed to the rat-nosed look of lesser Labs). So why ruin the ruse by revealing that his mother was a golden retriever?

Of course, for O and me to take an evening hike together is hardly unique, insofar as he walks me most every evening, the high point of most every day. The high point, at least, when the weather is pleasant and calming, or nasty enough to be exciting because it's scary enough to offer a reminder that nature always bats last: say, a wildly showy electrical storm, wind like a low flight of fighter jets screaming through the trees, a blinding white-out of blowing snow and swirling frozen fog. Barring any of that, during the moody holiday season—deep in the white gut of win-ter, with its foreshortened days, crackling cold nights, delaying snow, and precious little wildlife to animate the scene—a walk in the winter woods can often seem more effort than entertainment.

But on this good evening all is right in our pristine mountain world, and the uphill pull is unburdened joy. The weather is gentle for the last day of the year here at eight thousand feet in the Col-orado sky. The snow is dry and less than a foot deep (this is the fourth consecutive year of record-breaking drought), and Otis and I are hot to trot in celebration of another mostly good year lived mostly on our own terms in this mostly good place. It is nearly a quarter-century now since Caroline and I fled southern California with all we needed or wanted stuffed into my VW bus: camping gear mostly, plus two wooden orange crates holding 123 1960s and '70s vinyl albums (but nothing to play them on); a couple dozen nature, philosophy, and "back to the land" books; and clothing for all rustic occasions but none for job interviews. Everything else, what little there was, we'd sold or given away. Between us, we had $5,000 in hard-saved cash, good health, no debt, no worries, and, best of all, youth. Caroline was twenty-five. I was thirty-four. After years of slow-burning boredom and simmering frustration, our lives had linked and blended and now stretched enticingly ahead like a scenic mountain highway, where everything in sight is lovely but you can't see beyond the next hill or curve.

On the road, headed east, in search of the American West.

In search of a natural life.

It was August 3, 1980, that anxious day we fled Laguna Beach, where Caroline had enjoyed her teenage years as something of a hippie chick, although she'd been born in England. C's father was an Air Force intelligence officer who served proudly in World War II. I never had an opportunity to meet Stu Sturges, who hailed from Wisconsin and died of a cerebral aneurysm at the age of fifty-two, but Caroline loved him absolutely. In some subtle but vital ways I reminded her of him, which helped to balance certain worrisome aspects of my personal résumé—divorced, former Marine, and eight and a half years older than her. Caroline's mom, who just recently died, was definitively British and appropriately accented—the Queen Mother, her five daughters called her. Also a military brat, Patricia M'Cutcheon was born and raised in India. Since her father was a highly decorated British Indian Army officer, the family was modestly privileged within the raj. Because the Queen Mother and three of Caroline's four sisters resided in a cluster in southern California, together with years' worth of friends, C found it hard to leave. And in some ways so did I. Hard but necessary.

Like me, Caroline loved to camp and hike. Like her, I craved the serenity, purity, and unpredictability of real mountains. And most important to our deepening love, she, like me, had learned not to confuse quality with quantity in life or to let everyday distractions—such as career goals, car payments, and children—distract her from the pursuit of a genuine life. Almost immediately after meeting, we started scheming our escape to someplace quieter and closer to the natural world.

Our first hope had been Montana, and we'd landed in a place northeast of Yellowstone Park with Rock Creek rippling through, called Red Lodge. But the town was tiny and the county was poor and the people xenophobic. And no satisfying or sustainable work was to be found there for either of us. Nor did we really want to live in the town, or any town, no matter how quiet and quaint. Within months we decided to move on. Ironically, just a few years later, Red Lodge, like so many other quaintly charming Old West towns, would go and get itself Californicated. Yet Caroline and I had come from California to Red Lodge as the antitheses of Californicators; we were just plain fornicators, an unmarried couple searching for the good life as we had come to understand it: less of more and more of less.

And so it happened, having quickly gone bust in Red Lodge, that in December 1980 we repacked the old VW and took off again, this time slipping and sliding southward down the frozen spine of the Rockies to the San Juan Mountains of southwestern Colorado. To Durango, a place I had passed through many times since childhood but where I had never wanted to live. "Too close to the desert," I'd reasoned. The desert back then, before I'd read Edward Abbey's life-changing *Desert Solitaire*, was an alien place that scared and depressed me. But we stopped in Durango to visit friends, fellow California escapees (who have since returned to California and divorced), and we never quite got away. On a lark, Caroline applied one day for three different jobs—and was offered all three. A small local college that had been founded on the site of an 1800s military outpost called Fort Lewis, and so wears that odd name today, presented an opportunity for me to use my G.I. education benefits before they expired. And that was that. After a year of low-end rentals in town, we got married and moved up here to Spring Mountain, to our very own 1.3-acre lot in an aspen grove, prepared to camp out forever, if necessary, rather than ever pay rent again.

Spring Mountain. Okay, that's not its actual name. In fact, it's not really even a mountain. Technically, it's the bottom step up the side of a major local landform called Missionary Ridge. In private, we think of this place as Petersen Mountain. Nor is that vanity or possessiveness speaking. Rather, we nominally connect our surroundings to ourselves simply to register our heart-deep sense of *belonging* to this place, even as this place belongs to us. Not in title but in heart, where ownership really matters. The place evokes in us the Buddhist precept of *ahimsa*, "do no harm." Here, where our most numerous neighbors are not people but elk and bears and mule-eared deer. Here, where we've lived happily, for the most part, ever after and as free as we can be. Freer and happier than I'd ever dared dream was possible through all my agonizing years of adolescent Okie awkwardness and military service and aching, amorphous, urban anxiety and sullen social withdrawal and crippling anger and psychedelic "experimentation" (actually, I was an expert) and intellectual escapism and seemingly dead-end *searching* . . . without ever even knowing what it was I was searching for. In fact, I finally determined, the answer to *that* question fairly defined the quest.

In sum, I was pretty much like millions of other thoughtfully confused young Americans, baby boomers coming of age in the long, cold shadow of Vietnam. The difference was, I somehow avoided getting hooked on the pursuit of all the myriad "lifestyle opportunities" our culture proffers as the road to happiness— a blatant lie, yet a lie that most folks fall for to the point that the pursuit of trivial distractions, and working to pay for them, devours the best of their lives.

While my various intellectual and spiritual searches continue still today, as I hope they always will, I am no longer fueled by frustration. I am mostly a happy man. We are a happy family: Caroline, the mutts, and me. Long ago we made our decisions, just as everyone does. Only most of ours were different. And we abide by all of them still.

Like so many others, I fall easily into contemplative self-assessment during the stressful holidays. And the troublesome issue I find myself contemplating now, step by step up the mountain, is the issue I least want to think about, yet a problem no one alive can fully escape: money.

Everything, it is said, is relative. And relative to the American norm for my materialistic generation, I've been downright thrifty. I've bought only two new cars in my life. The first was a 1964 Mustang, for which I paid $2,300 in 1965, back in Oklahoma. The second and last was a 1969 Malibu, bought fresh out of Marine officers' school in Quantico, Virginia, for $3,200. It's been decades now since I've owned a vehicle that was less than a decade old and didn't wear at least a hundred thousand miles on its odometer, which by my lights is admirably low. Similarly, we never take a vacation that doesn't offer good hope of paying for itself—writing, speaking, teaching, robbing banks—and we always camp out. We camp not merely to save money but because for us, if it isn't camping it isn't a vacation. We have no addictions or expensive habits, no debt, no medical insurance, and we pay cash for all medical expenses. (I mostly use the V.A. hospital in Albuquerque, a lifesaver.) We live year-round in a 596-square-foot board-and-batten cabin I built with my own hammered hands, incorporating as many recycled components as I could scrounge or buy on the cheap: doors and windows tossed out in alleys in town; lumber and corrugated steel roofing stripped from a fallen-down barn; fiberglass insulation and an antique potbellied Monkey Ward woodstove rescued from a nearby ranch house that was being torn down.

Over the years, as money and time have allowed, or urgent need has demanded, I've improved the cabin: with enameled steel roofing to better stop the rain and slide the snow, an airtight woodstove that's safer, eats far less wood, and holds a fire all night, aspen tongue-and-groove interior walls in place of paperboard paneling, and—our one true touch of elegance—antique bird's-eye maple flooring, a generous gift from a generous friend. But back in the beginning, for the initial construction, rather than going for quality or speeding up the process by taking out a loan, we built only as fast and as fancy as we could afford on the cash-and-carry plan. True, our cabin—which we only half-jokingly call the Doghouse—is a claustrophobic cave by middle-class American norms. But middle-class American norms are frankly obese, and compared to how most of the rest of the world lives, our humble home is an elegant castle. Best of all, it's by-God *ours;* not the bank's or part of some hovering landlord's retirement scheme.

All of which is to plead that our ongoing fiscal woes arise not from foolish spending but rather from a long-standing preference not to squander our precious little time above ground in laboring to earn more than we need to live comfortably. Frankly, the Pavlovian pursuit and compulsive counting and thoughtless spending of mere money strikes me as deadly boring business. We have better things to do, Caroline and I, than to slave and save and earn and spend—working ourselves sick, as Thoreau quipped in *Walden*, "that you may lay up something against a sick day."

"Don't just exist—live!"

Back in midcentury Oklahoma, my fifth-grade homeroom teacher, Mrs. Edith Pryor, proclaimed that sage advice in flowing cursive on the big green blackboard, making quick barking sounds with the chalk. As banal as that proclamation may seem at first glance, its simple, self-evident wisdom has helped to shape my life, via a long series of decisions, into a form that I find valid, satisfying, and enough. From here in the midst of my so-called peak earning years, granted, that shape does not appear to include the possibility of retirement. Yet when you love your work—when life and love and labor and place all are of a piece—who wants to quit?

So forget filthy money. Away with soul-withering worry. This New Year's Eve, this final evening of yet another year of our whirlwind lives, we are healthy, happy, and celebrating—a boy and his dog striding up this comforting old mountain while ruminating on the past, pondering the future, and, with every step and breath, offering active praise for the blessings of the moment. And glory be, after the first hard few minutes and the catching of my increasingly elusive second wind, I sense that this is to be one of those sweet retro intervals when my aging mortal shell, rather than dragging behind and slowing me down, lifts me lightly along, like a buzzard climbing a summer thermal, up and up on a free ride to heaven. Suddenly I am young again, high as a hippie on the pure animal joy of self-powered movement. At least for the moment.

And what is life, really, but the moment?

Now is where the past leaves off.

Now is where the future begins.

Here and now is all and everything, and gone in a heart-stopping flash.

Of course, the unseasonably light snow eases my efforts more than a bit. Whether thanks to El Niño, La Niña, global warming, or mere meteorological serendipity, it's ten days past the winter solstice (Caroline's birthday) and this remains a blissfully, if worrisomely moderate winter here in the high southern Rockies, not even worth the weight and inelegance of snowshoes. It's convenient right now for all of us, this winter drought, but bad news come summer for our animal neighbors should the grasses and forbs, the berries and acorns once again wither and fail. Local reservoirs are running low. Wildfire is a hovering threat, and our water well (278 feet deep, but marginal even at that) might well run dry.

Yet, and as always, we'll deal with those hassles if and when they come. Worry is nothing but interest paid in advance on trouble. For now, we climb eagerly on, Otis and I, running occasional short sprints, choosing the steepest routes simply for the sake of their steepness, running uphill in the snow. While nothing in the physical (or any) realm is nearly so good as good sex, the so-called runner's high runs a fair second place.

As we near the top, ninety-five hundred feet above the sultry beaches of southern California and a vertical gain of fifteen hundred feet from the cabin—with only a few dozen minutes remaining in the day, less than a half dozen hours to go in the year, an unknown number of years left in our lives—a light of impossible beauty laminates the sunset sky. The churning, shifting spectrum of pastels—blue, lavender, purple, pink, red to fiery orange— seems almost sentient, somehow feminine, ineffably alive.

Twilights here of late, I've been noticing, evoke in their magical mood and eerie luminescence a Russell Chatham or Thomas Aquinas Daly landscape masterpiece. More than evoke; it's as if we have entered the living canvas, Otis and I, two white-whiskered Alices slouching through a crepuscular looking glass— moody but never maudlin, ethereal and sometimes spooky, quiet as meditation, this heart-cracking beauty of mountain and sky.

"Nature imitating art," some say of such sights, peering out on the world through windows smudged by human-centeredness.

To which I respond: Nature *is* art, inspiring, enabling, and informing *all* else.

"Nature is God's greatest creation," one friend proposes.

"Nature *is* God!" another friend rebuts.

When finally we reach our goal—a rocky point overlooking a snow-covered lake—I stop for a look around. The open-timbered bench marking the zenith of this smallish mountain, where Otis and I now stand, as I have said, is itself but a step up the face of a bigger mountain, and so on, up and up along a stairway to alpine heaven, ascending above and beyond modest Missionary Ridge to the dizzying Needles Range, there attaining fourteen thousand feet and higher, all within a couple dozen miles of here.

The awesome grandeur of such vertical landscapes makes one feel rightly small. And such feeling-smallness, by exposing the false front of our usual feeling-bigness, feels real good to me.

Impatient as a puppy, ever the anxious seeker, Otis flashes past, brushing against my snow-dusted pant cuff as if to proclaim, "Look at *me*, Dad! Here I *go!*" running in widening circles. On his third counterclockwise circumnavigation, the eighty-pound goofball surprises a congeries of ravens, which in their panicked flush startle the hell out of me, as I had neither heard nor seen them there, clustered on the ground behind a low rise to my right. Righteously alarmed, the overgrown crows hurl themselves skyward as one dark body, a flapping black cloud that rises in brief solidarity then flies abruptly apart, like a fistful of scarves flung into a wind.

How I do love ravens! At once the most clever, adaptable, and confident of birds and the most joyful heralds of death. Like Otis and me, ravens perceive themselves as far too handsome and wise for their humble lot in life as scroungers, kidnappers of robin chicks, and carrion eaters. Yet they, like O and me, don't merely endure but always find ways to enjoy. What most humans view as hardship, ravens see as play. Everywhere good I go, from Alaska to Mexico, ravens are there.

Even so—this late in the day, this deep into winter—these gregarious birds should by now have retreated to their nocturnal roosts to perch on limbs like so many lumpy black leaves, feathers fluffed for warmth, among the sheltering boughs of Douglas fir or ponderosa. Why haven't they?

Suddenly it occurs to me that these preeminent scavengers may have been feasting late on a holiday gift of frozen flesh. Dead elk or deer? Dead coyote? Dead . . . ?

Winter: the dying time of year.

It was near here, I'm reminded, and only last month that Otis and Caroline found a fresh elk calf carcass. Its rectum had been bored out—not by space aliens, as some alarmists have claimed when the same thing has happened to foundered cattle, but by various small scavengers, who enlarge the natural portal as necessary to gain entry into the body cavity, where all the good stuff is. Yet in the case of Caroline's calf, the two-hundred-pound animal's gut bag was lying outside the body cavity in a solid frozen wad, oddly unopened. Judging from the tracks, my observant spouse reported, a herd of twenty or more elk had recently passed through, running full-out. The calf, it seemed fair to surmise, had dropped out of that herd to die. Why had they been running? What had killed the calf? Why, how, and by what had its innards been pulled out, then left untouched? No other tracks were anywhere to be found.

Work obligations delayed my investigation, and I asked Caroline not to return in the meanwhile for fear that a mountain lion might be hanging about. By the time we finally got back up to inspect the carcass, a few days later, coyotes had come and gone, albeit in a strange sort of way. Coyotes usually eat every shred of an animal: meat, hide, hair, and all but the heaviest bones, which they scatter far and wide. But the calf's hide remained essentially intact, with head and lower legs still attached. So perfect was the inside-out skinning job that if you draped the hide over a sawhorse, it would appear almost alive. My favorite biologist, Tom Beck, says that sometimes in winter when coyotes find a carcass, they'll eat the softer innards and meat out of the frozen hide as if it were a shell, leaving the skin until the weather warms and thaws. Maybe that was it. But why didn't they get into the head for the brains, or carry the skull away as they generally do? The calf's eyes, always the first targets of winged scavengers, had, oddly, not been disturbed. That fact, and the lack of bird poop on and near the carcass, attested that birds had yet to find the prize, hidden as it was beneath overhanging boughs.

As Caroline insisted at the time, if we'd really wanted to find out what had killed the calf we should have returned the day she'd found it. By the time we got back, there was not much left to go on. Subsequent snows had erased all the older tracks, including hers and O's. As a last resort, I ran through a process of elimination, as I knew Tom Beck would do, to wit: All the bears were sleeping in their dens. To find a mountain lion up this high so late in the year would be unlikely if not quite impossible, since almost all the deer, their primary prey, had migrated to lower wintering grounds. Plus, lions always cover the remains of their prey with debris between meals, and this one was bare. None of the legs were broken or otherwise obviously injured. Sick? Possibly, but again not likely, given the large size of the young elk, which suggests that it was well nourished and healthy. Perplexing.

On closer inspection—prying the frozen hide from the ground and flipping it over—high up on the rib cage I noticed an isolated rip, one inch wide by three inches long, as if an arrow or bullet had passed through and the hole had later been enlarged by freezing or scavengers. This fit with the anomaly of the gut bag lying whole outside the elk. Perhaps, I angrily concluded, during the last rifle elk season, which had ended a few days before Caroline found the calf, some fool had shot, partially skinned and gutted, then inexplicably deserted the carcass. Abandonment of game meat is a moral and statutory felony, and the thought of that having happened here on our own little mountain preserve infuriated both of us, as if a thief had broken into our home. But then, we could be wrong. After all, there had been no human tracks nearby when C had first been there. Had the elk herd run through after the hunter had come and gone, obliterating his guilty prints? We'll never know for sure.

But the calf is down the hill a ways and the ravens are, or were, right here. So I hurry over to investigate. Approaching the spot where the birds had been ganged on the ground I find . . . nothing.

Who knows? Who gives a flapping croak? Not Otis, who has already whiffed some new and intriguing scent and is off hounding after it, headed conveniently down-mountain, the way we need to go. With twilight fading fast, I turn and follow his lead, the prints of my big insulated rubber boots shortcutting Otis's switchbacking slashes in the snow, like a drunken slalom skier. Dogs, like preachers, politicians, and real estate whores, never run straight unless they're being chased. But Otis has disappeared, coursing far ahead. Perhaps he's cut the pungent trail of a pine marten, like the one he and Caroline saw on this morning's walk together. In fact, Caroline admitted to having seen the sleek, cat-sized, tree-climbing, rodent-hunting weasel only after Otis had tracked its scent to the base of a tree and his animated excitement, urgent whines, and upward panting stare had lifted her gaze from its normally grounded fix. While a hunter, like me, peers up and away, scanning the horizon for broken hints of color, pattern, or movement, Caroline, a gentle gatherer, focuses closer at foot, stalking wildflowers, mushrooms, animal spoor, and other rooted prey. Alone, each of us is half blind. Together, we see near and far.

No matter. Wherever my dog-son has gotten off to, or why, he is out of my sight—an intolerable breach of Petersen doggy etiquette. I refuse to yell, clap, or wolf-whistle in the woods, any one of which would rudely shatter the tranquillity I come here for, disturbing the critters and destroying the very treasures I seek. Instead, I stop and peer around—waiting, watching, straining my ears into the ringing silence for the rhythm of panting breaths, the soft thuds of paws on the snow. I chuckle out loud when I catch myself sniffing the air, as if I were a dog or bear. This thought, in turn, reminds me of Dersu Uzala, the charismatic wild-man protagonist of Russian explorer V. K. Arseniev's 1910 classic adventure memoir, *Dersu the Trapper*, a mostly true story beautifully made into the 1975 Academy Award–winning film *Dersu Uzala*, by the Japanese director Akira Kurosawa. Dersu is an aging aborigine of a dwindling hunter-gatherer tribe, the Goldis, who are animistic (nature worshipping) foragers of the Manchurian taiga. The scene I'm recalling takes place one bad winter day while Dersu is out boar hunting with the captain. When Dersu misses an easy shot at an animal he can pungently smell but barely see, the old woodsman wails in pidgin Russian, "*Capitan!* My nose sees better than my eyes!" in sudden realization that he is going blind.

Or something quite like that.

The point being that that's the way our big boy Otis sees *his* world: nostrils first. Could we dwarf-nosed human animals experience for just one hour the world as a dog, deer, or bear perceives it—in shape-shifting layers of Technicolor scents, far more vivid and varied than even the most stunning sunset sky—that brief, epiphanous window of wonder would alter our outlook and actions forever. For all our manipulative cleverness, we really *know* so little of life.

Growing uneasy with Otis's ongoing absence, if not quite worried (he knows the way home from anywhere up here and would yelp for help if in trouble), I venture a soft, birdlike whistle, poorly imitating the bright spring rondo of a mountain chickadee. Inappropriate though it is for the bottom of December, it will alert Otis, if he hears it, that I am here.

Sure enough, within moments here comes the Oatsmobile, a graceful flowing streak of ink sluicing across the snow, sleek as liquid silk, contouring cross-mountain full-bore: big ears flopping, jaws agape and cheeks flared wide, gums spotted pink and black, long tongue lolling, ivory fangs flashing a delighted canine grin—four score pounds of pure animal joy.

As with the other animals in my life—and my life is peopled with animals—I envy Otis his freedom from burdensome ambition, from debilitating regret, pointless worry, and egoistic longing for public recognition and personal immortality. For him, life is *now*, to be *experienced*—chased, caught, and played with; rolled in or pissed on according to mood and aroma; chewed up and swallowed, digested, and always celebrated—not some Calvinistic adversary to be feared, conquered, intellectualized, rationalized, fantasized, or dogmatized.

Panting and pleased with himself—"Here I come, Dad! Such a *good* boy, me!"—Otis stiff-legs to a stop at my side and raises his snow-frosted mug for a pat. Which of course he gets, plus a kiss on the head (never will my lips touch the butt-licking lips of a dog) and a few soft words of encouragement to *Stay with me, knucklehead!*

Happily reunited, we hurry on through the gravy-thick dusk, suddenly eager for sight of the little brown cabin in the big white woods, that place so cozy, welcoming, and warm—warm, at least, if Chef Caroline hasn't neglected the woodstove again while preparing dinner. Tonight's holiday feast: a simple, celebratory banquet of Spring Mountain elk tenderloin, baked spuds and butter, sautéed morels (collected last spring both here and in Montana, dried for storage and rehydrated in red wine), a green vegetable, and a crisp salad tossed with vinegar and oil. And, of course, a glass each—or maybe, by God, two—of California Cabernet. (The last item for reasons of health, of course.) It would cost us more to drive the thirty miles round-trip to town and soak in fast-food grease.

Praise be to the inimitable, elemental, utterly essential pleasures of hearth, home, and family!

"What a boring way to celebrate New Year's Eve," some will protest, "just the two of you, *alone*, at *home!*" Yet we have tried the other way—the "traditional" American celebration so heavily hyped in screaming seasonal radio ads: "Come join the biggest and best New Year's Eve party *ever! Live* music! Door prizes! Big countdown to midnight! Bring *all* your *friends* and let's *party!*"

Jeez. Contrast that to this—up here in the cold, quiet dusk, versus down there in the "real" world of civilized, homogenized, capitalized culture. Down there, that is, in big-little Durangotown, hard by the mining-polluted Animas River. Río de los Ánimas Perdidas, River of Lost Souls, was so named, legend holds, by early Spanish explorers who lost members of their gold-seeking expedition to drowning while recklessly trying to ford the frigid, spring-flooded rampage; it's an apropos name yet today, considering how things have so recently gone to hell. Down there, where bars big and small are buzzing with booze-blasted patrons seeking momentary distraction and existential mollification via cerebral numbness amid the herded comfort of numbers: they're jumping tonight, all right, those lively liquor lyceums, filled to the gunnels with pay-to-play patrons drunk on the angst of another fleeting year done and gone, for better but mostly for worse, war and no peace in sight. Out with the old, in with the new . . . the unknown, unknowable, and clearly unacceptable. Down there, another year of too many lives lived in quiet desperation—if not quite so quietly tonight.

But perhaps I'm being too harsh. We all get by the best we can, and each to his or her own, so long as it hurts no one else (as driving drunk will surely do).

Joy and sorrow, pleasure and pain, love and loss and death: in *that* uncertain future, at least, we of the living are one.

Nor is it so simple a matter as them versus us, there versus here, town versus country, contrived versus natural. The real matter, to Caroline and me, is outside versus in: keeping *outside* of culture, if only just barely—watching, questioning, weighing—versus getting sucked back in, our minds and hearts slammed defensively closed, going with the muddy flow. Or maybe it's simpler even than that, and all inside of me. I've never been the sort, even when young and reckless, to care for the barroom scene, with its overamped music and crowded dance floors; the stifling stench of cheap aftershave, industrial-strength perfume, and raging pheromones; cover charges, drunken boring patrons, and steroidal bully bouncers. As my good friend George likes to joke (George always likes to joke): "New Year's Eve is *amateurs'* night. If the drunks don't get you, the police will."

Meanwhile, up here on the mountain, where nothing much ever happens, life is quiet, restful, filled with personal meaning, and the next best thing to free. Call it boring if you will.

Looking to our left, eastward as we go, light-years beyond the saw-toothed silhouette of the Continental Divide, we see Jupiter come awake: a blinking benediction in blue. At least I think it's Jupiter, not being much on stars (or planets either, obviously). I mean, there are so *many* of them. And all so far away, untouchable, ultimately unknowable, thus largely removed from my life. "One world at a time," said Thoreau on his deathbed to the hovering preacher. "One real world is enough," echoed Santayana a century later. I feel much the same. Yet how gratefully each night do I greet Orion (a bowhunter, like me), who at the moment, still hidden below the horizon, is gearing up with bow and dagger for another night's go-round with that ballsy old aurochs (a Taurus, like me), the two of them battling clockwise across the nocturnal firmament. Forever.

Shaking me from my reveries, Otis suddenly stops, goes stiff-legged, raises his muzzle, sniffs, and licks his slobbery chops—tasting some delicious promise that's as yet invisible to me. Explaining himself with an excited *Whoof!* he deserts me and bounds ahead, barreling down the hill. Following quickly after, I, too, soon smell the spicy incense of aspen smoke, perfuming the lucent night.

Almost home.

· 1 ·

By the middle of January each year, semihibernation becomes a comfortable routine. For winter weeks on end it's black-dark here before five-thirty, and you can listen to music and read only so many hours an evening under the glare of artificial light without getting headachy and fried, and we do not watch TV. So it is that we find our somnolent midwinter selves emulating our shaggy neighbors the bruins, who snore through it all in their snow-sealed dens, snug as bugs in bearskin rugs. It's easy to envision the snoozing lard-butts even now, since I once napped in a bear den myself.

"I know where there's a bear's den. You want to go with me to check it out?"

Our neighbor Patsy was phoning from her home two miles up-valley. It was late June and I trusted every word she told me because Patsy is a mountain gal, one of several hereabouts who put your mill-run Cabela's-clad dilettante "rugged outdoorsmen" to shame with their fearless foot-powered excursions into the wilds. No off-road vehicles, ATVs, snow machines, or GPSs for these ladies—Patsy, Erica, Nancy, my own Caroline—just balls of stainless steel. Few men their age (middle) would be able to keep up with any of them, much less dare to go where they go so often alone. My Caroline in particular . . . but she's another story.

Patsy went on to explain that during a hike the previous fall, the morning after a light snowfall, she and her mutt had just completed a long climb up a steep, north-facing slope when they'd cut a line of fresh bruin tracks cresting a saddle between low ridges and disappearing down a timbered draw. Since the bear had gone more or less the way they needed to go to get home, Patsy followed her dog as it followed its nose along the line of tracks until the trail disappeared into "a small hole under a big rock" in the midst of jumbled boulder slide. Since no tracks led back out of the hole, my neighbor stood wisely back. But her dog, doglike, ignored her commands to the contrary and snuffled right up to the black oval opening—where its nosy probing was stopped short by "a loud, bawling roar" from within. Taking the hint, they left the grouchy occupant in peace, and in a hurry, and Patsy hadn't been back since. I eagerly accepted her thoughtful invite, and an hour later we were on our way—Patsy, me, and her eldest son, Johnny. As we climbed, Johnny wondered out loud, and quite logically, "Why do bears hibernate in dens each winter?"

"That's a two-part question," I replied between uphill breaths, "requiring two answers."

Denning most likely evolved during the Pleistocene epoch (the most recent great Ice Age, spanning approximately 1.6 million to ten thousand years ago) for protection from predators in winter, a season of increased vulnerability. While humans were around then too, they don't likely figure into the deal, not significantly at least, since northern foraging peoples specialized in locating and marking active bear dens before they were sealed by snow. Returning in midwinter, these hungry tribal folk would dig out, kill, and eat the occupants with gusto. Thus did denned bears supply early humans with a bulk source of superb nutrition at a time when little or no other fresh meat was afoot. Since such a practice works hard against the effectiveness of denning as a survival tactic, the security motivation for denning logically owes not to human hunting pressure but to such four-legged threats as wolves, which are active all winter and occasionally attack and kill young bears, including even grizzlies. A subterranean den with a discreet entrance concealed by deep snow provides a snug, secure, and defensible nursery for naked and helpless bear babes, which are typically born in mid-January. The average litter is two cubs, a girl and a boy.

Hibernation, as distinct from denning, is an ingenious strategy used by many creatures to avoid winter starvation. In the case of northern bears, winter is a time when there's rarely enough food around to replace the calories that would have to be expended in battling snow, icy water, and deep-freezing cold. With the exception of the purely carnivorous polar variation of the brown (grizzly) bear lineage, all North American bruins are omnivorous and, necessarily, overwhelmingly vegetarian. And precious few veggies grow during an Ice Age winter.

Grizzlies, having evolved as ursine backhoes, routinely undertake major den excavations, often tunneling into a hillside beneath the roots of a massive tree. But black bears (climbers by nature) opt for less labor. Locally, the favored blackie denning site is a natural cavern in a rockslide, which the seasonal tenant improves as needed. It was to just such a place that Patsy had trailed her bear.

———

After an hour of fighting our way through head-high, bug-infested oak brush, dodging over, under, and around blowdown timber, we arrived at the foot of Patsy's boulder field, which forms a steep lumpy river of rocks a few hundred yards on a side, mostly grayish granite boulders.

"Well, it's up there *somewhere*," said our guide, noting that everything had looked different last October, then freshly covered in snow. We decided to spread out and search independently, and it was Johnny who finally scored. What had attracted his sharp young eyes was a small mound of reddish dirt that "looked out of place" among the gray rocks. As he approached to investigate, the black eye of the den entrance winked at him from behind the earthen berm.

"You sure it's safe?" Patsy inquired as I prepared to crawl inside.

I assured her that it was, explaining that in the most exhaustive study of western black bears ever conducted, Tom Beck, who recently retired as senior research biologist for the Colorado Division of Wildlife, had made a career of crawling headfirst into occupied bear dens in winter. The animals whose homes Tom was invading had been livetrapped the previous summer and fitted with radio collars, then released and monitored from a distance (often from the air) until they went to den. The den sites were then plotted on topographical maps, allowing Tom and his team to visit them in winter. Once inside, Tom would jab the drowsy occupant with a syringe attached to the end of a pole and filled with a powerful tranquilizing drug.

"The needle jab," says Tom, trotting out the Floridian swamp-rat patois of his youth, "tends to wake them suckers *right* up." It also tends, within a minute or two, to put 'em right back down. "And that minute or two," Beck suggests, "can get *real* interesting."

As soon as the bruin was out, Tom would tie a rope to its leg and guide the limp body as his helpers dragged it into the sunlight to be weighed, blood-sampled, ear-tagged, and to receive replacement radio-collar batteries or have the collar removed at the study's end. It's critical, Beck emphasizes, to "process" the animal as gently and quickly as possible in order to avoid causing it harm. Finished, the researchers would tuck the beast comfortably back into its den, repositioning it precisely as they'd found it. "It's a job best done," Tom advises, "before your bear wakes up."

Indeed, as I have seen for myself.

A few years back, I helped a game warden friend (as a toddler helps his dad mow the lawn) trap and relocate a "problem" bear. (Most often, in fact, people are the problem.) This one had smashed through a flimsy backyard fence and killed a pygmy goat in a subdivision near here, as the residents watched in shock. Tearing its victim in half, the bruin absconded with the front end, leaving the prime hinder bits for later. District Wildlife Manager Cary Carron arrived at the scene an hour after the crime, towing a culvert trap on a trailer. Using the smelly remains of the little goat as bait, he set the trap and left. The bear obligingly returned and got itself caught that same night. Having nothing better to do with its time, the big male blackie ate the bait while awaiting our arrival.

After hauling our prisoner eighty miles to a new home on public land far from the nearest subdivision or bleating pet goat, Warden Carron opened a small lid on the top of the trap and jabbed the bear with a dose of tranquilizer. By now, understandably, our hairy friend was a wee bit out of sorts, roaring and swatting at its enclosure. But soon the tranqued bruin quit complaining and collapsed.

Working with a sense of urgency, we opened the cage and hauled the beast out so that Cary could insert a numbered ear tag that would identify the animal as a previous offender should it get into trouble again. That took only a minute, after which we dragged the goat-stinky mass of greasy fur to a nearby brook and into the cool shallow water, in hopes of speeding its recovery. The tactic worked all too well; the three-hundred-pound teddy came promptly awake, wobbled to its feet, looked groggily around, spotted us, snarled, and charged. We, of course, ran like hell for Cary's truck. In its normal sober state, the big fellow could easily have overtaken us. But after only a couple of bounds our pursuer, not yet quite up to speed, stumbled, tumbled, and fell. Not for long, however: just as Cary and I reached the safety of the vehicle our pursuer stood again, shook like a wet dog, flashed us a final threatening glare . . . and shambled off into the sheltering woods.

But back to Tom Beck and his den-raiding routine: with a "processed" bear snugged back into its winter quarters, the researchers would reseal the entrance with snow and depart. Most often, Tom speculates, the victim bear "takes it in stride as just an annoying dream."

It's a rough research regimen, to be sure. Much to his credit, as the years, bears, and occasional injuries to animals accumulated—most hurts happened when a bruin got a foot caught beneath a heavy falling guillotine trapdoor—Beck became increasingly bothered by what he and his fellow researchers were doing. His first major act of constructive rebellion was to design a kinder, gentler trap, which ensures that no harm will befall the bears. When remote infrared camera technology came along, Beck promptly tried it, embraced it, and encouraged his peers nationwide to do the same. While livetrapping, radio-collaring, and den invasions remain necessary in some research situations, infrared photo technology has substantially decreased the need to detain and manhandle bears. Now they come to a scent bait suspended on a cable beyond their reach and get their pictures taken repeatedly, day or night, with no humans present and no food reward to ruin them. Often that's enough.

Even so, before his research and career were done, Tom Beck had crawled into nearly two hundred occupied bear dens. While he enjoyed many scary moments in those moist dark holes, he managed to live and tell. Happily for me, I number among the best told of. And that, in turn, allows me to tell others, like Johnny and his mom, with the confidence of one who knows from personal experience. And, darn it, I could have *had* that personal experience, several times over, had I only accepted Tom's repeated offers to tag along on his winter den-crawling expeditions. In a fit of generosity, he once even offered to let me be the "needle guy." Tempting, of course. But the timing was never quite right.

And now Tom Beck is retired.

So it is, in part to compensate for all those missed opportunities, that I never bypass a summer-empty bear den without investigation, getting down on hands and knees to have me a peek inside. Which is generally as far as it goes, as far as I *can* go, since few dens I've found have entrances large enough to admit a human adult, even a narrow one like me, without some shovel work. According to Tom Beck's data, Colorado black bear den entrances range in size from a record height of twenty-eight inches to as low as nine inches; the average is in the teens. These portals, says Tom, "are never any bigger than just big enough for the bear to squeeze itself through." Thus, the bigger the door, the bigger the bear. The oval eye that Johnny spotted that summer afternoon was not quite two feet wide by sixteen inches high at the apogee of its upper arch (incredibly, I'd had enough forethought for once to bring along a tape measure), tapering to half that at its edges. As I say, I'm a thin man—160 pounds spread across six vertical feet—yet I could barely shoulder through.

But once I got inside and turned on my flashlight . . . what a difference! With three and a half feet floor to ceiling, I could sit
upright. The cavern was eight feet front to back—from entrance to
sloping rear wall—and almost twelve feet wide. If push came to
shove—say, you were caught out in a killer storm or on the lam
from the FBI—four adults could stretch out comfortably. The interior was surprisingly clean and clean smelling. The dirt floor (from
which the little earthen berm out front had been excavated) was
thinly lined with a matt of fir and spruce boughs, their needles
still pale green. The ceiling and walls, formed by the concave bottom of the massive overlying boulder, had been rubbed smooth
in places by generations of occupants—over hundreds, perhaps
thousands of winters—scratching their bristly backs. Individual
strands of long, wavy, silken guard hair clung to the entrance and
ceiling. Woolly clumps of dense winter underfur lay clotted among
the evergreen boughs. In all, it almost felt like home.

After I'd had a good look, feel, and sniff around the bear's winter digs, Patsy used my camera to snap a couple of pictures as I
emerged from the den, squinting in the glaring light. When neither of my companions expressed any interest in taking a tour of
the den, we headed back down the hill and home.

A few days later, I returned to the den alone and wormed my
way back inside. There, I stretched out full length on my back,
rested my head on my day pack, puffed a few puffs on my old
briar pipe (an experiment to check the air circulation, which
wasn't very good), and enjoyed a dreamy nap.

· 2 ·

All of which reminds me, as I was saying: we sleep a lot in winter
here. Well rested, most mornings I rise early and get right to work.

After dragging myself away from Caroline's magnetic warmth, I pull on robe and moccasins, scratch Otis's ears and let him out to conduct his morning pee patrol around the boundary of our magnanimous postage-stamp estate, stir the ashes in the wood-stove, top the glowing embers with a few finger-diameter kindling sticks, add some larger splits, open the damper so that air rushes in beneath the coals and fans them back to flame, close the stove door, put on a pot of coffee, and wash my face and hands in fifty-four-degree well water, the temperature at which it comes from nearly three hundred feet belowground. While we do have hot water these decadent days of late, I still require a cold splash for a wake-up.

When Caroline and I first moved up here from town—on April Fools' Day, 1982—to act out our *Mother Earth News* "get back to the land, do more with less, take control of your own life" ambitions, we had no electricity, thus no running water hot or cold, save what we hauled in and heated on the woodstove. Boldly challenging my lifelong aversion to debt, we'd signed a $5,000 loan carried by the seller (over three years, plus $500 cash down) to buy this wooded bit of mountainside, tucked covertly in a high back corner of the oldest and (at the time) least developed summer-home subdivision in the county. Back then, in fact, the whole region was only lightly peopled in summer and all but deserted in winter, and we innocently assumed it would stay that way. Having fallen in love with the dense grove of quaking aspens that shades most of the parcel, and having camped here a few pleasant nights to "get the feel" of the place, we took the leap, borrowed, and bought.

That was autumn of 1981, when it all began. Over the winter we scraped together another $400 cash to buy a long-abandoned 1950s-vintage eight-by-twenty-four-foot travel trailer complete with a decade's depth of wood rat turds. After cutting the fewest possible trees to open a narrow two-track lane down from the dirt access road to the center of the property—with aspens, ponderosa pines, and white and Douglas firs towering all around and an oak-brush hill rising steeply on the north—we hauled the trailer in with a pickup, set it up, cleaned it up, and moved most eagerly in. In doing so, we became only the fourth year-round "household" on the mountain (in fact, two separate mountainside slopes divided by a big creek valley), and none of the other three were within sight or shout. No penned-up or chained-out dogs barking and yapping annoyingly. No delinquents, juvenile or otherwise, buzzing around on motorized toys. No having to listen to somebody else's music played too loud, as had been the case in town. No traffic sounds. Clean air. Quiet, private, safe, semiremote in summer and all but inaccessible in winter, rustic, modestly rugged, and affordable even for the low-income likes of us. Our own Walden Pond, as it were—minus, of course, the pond.

Across the next fifteen years, until the human invasion of the mid-1990s, it was almost paradise here, though the sledding was hard in winter. But even at its hardest, it beat the pants off town.

While still living in town, we dubbed our final rental house there the Slave Quarters, in honor of its cramped size, tarpaper exterior (the owner had stripped off the original siding but never quite gotten around to replacing it), and dirt-alley placement behind one of the biggest nineteenth-century Victorian brick mansions on upscale Third Avenue. And the landlord, most assuredly, saw himself as Master.

Yet even the Slave Quarters was an improvement over our original Durango digs—a second-floor efficiency apartment in the Swiss Chalet, a second-rate motel a mile west of town, where the winter sun never shone, a cold wind blew nonstop, and the parking lot ice never melted. As soon as we could, we moved from there to the Slave Quarters, absorbing a rent increase from $125 to $195 a month, plus utilities. Accordingly, as soon as we could, we moved again. Up to Spring Mountain. Up to utopian here. And here, by golly, we got along just fine without electricity, indoor plumbing, or even a telephone.

If it weren't for the need today for a big, 240-volt submersible pump to lift water from a deep well (drilled and plumbed in 1986 at a cost of $3,500), we could have gone juiceless forever. (With the help of a Radio Shack adaptor, I could recharge my only utterly essential electrical appliance, a laptop computer, from the cigarette lighter in the pickup truck or a single-panel photo-voltaic converter.) Likewise, in those young and hardy days—except in winter blizzards—we hardly missed indoor plumbing. In fact, we rather enjoyed the outhouse adventure, aware that for millions of years and until just recently, everyone everywhere—kings and queens and holy messiahs alike—lived without water faucets or flushing commodes, as millions worldwide still do (if relatively few by choice).

Of course, when you have the affordable option at your fingertips, "*could* go without" versus "go without" is no contest. Caroline and I not only appreciate hot running water, we also love music played loud on a good cheap stereo and are blessed with a synchrony in tastes.

"What kind of music do you like?" someone occasionally asks.

"*Good* music," we answer as one.

And good music is generally enough virtual entertainment for us. Except for the winter Olympics, I haven't watched TV for thirty-five years, and I can't say I've missed a thing. Supine on my deathbed reflecting back on my small life, I doubt I'll exclaim, "Damn, if only I'd *watched more TV!*"

Neither does commercial radio get an airing here. Aside from word of mouth passed among friends, our primary tap into what's going on out there in the "real" world of economic wars, religious terrorism, and chimpanzee politics is public radio. NPR's evening *All Things Considered* and *Morning* and *Weekend Edition*s are our favorites, and best of all is the wise and wizened voice of preeminent political commentator Daniel Schorr. Dan is to radio as Hunter S. Thompson is to print, the two of them providing some of America's most honest and informed political criticism. But even public radio quickly becomes repetitive, boring, and largely pointless when "big news" (meaning always *bad* news) is going down. Five or ten minutes of radio news once or twice a day is generally more than enough, no TV or newspapers wanted.

Of far more interest here on Spring Mountain is the chittering, gossipy news being broadcast from just outside the north-facing kitchen windows by station WBF (winter bird feeder). Regular commentators include Steller's jays in stately powder-blue vests, sooty-headed, high-crested, bright-eyed (an illusion owing to their white "eyebrow" streaks) birds as raucous and temperamental as they are lovely; black-hooded Oregon (winter only) and gray-headed (year-round) juncos; nuthatches (white-breasted, red-breasted, and pygmy, tree-trunk-crawling woodpecker wannabes); and cheery chickadees (mountain and black-capped varieties). All of them scratch out a semihonest living in the snow below the recycled tonic-bottle seed dispenser suspended with baling wire from the lowest limb of a slender aspen whose growth was long ago stunted by a severe bark-shredding one night back when I was green enough to wilderness ways to lash to that innocent trunk the meaty rib cage of the first elk I'd ever killed, "to see what comes to check it out." What came, of course, was two hundred pounds of ursine trouble.

Beyond and far above the feeder tree, casual flocks of common ravens cluck and caw bemusedly as they seesaw through the icy morning sky, headed who-knows-where in eager anticipation of another day wisely invested in eating, playing, and thoughtful conversation. From the creek valley below rise the piercing *Maaag! Maaag!* pronouncements of black-billed magpies: big, visually stunning piebald birds with blue-green iridescent wings, long slender tails, snow-white shoulders and bellies, anthracite breasts and hooded heads, every ornery inch of them gleaming like the most precious jewels, which to us they are. This so-called weed species is increasingly abundant here in winter, though we rarely see 'pies this high in summer, unless, of course, there's carrion around.

· 3 ·

After checking in with the birds and seeing to routine chores, I shuffle over to Angel dog's bed in the southwest corner of the living room and sing her some silly little tune, whatever oozes from my sleepy brain. Not much of a music critic, Angel yawns, grins, and stretches gratefully awake.

With the livestock all thus roused, I open every curtain in the cabin, of which there are many, thanks to Caroline's construction instructions back when I was cobbling this shack together. My wife's "I want *lots* of windows" was a mandate that cost me extra work and money at the time but has since well proven its worth, as the light and views provided by all that glass relieve what otherwise would be a depressingly isolated darkness in a woody cabin cave.

When the coffee goes good and black, I pour two mugs and take one to the queen in waiting, reposing prone in her quilted throne, covers pulled over curly blond locks, another angel feigning sleep, awaiting caffeine and kisses. By now it's time to let Otis back in, let Angel out, let Angel back in (in her dotage, she can't take the cold for long and gets right down to business), feed both mutts, return to the living room, and plop down in my duct-tape-reupholstered chair (brown tape, of course, to match the genuine Naugahyde). Thus settled in, I sip coffee and read for a few lazy minutes, with radio and birds chirping softly in the wings.

We're the richest po' folk I know.

Some among our big-city friends think and speak of Caroline and me as wilderness ascetics. As viewed from a Los Angeles, Chicago, or Manhattan high-rise, we surely must be; to most people, wilderness is relative. But asceticism has never been our thing. We do not seek to absolve our sins through self-denial, but merely to control our own days and destinies by controlling our material consumption, financial encumbrances, and work and time obligations; to straddle the clean, sharp edge—geographically, culturally, and spiritually—between the human and the natural worlds, selectively gleaning the best (for us) from both. And we've pretty much made it work. We can walk out our door—anytime, any night or day—and up the mountain, not so awfully far, and be in a wild forest pulsing with life and mystery. After one strenuous day's hike from home, we can camp for the night within the 488,200-acre Weminuche Wilderness (say, *Women-ooch*, named for a local band of Ute Indians), the largest and arguably the loveliest public commons in Colorado. The same distance in the opposite direction—thirty minutes by pickup truck—puts us on Main Street of clang-bang boomtown Durango, where your dollars and daughters are always welcome. We go one way for wilderness, another for cultural cacophony, as we so choose. We're edge dwellers, not wilderness wildings, although we wish we were.

· 4 ·

The simple life.

While I like to think I live it, even just defining the term is far from a simple task. In a recent exchange of letters with a dear friend, Flo Shepard, the topic of voluntary simplicity arose, giving her yet another opportunity to scold me with compliments, as is her motherly way. "A simple life," she wrote, "is one where the guy goes to work each day and doesn't have to think about what he's doing or why he's doing it. Your life is not so simple. It's diverse, challenging, complicated, reflective—somewhat like the life of a primitive."

At this point I must interrupt to interject that Dr. Flo's late husband, Dr. Paul, dedicated his special genius to assembling a formidable body of scientific evidence in support of his conviction that the most "fully human" people who ever lived were our preagricultural hunter-gatherer forebears of the icy upper Pleistocene and earlier. Through all this time, wherever they lived, all people on Earth lived similarly: tribally, with a foraging economy and an animistic (nature-centered and Earth-bonding rather than heaven-bound) worldview. These truly human lives, as Paul Shepard meticulously chronicles in a score or so books, were stone-simple materially yet richly diverse, purposeful, relatively easy, and solidly grounded on planet Earth. Thus Flo's complimentary use of the often pejorative term *primitive*. Her letter continued:

"You tend to portray simplicity as always escaping from or rejecting something, making choices *not* to do something rather than emphasizing the positive fulfillment you feel in, say, your marriage and the various causes you champion and your hunting and writing lives. You joke that you haven't had a 'real' job in years, and that you write because you're 'otherwise unemployable.' But living as you do out there *is* a job. You have your work cut out for you because you've cut your work out for yourself. It takes a lot of determination and focus to stick with such a commitment. And speaking of focus—you certainly have it, demonstrating concentration to the exclusion of others, the world, even your own welfare (but never Otis's). Do you realize that the state you are in is the reason people go into meditation? Only they try to be empty, and you are full."

"Full" indeed, my dear. Yet opinions vary greatly concerning just what it is I'm so full of.

In late winter 2002, like thousands of Americans who live in places where urban smog and artificial light haven't yet erased the night sky, Caroline and I dragged ourselves from bed at three A.M. and sat outside for two frigid hours watching the Perseid meteor shower. Yet after only a few minutes I surprised myself by realizing that I was already beginning to tire of the visual bombardment, spectacular and rare as it was. Concurrent with this realization, it struck me that a lone shooting star is in fact more precious and exciting than the Perseids' staggering nonstop abundance.

Spontaneity, unpredictability, rarity, ephemerality, mystery: the main ingredients of magic.

Looked at from this peculiar perspective, the Perseids can be viewed as a pyrotechnic metaphor for human materialism, which helps to explain why so many among the very rich seem pathologically driven to strive unendingly to get even richer, to acquire ever more money, power, *stuff,* in an addict's effort to keep boredom, emptiness, loneliness, and the ugly naked truth at bay. To the woman or man of modest means and needs, simple pleasures and satisfactions are manifest at every turn.

> *How wondrous, how mysterious!*
> *I carry fuel.*
> *I draw water.*
> —LAYMAN P'ANG

"To reduce wealth to money and possessions is an incredible underestimation of our emotional life," says Arne Naess, the Norwegian Edward Abbey and the father of deep ecology.

And an incredible waste of our emotional lives as well.

Henry David concurs in spades, noting that "most of the luxuries, and many of the so-called comforts, of life are not only not indispensable, but positive hindrances to the elevation of mankind."

Indeed, it is the Perseid bombardment of insignificant material and time-eating distractions proffered by our dazzling culture that clutter and confuse us and delay or prevent us from tending to the simple essentials of real and rewarding inner and outer lives.

Equating the simple life to the good life is a cherished American tradition. Of course, when I variously refer to semipoverty, semi-elective semipoverty, or self-induced poverty, I am not speaking of deep, debilitating, generational, inescapable, humiliating, alien-ating, soul-bending, body-wasting, imprisoning, can't-make-the-rent-or-feed-the-kids, down-and-out murderous *poverty*. Rather, I'm speaking of (and, I presuppose, speaking to) those like C and me who have or once had a choice and have chosen to reject or at least minimize the get-all-you-can paradigm of our "grow or die" economic culture in favor of, as a guiding philosophy, learn-ing to be happy with only what you need, thereby escaping the worst of the Sisyphean rodent race.

Not extremism in any direction but balance; that's the ticket. As put metaphorically by Alfred, Lord Tennyson: "The happiness of a man in this life does not consist in the absence but in the mastery of his passions."

Or as stated by smooth-tongued Aristotle: "The man who indulges in every pleasure and abstains from none becomes self-indulgent, while the man who shuns every pleasure, as boors do, becomes in a way insensible; temperance and courage, then, are destroyed by excess and defect, and preserved by the mean."

Indeed, chasing the good life by way of voluntary simplicity is an ancient pursuit. Older by far than Aristotle. Older even than Buddha. And so very much older than sweet baby Jesus. Here in

America, it began with the first illegal (from the native inhabitants' point of view) aliens, the so-called Puritans. Not long after that unmitigated mess, the pursuit of simple American living became far more attractive via Jeffersonian idealism, which warned that "desire and fear are the two principal diseases of the mind," then went on to full fruition in the New England transcendentalism of Thoreau, Ralph Waldo Emerson, Mary Moody Emerson (Ralph Waldo's wonderful aunt), and other modestly privileged philosophical intellectuals of early-nineteenth-century Concord, Massachusetts. Then and there, in fact, was when and where the premier precursors of the hippie communes of the 1960s and '70s blossomed; and, like their hirsute reincarnations 130 years later, most soon wilted and died.

Could those communal failures early and late, I've wondered, in part be attributable to the possibility that simplicity, in order to thrive in a culture that embraces capitalism as its national religion, must be an individual or at most a family endeavor, rather than a large-group undertaking? A pursuit powered by personal spirituality rather than communal dogma? Large numbers of people complicate things. Personalities conflict. Energies differ. Sexuality confuses. Tyrants emerge. Group dynamics are never simple, especially among would-be individualists.

It strikes me that the straightest path to a life of satisfying simplicity is neither a complicated group effort nor a blanket denial of the material world. The path, rather, is marked by intelligent *balance*—finding a complementary and comfortable mean *between* the material and the spiritual, between nature and culture, between personal and social, with plenty of time left after each day's work in which to socialize, play, meditate, make music and love, and, of course, to enjoy a nice walk. Thoreau dubbed such a middle road a "border life" (on the edge) that picks and chooses intelligently and independently rather than following blindly.

Among twentieth-century America's first and most forceful

spokesmen for the need to simplify our lives was social critic Lewis Mumford. Mumford's writings (*Technics and Civilization*, *The Culture of Cities*, and others), beginning in the 1920s, were sharply critical of the inhospitality, inhumanity, and unnatural-ness of modern industrial culture and urban and suburban resi-dential and work environments. But rather than issuing a call for thoughtful Americans to flee the crowded and un-natural cities in favor of a slower-paced and saner country life, as was the fash-ion among other social critics of the time, Mumford preached that America must "remake the workaday world so that people will not *wish* to escape from it!" Toward this end he argued con-vincingly the merits of Thoreau's balanced border existence by asking rhetorically, "How many men sweat in their offices so that they may give their wives a private car, a house with multiple bathrooms, or expensive furs! How many men whose wives would be far more happy, far more richly satisfied, with a little more of their husband's time and a little more of a lover's attentions!"

More than a few, now as then. But it's even sadder that we must also ask how many wives *drive* their husbands and *them-selves* to work incessantly in order to have those cars, those mul-ticommoded homes (if rarely, in these politically correct days, the furs). How ironic that we can look back with scorn and deri-sion on first-contact American Indians who so gullibly swapped furs and other valuable (that is, hard to come by and useful) pos-sessions, even sometimes their daughters and wives, for beads and other gaudy doodads. So far as I can tell, it's the selfsame trinket mentality at work now as then.

Every time I find myself weighing the rewards and challenges of simple living, which is fairly often, I come eventually to think of President Jimmy Carter. While mean-spirited political critics continue to deride "Peanut Jimmy" as an ineffective foreign policy and economic leader, Carter was easily the most honest, good-hearted, sane, and humane president I have known in my life. I can even forgive his mildly annoying penchant for name-dropping (God, Jesus), since Jimmy is among the relative few who truly walk the Christian talk.

He was, simply put, better than we deserved.

Speaking on a straightforward and commonsense level that nonetheless proved incomprehensible to most Americans, Carter cautioned that "owning things and consuming things does not satisfy our longing for *meaning*. We have learned that piling up material goods cannot fill the emptiness of lives which have no confidence or purpose."

But as good as this sounds, Jimmy was wrong on two counts. First, we have *not* learned that happiness, much less meaning in life, cannot be bought. And second, piling up material goods clearly *can* fill the emptiness of lives too shallow to know the difference.

And that's a majority in any town, ain't it?

· 5 ·

Fresh-fallen snow on the ground this morning, icing on the cake. Around the cabin, these few new inches of white politely hide a growing accumulation of unsightly yellow dog and Dave stains. All around us, the thatchwork boughs of hardy evergreens strain to support cumulative tons of suspended snow. Sometime during the night, as we slept, the gentle storm came and went in perfect silence, leaking the gift of precious moisture on its way northeast to the alpine peaks of the Continental Divide, where all clouds congregate, in all seasons, to dump their largest loads. Typically, if we get inches here, the Divide gets feet. And when we get feet—well, at least the skiers are happy.

I'm happy too, in a warped sort of way, when a super-heavy

snowfall forces me out of bed, out the door, and up on the roof to shovel snow at midnight (to keep the cabin from caving in). Adventure is mostly a drag when it's happening, and midnight roof shoveling in a blizzard can be downright miserable. I render it bearable by fantasizing escape to some sunny such paradise as Tahiti or Tortola and pondering the hereafter (Tahiti or Tortola, minus modern development, would suffice) should my ticker run out of tape or should I slip and slide off and be buried waist-deep and headfirst. A couple of times, in fact, I have slipped and shot right off the roof while shoveling snow in the dark. Happily, the lower roof edge is only ten feet above the ground and the accumulation of roof-slid snow there served to cushion my landing. The trick is to try to hit feetfirst while clamping your legs tightly together. With luck, you'll sink in only waist-deep and can wriggle and pull yourself out. The real trick, of course, would have been to build enough pitch, or slope, into the roof that snow would slide off on its own, alleviating shoveling altogether. Alas, it's way too late to turn back now.

But no such adventure this time; these fleeting few inches will soon be gone. The morning is brilliantly quiet, clean, and cold, the forest glittering and pure. As the sun tops the last ridge to the east and lends its warmth to the air, the tree-trapped snow—wet, dense, and bonded by freezing—begins to thaw and crack. Every so often a big, heavy clump breaks loose and crashes down, causing a cascading tree-branch avalanche as it goes: *Whump-whump, WHUMP!* A stroll in the woods on such a morning can be a bracing experience: button up your collar; hold on to your hat and brace yourself to be clobbered, engulfed, momentarily blinded, and perhaps even knocked to your knees by any number of utterly unpredictable tree avalanches. Happily for me, and by her own decree, Caroline is the morning walker here, no matter the season or weather. This morning, in order to break trail in the raw, new snow, she went out on snowshoes.

Which prompts me to grumble that no matter what the glossy

magazine ads may claim in an effort to portray snowshoeing as sporty and glamorous—or the rave-review articles written to support and recruit those ads—the devices themselves are neither sporty nor glamorous. Neither are they even a particularly energy efficient means of snow travel, compared to cross-country skis. What snowshoes can be, as they long have been for us, is utterly essential. Once, long ago, during the only winter in which we ever took an extended trip together (someone has to be here, remember, to shovel snow off the roof), we arrived back home— that is, at the bottom of the final steep access road—to find a three-foot depth of unplowed snow. Happily, still being something of a Boy Scout, I had tossed my snowshoes into the truck before we left, just in case of such a return. Feeling smugly prepared, I strapped them on and started stomping trail uphill, with Caroline following behind. It worked for a while, but halfway up we hit a soft spot and—*whump!*—C dropped through and found her five-foot, one-inch self stranded, utterly stuck in the snow. I could have dragged her out, but she'd likely have gotten stuck again. There was no choice, we agreed, but for me to take the flashlight and trudge on up, then down the other side to the cabin, there to shovel the snow away from the door, remove my snowshoes, go inside and retrieve C's snowshoes, put my own back on, and stomp back down to where she patiently waited, alone and half buried for twenty bone-chilling minutes in the obsidian dark. On my return, I stomped out a firm spot all around her hole and hoisted her out. Sitting, she strapped on her shoes and we slogged back home, built a fire, and fell asleep, exhausted.

Exhausted but home safe.

Certainly, the inelegant new high-tech shoes with metal frames and synthetic support beds are vastly superior in performance, if not aesthetic appeal, to the traditional wood-and-rawhide jobs you often see hung decoratively over gas-log fireplaces in mountain-town bars, restaurants, and trophy "homes" (most, in fact, are warehouses for conspicuous wealth). The superiority of the new models is due largely to their metal cleats, which provide firm traction, and bindings that actually bind, both of which improvements could easily be appended to the traditional woven models, though I've never seen it done. Still, no matter how they're dressed or hyped, snowshoes are tools, not toys. Realities rather than dreams.

This morning, like every morning, Caroline went and returned. Over steaming jasmine tea (I've worked three hours by now and according to my labor contract with myself am entitled to a tea break), my partner in this life of wee adventures recounts the high points, and the low, of her snowy morning's walk, to wit:

While following Otis along a twisting game trail—visible to the familiar eye as a shallow linear trace, or dip, in the unbroken snow, frequently contouring a hill—my wife noticed a pair of "bony little feet" projecting upright from a lump of snow beneath a big Doug fir. Grasping the skeletal digits, she gave a gentle tug and out popped—a chickadee, not yet stiff or even cold, but convincingly dead. The tiny bird had apparently been avalanched from its perch and buried alive just minutes before C had found it.

Imagine: You are that tiny bird, patiently enduring the long frozen night, as you have so many nights before, huddled among the sheltering boughs of a friendly tree, your downy underfeathers erected for warmth, uncomplainingly waiting for the snowfall to end and the morning sun to dawn. Finally, here comes ol' Sol, warming your pewter breast and the pea-sized heart within. Any moment now, you'll stretch your wings and away to another day of meaningful work and untold adventures, free as the proverbial bird.

And then . . . *fwump-fwump, Ka-WHUMP!*

All is dark and cold again. You are trapped upside down (as if you'd fallen headfirst while shoveling a cabin roof). You can neither move nor breathe. Slowly, your panic subsides . . .

Nature isn't always pretty, but she darn sure always works. And rarely is there waste. Knowing and respecting nature's rule of recycling, Caroline placed the little feathered body in the snowshoe trail behind her, where some hungry scavenger—raven, magpie, coyote, fox—would soon happen across it, or perhaps already has, converting the death of another into life for itself and, come spring, its young. "Born again," that chickadee shall be, or close enough for the likes of me. I mean, why would anyone want to go on, and on some more, *forever*, with no chance of release?

It is only the promise of death that makes our lives worth living.

· 6 ·

Late winter, late night, midlife.

My sleep having been interrupted by an increasingly pressing concern, I rise in the chilly dark and stagger naked toward the bathroom—a short trip—bouncing from wall to door, feeling with a toe for the smooth porcelain cold of the toilet bowl. It's a relatively recent concession to midlife and wife, this water-wasting contraption. For well over a decade here we got on fine with an outhouse, though it tended to induce constipation in city visitors, particularly the girls. And even for us country bumpkins, an inside outhouse on a subzero February night such as this, I admit, is a welcome luxury.

Done with that, I stumble on, navigating semivisually, my eyes gradually adjusting to the opaque cabin interior. Another short trip, around a corner and up one step, and I'm in the living room, which we jokingly call the great room by way of celebrating its 146-square-foot greatness, with a wood post in the middle. (Having neither the desire nor the money to hire a bulldozer to come growling and farting in to gouge out a level building pad—thereby forcing the mountain to conform to our wants—I conformed the shack to the mountain's natural slope, necessitating a modest split-level.) But the joke—of semielective semipoverty—is on no one but us, and we don't often mind.

Living this way was and remains our decision, and I'm frankly proud of our snug little abode, having built it entirely myself. Which is to say, I looked at our bank account and the lay of the land, weighed my meager skills, explored the possibilities, sketched some plans, gathered some basic tools (handsaws, portable electric circular saw, hammer, level, paintbrushes, the absolute minimum) and enough rough-in materials to get started, dug the holes (by hand, with an old-fashioned posthole digger), and set and cemented the upright support posts (rot-resistant redwood with their bottoms dipped in motor oil as preservative), sawed every board, hammered every nail (and quite a few fingers), and can personally lay claim to every single mistake.

My biggest, most frustrating and laughable goof happened one day when, after setting a row of upright four-by-four-inch support posts in concrete and trimming their tops to the appropriate height to hold the topmost roof beam, I realized I'd somehow cut one post a foot too short. What I should have done right then was to pull the short post out and replace it. But I was stupid and lazy and broke and decided instead to trim all the other posts to match. This bit of idiocy resulted in perpetual payback, since it lessened the slope of the roof sufficiently that snow is reluctant to slide. Thus the perpetual necessity for my winter rooftop acrobatics.

Even so, I trust you can imagine the satisfaction and pride that comes from constructing your own shelter and living in it year-round, year after year, mortgage-free, snug against the worst weather nature can throw your way. It was, necessarily, a long-term project, my cabin-building gig, progressing as time and cash allowed. I began in 1982 and had it essentially completed, as a structure at least (minus indoor plumbing and other such luxuries), five years later. Caroline's contribution was to work a series of dead-end jobs in town to keep us going while I goofed off sawing and hammering, teaching part-time at the local ski college and trying to learn to write for money. Since the cabin's initial "completion," as I've already boasted, I've made gradual improvements, until today we can declare that yes, we may well live in what some consider a shack (with a nod to Aldo Leopold), but, by George, it's *our* shack top to bottom. Building your own gives the term *home* a whole new depth of feeling. From hamburgers to houses, everything tastes better when you make it yourself.

Here in the many-windowed great room the mood is notably lighter. The moon this sparkling February night, hung high and heavy in the west, is plump and bright as an incandescent egg. Floating eerily above a darkly silhouetted horizon, this midnight orb paints a luminist scene stirringly similar to the original Thomas Aquinas Daly watercolor *Beaver Ponds with Rising Moon*, which watches hauntingly over this space. Aided by the moonglow, I open the woodstove door, stir the ashes to excite them a bit and create more light, grab an armload of aspen splits from the bin nearby, and arrange them in the stove just so—crisscrossed to allow air to circulate and feed new flames. Such nocturnal stove tending is standard winter routine here, where wood is our only heat. And we like it fine that way. In fact, for me, it's a lifelong dream come true.

In midcentury Oklahoma, when and where I grew up, nobody I knew heated with wood. Nor did anyone I knew in our middle-class world even have a recreational or decorative fireplace. In that robust postwar economy, people were busy modernizing their homes, disguising lovely old log or frame houses with tacky asbestos shingles, trying to appear with-it and prosperous. And in that oil-rich region, back then, natural gas was so incredibly cheap, and romanticism and nostalgia for "the good old days" in such short supply, that it just didn't make sense to heat with wood.

Coming from such a smoke-free background, I can't say where I got the bug for wood-burning warmth, but I had it from the start. While still a boy I went camping every chance I got, winter as well as summer, and the heart of each campout was a prolonged evening fire. Jumping ahead several years, past the Marine Corps to Laguna Beach—where it rarely gets cold enough to justify heat but people have money and fireplaces are much in style—I used to walk around town at night, to and from my cell in the moldy basement apartment of a turreted mansion I call the Castle on Catalina Street, three blocks from the ocean, breathing deep the tangy scent of orangewood and eucalyptus smoke rising invisibly on the damp, heavy air. Even then I rarely envied other people anything, but someday, I promised myself, I too would enjoy the anachronistic pleasures of a campfire inside my home, and not merely for recreation.

Wood smoke, to me, has always smelled like . . . romance? Yes, that's the word, *romance*, evoking not only flickering memories but the actual gut feel of a thousand campfire nights relived: glowing coals, sizzling meat, potatoes baking amid winking embers, the creature comfort of radiant heat, the hypnotic gyrations of animate flame, the security of light in the darkness, smoke like incense, quiet reflection alone, or good conversation with friends.

Back then, fantasizing the life I now lead, even chain saws seemed somehow romantic—an ugly tool to help build a beautiful dream.

Now, recalling such feelings on this winter night, my mood goes soft and weird, and rather than shutting down the stove and returning to bed as usual, I swing the glass door open wide, step back, and sink into my chair to enjoy—just for a moment, I tell myself—the original midnight matinee.

Logging on, as it were, the good old-fashioned way.

Meanwhile, outside in the brittle cold—not real near but not too far—a lonesome hooter calls. Moments later—not too far but not real near—its query is answered in kind. I smile, happy to hear them at it again, "twitterpating," as the professorial owl in Disney's insipid, insidiously antinature *Bambi* sweetly euphemizes wild-life courtship and copulation, denying the existence of pure animal lust. In fact, those two great hornies out there sweet-talking in the frozen night have been at it since Christmas, their kind being among the most eager twitterpaters of all North American birds. By early spring, while snow still falls here high in the Rockies and smaller migratory neotropicals still bask in warm southern climes, these consummate predators of the night will already be tending a brood of chicks. Which is to say, in starkly un-Bambified terms, that the parent owls will be feeding their voracious clutch the warm, bloody, and often still-twitching bodies of Thumper, Mickey, and other cute little beasts. This is good news or bad, depending on your place in the food chain.

· 7 ·

The flickering stove fire, struggling to rekindle itself, is visually warming, though I'm sitting too far back to feel much of its heat and as naked as the night I was born, oh so long ago. Squinting at the indoor-outdoor thermometer on the north wall, I read the chilling news: five below out yonder with the conjugal owls, a relatively cozy forty-eight here in the Doghouse. Suddenly it occurs to me that if I'm going to stay up, which it now appears I am, rather than sitting here shivering I could go put on some clothes, like a civilized person, or at least move closer to the stove, like a wise Neanderthal. In a sleepy compromise I grab robe and cap from hooks on the wall and scoot a bit closer to the stove, basking in its ticking glow.

That's more like it . . . staring into—not merely at, but *into*—the dancing flame.

It's a universal human predilection, I suppose, this Promethean infatuation with carbon-fueled combustion, ingrained in our forebears as part of the fiber of our wild human roots. Gazing reflectively, romantically, dreamily into bright leaping flames—pyromancy, we might dub it—connects us viscerally, palpably, and most certainly spiritually to our formative past, rekindling that magical human trio of myth, imagination, and utility. Yet it's not so much the dancing flames that hold me here in the chilly great room now, nor the mesmerizing glow of the nearly full moon, amber and bracing as sour-mash whiskey, but something about one of the aspen splits I just put on to burn. As I eased it into the stove, by the yellow-red glow of moonlight and coals, I recognized the split as an individual among its thousands of near twins in the firewood heap outside: a stick with a stirring story.

Quaking aspen (*Populus tremuloides*), like no other tree I know, is a storyteller, a sylvan logbook of recent local life. Recorded in its tabula-rasa bark, soft and powdery white, are rousing tales of deer and elk—written in the dark thick scars of autumn antler rubs, in the oily smears of sebum secreted by preorbital glands and deposited by face-rubbing, in the denticulate scarring of winter bark gnawing. The tooth scars are products of the happy fact that the green, easily accessible underbark of aspen has a nutritional value for wild ungulates approaching that of prime grass hay, providing an ever-present source of emergency rations that often defines the difference between winter starvation and survival until spring.

As a matter of fact, the caloric severity of a given winter can be judged in hindsight by the extent of the elk's aspen gnawing. While starving elk are blessed to have it, aspen bark is not a frontline food when better is available. With living, standing trees, the damage is generally limited; elk rarely girdle a live aspen—that is, remove the bark all the way around, thus dooming the tree to infection, starvation, and death. Instinctively, the giant deer "know better," intuitively aware that such shortsighted greed—as routinely practiced by humans through clear-cut logging and other gluttonous resource mismanagement—will work against them in the long run. With limited barking—a gnaw here, a nip or nibble there, rarely totaling more than one square foot per year per adult tree—the shallow wounds soon darken from white to gray, harden, and self-seal like the scars they have become. All is healed. But with freshly fallen live aspens—blowdowns—winter-hungry wapiti exercise no such restraint, consuming every shred of accessible bark, eating the doomed tree bare. And why not? So which, in the big picture and the long view, is the more "intelligent" species, us or the forest beasts?

Porcupines likewise autograph aspens, with sharp climbing claws and bark chews. The porky, by choice, prefers pine bark. Hereabouts, ponderosa is its favorite; in lower elevations it is piñon, also known as dwarf, pine. But sometimes—I've seen it most often in late winter—the spiny little beasts take a hankering for tender-skinned aspen saplings. These slow-witted, short-sighted rodents, unlike the prudent elk, blithely girdle and kill tree after youthful tree. Sometimes, as happened just behind the cabin several years ago, a single night's work by a single porcupine can stifle the regeneration of an entire aspen clone. This perplexing tree-killing behavior prompts us to wonder, Why does this creature even exist? What is its positive role in the ecological scheme of things? Why did it evolve with the apparent single-minded goal in life of debarking and killing as many trees as possible?

I've given this prickly mystery considerable thought. Although my theory is neither supported nor refuted by research, it strikes me as logical and obvious that under the pristine conditions in which porkies (and the rest of us animals) evolved—here in North America, that is to say, before European settlers began clearing extensive tracts of forests for farm fields, before clear-cut logging and the suppression of the small, ground-debris-cleansing, lightning- and Indian-ignited fires that traditionally swept through the ponderosa-and-aspen biome every few years and, in so doing, prevented major conflagrations—the bark-eating, tree-killing porcupine I reckon helped thin dense climax forests and create essential snags. This in turn provided essential food and habitat for many forest creatures. The porcupine's tree killing, therefore, not only facilitated healthy forest regeneration but, through spotty thinning, allowed sunlight to penetrate and nourish the growth of brush, forbs, and other understory vegetation upon which myriad wildlife depend for food and shelter. Today, our activities have reduced these once useful creatures to "pests" . . . just as we've done to ourselves.

Porcupines and elk are hardly the only aspen forest denizens to mark their passage on the impressionable white bark. In the process of shedding their lower limbs as they grow, top-heavy ("apically dominant" in biospeak) aspens scarify themselves, often in provocatively humanlike fashion; their limb stubs and cavities bear eerie resemblance to winking aspen eyes, erect aspen penises, open aspen vulvae. And people, too, love to carve on aspen bark.

But for me, the most exciting aspen art of all—as borne out by the log I'm now watching burn in my stove—is the work of climbing bears.

· 8 ·

Black bears, like their grizzly cousins, court and breed in June and July. Afterward, thanks to a marvelous evolutionary adaptation called delayed implantation, the fertilized female is able to go about her survival-essential summer business of eating and putting on winter stores of fat without the nutritional distraction of fetuses growing inside her. Come fall, as denning time approaches, the fertilized eggs, called zygotes—one per pending fetus—which until now have languished in dormancy in the mother's fallopian tube, attach themselves to the uterine wall, and the long-delayed pregnancy takes off.

But the marvels of delayed implantation go far beyond mere timing. In addition to her own physical needs, a hibernating mother bruin must produce enough rich milk to nurse a litter of hungry cubs for at least three months, in most parts of North America, before emerging from her den in April or May. That's a lot of calories, to be rendered entirely from stored body fat. And that's a lot of fat. Should she run short, the nursing mother's autonomic self-preservation mechanisms would kick in, her milk production cease, and her cubs starve to death. Such a nutritionally depleted sow might also die in the den along with her cubs. To prevent such disasters, delayed implantation comes riding to the rescue. If a fertilized sow suffers a bad nutritional summer— say, due to a late frost that stifles the fruiting of such critical predenning staples as nuts and berries—and thus is forced to den without the caloric surplus necessary to see herself and a litter of cubs through the winter, the dormant zygotes will not implant, effectively terminating the pregnancy before it begins. No muss, no fuss, no pain, no conscious emotional loss. Relieved of the pro-tracted nutritional drains of pregnancy and nursing, even a skinny bear, if otherwise healthy, will generally make it through the win-ter to breed once again, eat, and perhaps grow fatter the following summer. After this ingenious fashion not only does delayed implan-tation help ensure the survival of the species, it also keeps bear numbers in tune with the fluctuating ability of their habitat to support them. If only we humans were so blessed!

At birth, black bear cubs are tiny, blind, nearly hairless, and utterly helpless beyond the instincts to snuggle up to Mom for warmth and to nurse. Which instincts, happily, are all they need for now. By the time the new family emerges from the den in the green-up prime of spring, the same cubs that began life a few months before as eight-ounce rat-balls will be fully furred, have ballooned to five pounds or more, and be ready to roam, romp, and—though nursing will continue for some months more—start learning to find, select, and eat solid foods by imitating their mother's choices, including grasses, sedges, wildflowers, bugs, baby deer and elk, carrion, and, when times are hard and people are careless, human garbage.

But bears mature slowly, and cubs of the year—*coys* is the bear watcher's acronym—are ever at risk of being killed and eaten by predators. Ironically, the greatest threats to young cubs are males of their own species. Depending on where the black bear cubs live, other potential predators include grizzlies, wolves, wolverines, coyotes, cougars, eagles, and automobiles.

And so it has evolved that in an effort to defend her cubs against the threat of predation, among the first lessons a black bear mom teaches her brood after they abandon the den in the spring is to view trees as ports in a storm and climb them *instantly* when they feel threatened, or at her vocal—and, as I have wit-nessed, silent body-language—command. As the little buggers grow, this life-essential skill gets practiced a lot, often as not just for play. And when the climbed tree is an aspen—white as bleached parchment, smooth-skinned, soft-barked—scars will tell the story. That "here a bear climbed a tree" is obvious. Beyond that, the "Who done it, when, and why?" takes a bit more sleuthing. The interpretive dilemma is that as an aspen grows, the slashes cut by climbing bears stretch endlessly, making it difficult to say whether they were made recently by a big bruin (unlike grizzlies, all but the most obese adult blackies maintain their climbing skills and readily go to tree when threatened), or long ago by a cub. Personally, I can live with such unknowns. In fact, at this point in life's game, I'm not sure I could live without them.

Whether the work of cub or adult, the bear-scarred aspen split that has captured my focus and imagination tonight, an eighteen-inch section of a forty-foot trunk, tells eloquently of a bruin's brief embrace; of thickly muscled arms hugging the slippery upright pole in a wild and fierce surround; of scimitar claws ripping the tender bark, incising five curvaceous slashes, each several inches long and a quarter inch deep, as the bruin descended, slipped, slid, gripped tighter, dug in, and arrested its fall. I have seen such aspen acrobatics in action, several lucky times. And in every case the climber was a coy or yearling. The most recent such demonstration took place just last fall.

· 9 ·

On a perfect evening in September, I'm approaching the lip of a ledge above a small secluded pool of natural water we call Hillside Spring, two miles up the mountain. As always, I stop to listen before starting down the game trail that leads to the spring . . .

and hear loud splashing below. Instantly, the ancient wild vibes kick in: fast shallow breathing, heart audibly pounding, whole-body trembles, keenly focused alertness, with the larger world tuned out. Hunters know this familiar affliction as "buck fever" and struggle to overcome it in order to think and shoot straight. Psychologists and ethologists (students of animal behavior) refer to this autonomic survival response as the fight-or-flight syndrome. By any name, it provides anyone who's experienced it with gut-churning proof that we remain, in our deepest genetic core, wildings that evolved not only as predators but also as prey.

Dropping to hands and knees, I creep toward the rim, hoping to sneak a peek, size up the situation, and calculate my next move. But before I get there the splashing stops, succeeded by the thudding, rock-rolling sounds of something big moving up the slope toward me. The trail will bring the unknown creature to the top of the rim directly in front of where I now crouch, and only a few yards away.

Adrenaline whines through my veins like the chemical electricity it is. I wait. Soon enough, a patch of beige appears behind a bush at the top of the ledge, and I think, "That's a mighty short elk."

A moment more and the low-rider elk morphs into . . . a bear! A startlingly huge bear at that; in fact, this is easily the *biggest* black bear I have ever seen in Colorado—grizzly big or bigger, at least four hundred pounds. I note a milk-chocolate torso, dark lower legs and face, with a broad flaxen saddle across the shoulders and back; with long wavy hair, this bear is fall-fat and gorgeous—it's got the classic grizzly look.

Alas, as grizzled as this bear is, and as much as I wish it were, it is no grizzly. What it is is an exceptionally big black bear, a monstrous old boar, the King Ursid of Spring Mountain, without doubt.

But no sooner do I think these definitive thoughts than two tiny coys come bouncing up the hill to the big "boar's" flanks.

Incredible as it seems, there is no room for doubt: this mountain of a bear is a girl.

Bears of all species normally exhibit pronounced sexual dimorphism—that is, the males grow considerably larger than the females. From the time a sow reaches breeding age, her growth slows or stops as her excess "growth calories" are kidnapped by an almost continuous cycle of cub production and nursing. Contrarily, growth in male bears is generally limited only by longevity and nutrition. Thus, the standard gestalt interpretation for adult bears is that small to medium means female or young male, large means mature male or big female, and huge means king of the mountain. But clearly not always.

How I love it when nature breaks the "just so" shackles we try to force her into!

And no sweat, I assure myself, recalling the counsel of my biologist buddy Beck, who maintains that healthy, truly wild black bears, including sows with cubs, are rarely a threat to human adults, so naturally timid is the species. (Except in Alaska, where they are often quite aggressive.) Besides, even as close as she is, I'm downwind, dressed to blend in, motionless, and kneeling. The sow will likely stroll right on by without even noticing me, as females generally do.

No sweat.

But I don't even have time to finish these optimistic thoughts before the bear alters course ninety degrees starboard and—coincidentally, still oblivious to my hunkering, trembling presence—starts straight for me. The two coys, their fur wet and matted from their recent romp in the pool, follow their mother close at heel. With no time to indulge the luxury of inaction, I do a quick-draw for the pepper-spray canister riding ready in a holster on the right side of my day pack. For once, I have the noxious stuff where I need it, when I need it. In a flash it's out, safety off, and aimed bearward. Although Tom Beck's studies suggest that pepper spray isn't as effective against black bears (and even less so against lions) as it is against grizzlies, it will at least temporarily stop and disorient any animal with eyes, mucous membranes, and lungs, allowing you time to get someplace else.

My sudden flash of movement wins the big bear's instant attention, stopping her cold just ten feet away. Rather than instinctively charging, as a grizzly sow, being hardwired for an offensive defense, would have no choice but to do, my adversary stands and glares at me through eyes far too small for her wash-tub of a head. At the same instant, and with neither grunt nor glance from Mom, the cubs rocket up separate aspen trees to bawl and thrash about in histrionic terror, like giant freaked-out squirrels. I study the sow's eyes and face. We are so close now that I imagine I can smell her chlorophyll breath. Studying hackle hairs, posture, head position, I search for body-language clues to mood and intent . . . but I find her, like all females, essentially inscrutable.

Enough. Squatting here trading stares with a really big bear is foolish. As with mountain lions, a majority of human victims of bear attacks are children and small adults. Bigger is more threatening to predators, thus safer. With no further ado I smoothly stand and in the same motion take a first step—not directly away, which might trigger the bear's predatory chase instincts, and not directly toward her, which at this intimate distance could prompt a defensive attack, but at an oblique angle away. My bear spray, meanwhile, remains aimed point-blank at her nose. In response to my confident movements—precisely as Tom had predicted for such circumstances and I had desperately hoped—the sow blows a tremendous *Whoof,* swaps ends to show her fat, furred fanny, and bulldozes back down the hill she just came up, roaring and huffing ferociously, albeit in faceless retreat.

Unceremoniously abandoned, the cubs detree at terminal

velocity—each autographing its aspen with a series of elongated, slip-sliding claw marks as it drops—and hit the ground running, bleating like terrified lambs as they chase after their moaning mom.

As I listen to the fading sounds of the three fleeing bears, I smile and give thanks for such moments of wild abandon as this, which lift us from our daily drudge and put us up on the silver screen, rather than out in the audience getting fat on popcorn.

It may be safe and it may be comfy, but you don't find relief from super-civilized boredom while sitting indoors—precisely as I'm doing this cold winter night, reliving summer in memory.

Thus does the burning aspen log with its intriguing scars speak to me in the feral language of metaphor.

Or at least so in my dreamy state.

But as tenacious flames probe the rounded, bark-on side of the half-moon split, searching for chinks in the cellulose armor, the wood begins to speak audibly—snapping, popping, hissing. It's reciting, I fancy, its own eulogy: a swan song of seasons turning; of the warm caress of summer sun and the cold wet weight of snow; of patient, annular growth and wooden resolve; of leaves like serrate hearts, sprouting, greening, maturing, then dying and turning to gold; of a bear's ups and downs and the wounds it left behind—hardening, graying—a visual metaphor for the bittersweet brevity that makes all life so precious.

The summer after the bear-scarred aspen fell, I found its long white corpse, like a giant stick of chalk, lying leafless in the woods. After amputating its limbs—too small for firewood and better left as forest mulch—I sawed the trunk into manageable lengths. Noticing the bear scars, I cut carefully around, leaving them intact without thinking why.

Only now do I know.

And so it is on this February night, as I sit here contemplating the shaggy beast who left that cursive autograph, that I can't help but wonder: Where are you now, friend bear? Grown old and died naturally? Killed by hunter, government trapper, predator-phobic rancher, vehicle collision, or habitat destruction? Or—a more pleasing supposition—snoring snugly in your den, somewhere quite nearby?

· 10 ·

After sawing up the blowdown tree (aspens have shallow roots, prefer moist soil, are susceptible to structural disease, and thus are relative pushovers for a good stiff wind), I wrestled the heavy, post-length logs into my '79 Toyota (with nearly half a million miles on her odometer, she smokes a bit but keeps on truckin'), coasted down the dirt forest road, motored a ways on county asphalt, got out and locked the front wheel hubs, got back in and shifted into low-range four-by-four, and switchbacked slowly up another unpaved road to home. At the cul-de-sac above our property, I reenacted a ceremony I've enjoyed countless times over our years here, a sweaty sacrament of the sort Pulitzer-winning poet and roadkill carnivore Gary Snyder rightly honors as "real work."

Alas, it strikes me as sad that so few of us anymore can count our daily labor as real—in direct relation, that is, to our personal lives and spiritual and material needs, and thus filled with meaning and joy.

But the realest sort of work this is, getting in your wood, though overtly dangerous and brutally hard at times. The next step in this oft-repeated cycle is to unload and saw each log into eighteen-inch stove lengths, obeying what I think of as the "rule of eighteen," deriving from the convenient coincidence that a) our woodstove is happiest with eighteen-inch logs; b) eighteen inches is the active length of my chain saw's cutting bar—big enough for serious work yet not so big as to be unduly tiring, unwieldy, and therefore unsafe; and thus c), simply by holding the bar momentarily over a log before making a cut, I get consistently perfect stove lengths.

And what else? I know there's a "d" out there somewhere. Indeed, shortly after we moved here, when we still knew next to nothing, a neighbor came to introduce himself one day just as I was attempting to split our first winter's firewood. After cutting a tree's worth of aspen trunk into stove-length logs, I'd turned one on its end and started whacking away, attempting to split it in half lengthwise. My maul was new and sharp and the soft wood should have opened with ease. But it didn't. Rather, the log bounced an inch off the ground every time I hit it, preventing the maul from sinking in. When I repositioned the fallen-over log back on its end for another whack, the neighbor gently suggested, "If you'll put another, larger-diameter log between the ground and the log you're trying to split, it will eliminate the bounce and save you a lot of work." I did, and it did. So there it is, the fourth and final element of the rule of eighteen for efficient firewood making: place your rounds atop a larger upturned "anvil" log for splitting. And for average-sized people, the anvil works best when it stands about eighteen inches high. Not only does using an anvil log make splitting more efficient by eliminating bounce and allowing maul to contact wood at the apogee of speed and momentum—just below vertical in the downward-swinging arc—but it's also safer, since you're far less likely to miss the log or glance your maul off and into leg or foot.

Once I've resharpened the chain's seventy-two teeth freehand with a round file (after a while your hand and eye learn the correct angle), I clean the trusty old Stihl 034 (in chain saws, all the best are made in northern Europe) and set it aside to cool. Meanwhile, I haul out the maul and get to splitting.

A maul is nothing but a fat-headed axe with extra weight—eight pounds is perfect for me—to enhance inertia and cleaving power. The exaggerated wedge shape of the head—a fat V—also helps split a log apart as it passes through. I prefer a fiberglass-handled maul, since wooden handles, even tough old hickory, snap like matchsticks with serious use. With the relatively soft aspen and ponderosa pine we mostly burn, the splitting can begin as soon as the cutting is done; no need to wait for drying, frost curing, or checking (when the end grain starts to split), as with denser hardwoods. Of course, if you have the luxury of time, dry wood often splits more easily. Depending on their diameter, log sections up to two feet thick get whacked into half-, third-, or quarter-round splits. Really massive, lower-trunk logs may require you to chip around and around their edges, cleaving off narrow splits until the core has been whittled down sufficiently to be split in the normal fashion.

With the load of wood all split, I pitch the hundreds of pieces into the truck, back down the drive to the little grassy clearing among the trees that we call a yard, and stack (or toss, depending on mood and time constraints) the latest haul atop the growing heap of former local forest that warms us half of every year, body and soul.

I'm romanticizing here, of course. But not by all that much. Getting in your wood is hard, repetitive, and dirty work. The payoff, however, lasts all winter, and it's absolutely true that self-got firewood warms you body *and* soul. With each stick of fuel I feed to the stove—as with each bite of elk or mushrooms or other wild foods I collect and feed myself—I am warmed not only by caloric combustion but by the inimitable pleasures of having provided for myself and my family. No middlemen wanted or needed.

Locally grown and organic. Free-range. The use of fossil fuels for farming and transportation eliminated. And, once you're minimally equipped, very little money required.

Such work—real work—no matter how dirty or hard, is always labor-free.

As I sit and rock and watch firewood transformed to fire, smoke, heat, light, and ash, I reflect in respectful reciprocity on the once-living being from which this fuel was cut—its past, present, and future foretold by biological imperative. Maybe it sprouted from seed or, as is far more common with aspen, suckered from a parent root; then it proceeded to branching, budding, growing slender and tall and crowned at the top, young, strong, smooth-skinned, and limber, a straight and handsome young tree. Yet it collected scars even in its prime; and heart rot, like a time bomb, lurked, insidiously working deep inside. Inevitably the aspen aged, wrinkling, stiffening, weakening, leaning, destined to let go of life and crash back to earth one moody day or night . . . eventually, perhaps, to be found, thanked, dismembered, and hauled gratefully away by some happy woodsman, facing its final fate: to be devoured by the all-consuming, inescapable pyre of death feeding life. Up in smoke. And when it's done, when *I'm* done, my ashes, like those I'll shovel tomorrow from a cooling stove, will be returned to the forest and scattered, painting dark linear patterns on clean white snow—bear-claw scars on aspen bark—melting with that snow in the warmth of spring, seeping into the forest duff to nourish the growth of . . . what?

An aspen sapling, I can hope.

With a sudden eruption of combustive energy the fire flares high, every last log in perfect synchrony—crackling, sparking, shocking my wandering thoughts back on track, bringing me indoors again, to the exciting here and now. But soon the brief pyrotechnics die down and my mind drifts outward again, back to this morning.

It was early and I was listening to a news commentary by NPR's *Morning Edition* host Bob Edwards when his Kentucky bourbon voice was interrupted by a cacophony of screaming jays, somewhere near outside. Knowing from experience what such an outcry almost always implies among Steller's jays, I dashed to the west-wall windows and peered out and around, searching for the mobbing birds and sloshing hot coffee on my crotch in my haste. The excited jays were ganged near the top of a ponderosa, some eighty feet up, just twenty yards from the southwest corner of the cabin, overlooking the snow-shrouded grave of Amigo (our first dog here). Although I could see flicks and blurs of bluish movement, my view of the high-perched birds was mostly blocked by the roof's overhang and a yard-long drape of icicles. As I visually probed, hoping for a glimpse of the villainous character I knew had caused the stir, I noticed something as lovely as it was unlikely: a butterfly—small, blue as an October sky, floating lightly along, not pumping its wings but free-riding on a gentle breeze.

This, I knew, simply could not be—a butterfly at eight thousand feet in the Colorado Rockies on a February morning at two below zero.

And then I saw that it wasn't.

What it was was a powder-blue breast feather, fluffy as eider-down and no larger than a nickel. Then another. Soon, a whole parade of these dainty angels of death came gliding across my view, drifting lazily down from left to right, settling gently atop the snow, forming a line marking the unseen winged hunter's route of departure as it struggled away with its breast-torn prey.

Still hoping for a glimpse of the hawk and its breakfast, I rushed outside—where my rawhide-soled moccasins slipped on the snow and I fell to my knees with a curse and lifted my face skyward in desperate faith, like some crippled, crawling pilgrim . . . but too late. The assassin—a Cooper's hawk, most likely—had already flown the coop. The deed was done, the drama ended—until, of course, the next time. For life to continue, death must always have a next time.

Cleansing winter: so lovely, pure, and unforgiving.

That little drama, as I say, played out earlier today—or, to be chronologically precise, since it's long past midnight now, it happened yesterday morning. Meanwhile, tonight—which technically is tomorrow morning and brings us, thus, back around to early today—I slump ever lower in my chair as grogginess and gravity conspire to drag me mentally and physically down, down. My thoughts, already weak and dim, fade like the flames in the neglected stove . . .

Just in time to save me from a nodding nosedive onto the hardwood floor, I'm roused by a slow, sibilant sizzle, *Sssshhhhh*, issuing from a shadowy corner of the silent room, musical as an angel's fart yet rancid as death's own breath. Now comes a low moan, a muted shuffle, as ancient Angel dog, still asleep but ill at ease, shifts arthritic bones on her padded bed.

Angel: huge, old, and increasingly in the way (like me), she (like me) long ago showed her tail to a poor first draw in life, striking out in search of something better, going it alone, risking all, appearing here one summer day a few years back. At first we tried to ignore the scruffy beast, trusting she would go back home, wherever that might be. But Angel knew before we did that she *was* home. And therefore she persisted, day after night— right ear erect, left ear limp, brown eyes pleading, begging to be taken in.

And so, in due time, we took her in. After all, it's not every day you find an Angel on your doorstep, 110 pounds of grateful love.

And so it goes: you get your mutts for free, then break the bank to keep them running.

· 11 ·

Yet again the woodstove speaks, and this time its message is urgent. What little remains of the bear-scarred log has just exploded—a pocket of trapped core moisture, I suppose; heartwood, heart's blood, expanding into vapor with the calamitous energy of ultimate expiration, hurling glowing shrapnel out the open stove door and across a throw rug. Thin, cheap, and tattered (like me), that old rag of a rug is all that lies between fire and a flammable floor. To save the rug, the hardwood flooring beneath, and perhaps the cabin from catastrophic conflagration, I drop from my chair to my knees and snatch up the livid embers, one at a time, tossing them back into the stove. In a moment of ironic mirth, I grimace to think I'm emulating those tropical foreign fellows who dance barefoot across carpets of glowing coals in order to prove . . . well, *something*.

In the end, the Doghouse is saved by the skin of my hands. And no big deal: a few tips snipped from the ever-ready aloe growing on a south-facing windowsill, sliced open, applied as a poultice, and taped in place—a sure cure for the blistering wages of groggy stupidity.

With the indoor temperature having soared to a steamy fifty-nine, I arrange a fresh load of three aspen splits and one slender limb of oak in the stove, close and latch the door, set the spin-draft for a low slow burn, pet a snoring Angel (she stretches, quivers, and farts again in dreamy appreciation), then slouch at

long last back to bedroom and bed. As I ease between the flannel
sheets, Caroline, my own Sleeping Beauty, greets the cold press
of my skin with a warm and welcoming sigh. I snuggle even
closer. So does she. I am ice; she is fire. Our thermal dynamic is
perfect.

On the floor in a bedroom corner, curled like a furry fetus on
his own comfy bed, Otis snuffles, shifts, and moans, utterly content. Homeostasis returns to the little cabin on the big mountain
in Colorado. Not a creature is stirring, not even a hantavirus-
harboring deer mouse—the latter thanks to our vigilant guard-
ians the foxes, coyotes, falcons, and hawks. And the owls, of
course, who-who have long since fallen silent, enjoying some
dynamic snuggling, perhaps, of their own.

· 12 ·

According to the little plastic thermometer dangling from the
zipper of my day pack, the temperature on this fog-shrouded
morning in early March is a perfect twenty-three. Perfect because
it's cold enough to keep the several inches of new snow that fell
last evening (atop a two-foot base) from going slushy too early in
the day. Perfect also for brisk outdoor exercise; a few degrees more
would be verging on too warm for comfortable cross-country
skiing.

Finding affordable outdoor fun—even such "glamorous" fun
as skiing—is generally just a matter of avoiding the herds, who
love to line up and pay. For this event, on this transitional morning between winter and spring, I've driven less than four miles
from home, into the mountains northward, where the snow is
sufficient for skiing in spite of the winter's drought.

My companions on this little adventure are Nancy (her husband and my good friend George, poor fellow, is in town tending

his bread and butter, the Southwest Book Trader) and Branson Reynolds, a master photographer of southwestern landscapes, Native American people, and naked ladies (none of whom, thus far, have been Native Americans). Caroline is gone for a while and dearly missed, visiting family in Laguna Beach. Our plan is to make a relaxed climb three miles up a snow-closed national forest road, break there for refreshments, then ski the downhill run—steep all the way and curvaceous as Branson's figure models—as fast as our long, skinny planks will carry us. Tractors going up, sports cars coming down.

By the time Nancy and Branson get their lovely, slick-bottomed wooden skis waxed for climbing, I—equipped with a gnarly old pair of five-dollar garage-sale waxless laminates with built-in snow-grabbing scales; good, low-end technology—am a quarter mile ahead. A gentleman always, I stop and wait for my companions to catch up. The fact that Branson has the brandy flask and Nancy is toting our lunches has nothing to do with this courtesy.

The remainder of the morning is much the same: I climb steadily while my friends slip, struggle, speak naughty words, and stop repeatedly to mess with their waxes as the snow conditions change. I wait again. They catch up again. And so it goes.

I'm not trying to outshine my friends and couldn't if I wanted to. Both are far more experienced skiers. Since it's so steep at home, Caroline and I find snowshoes far more practical than skis. Which is to say, we don't ski often. My advantage this morning is purely technical in that scaled skis have the distinct uphill advantage of what Nancy calls "training wheels." Our differences don't really matter. We laugh and joke and have a grand old time in spite of the inequities of our equipment—for everyone knows that payback lies ahead.

As the morning progresses, the fog slowly lifts and dissipates. Soon, visible rays of sunlight are fingering down all around and the sky, fully revealed, has the blue-green sheen of polished turquoise, like a tropical sea.

We ski on. While our legs and lungs do most of the work, our arms share the load by planting long, basket-bottomed poles firmly in the snow and shoving down and back. Done well, the combination of arm- and legwork is poetry in graceful motion. No other physical activity, not even swimming, exercises as many muscles as thoroughly in so short a time while giving so much pleasure in the doing. When you're really into it, your heart and lungs shift into overdrive and stay there as you flick or, on steep climbs such as this, slog along.

In due time we reach our goal, a level spot in the road where a summer foot trail, now obliterated by snow, snakes off toward an alpine beaver pond. After packing down a place to sit, we step out of our bindings and off our skis and plant them upright in the snow alongside our poles, then unfold a big plastic tarp and plop ourselves down for lunch. Nancy produces the main course, turkey sandwiches. I contribute a thermos of coffee. Branson hauls out the flask. For water we eat snow.

Life is good, and save for a quarter's worth of gas, this day is utterly free.

An hour later we're well rested, bellies comfortably full, moods as mellow as cognac. With the sun booming down from a cobalt sky, the temptation is to strip to our Skivvies and lie back for a snooze. The midday sunshine, however, is a decidedly mixed blessing, for already the snow is glistening with a thin film of meltwater, promising, should we dally much longer, a sticky and sluggish downhill run. So we stand and prepare to deliver. While Nancy and Branson scrape their skis clean of this morning's soft gripping wax and apply a hard, fast wax for the downhill race, I step aboard my waxless wonders, snap down the wire boot-binding bails, and push off, looking for a bit of a lead. But my advantage soon proves insufficient. From close behind I hear Branson's shout of "Payback, sucker!" as he and Nancy come sizzling past—*Ssstt! Sssstt!*—crouching low, poles tucked under armpits, leaning artfully through the bend ahead and out of sight. Everyone hates a showoff.

Alone again at last, I stoically plug along, moving mostly under my own power, the friction of my skis' scales fighting gravity and working hard against me. Not once do I get a fast, free ride of more than a few dozen yards. Oh well. No magic works all the time, and I comfort myself with the thought that even as I poke—not effortlessly, yet easily and with a great deal of joy— down this lonely, lovely mountain road, basking in the warming glow of restorative sunlight and exercise, my fast-lane companions are standing in the chilly shade beside the truck, stamping cold feet and waiting.

For I have the keys in my pocket.

So goes a typical morning of cross-country ski touring, mountain style. Not a penny have we spent for admission nor a lift line have we stood in; neither long drive nor crowded parking lot nor designer-draped tourists have we suffered. Just God's own carpet of white beneath our skinny skis, a broad blue sky above, and the blessing of time spent among best friends in the very best of places—the free and natural world.

Even so, I admit to being tired of winter by now, eager to put away the snow shovel and get back to walking on nice dark dirt and rock. Happily, we haven't much longer to wait.

· 13 ·

For the past week of evenings, in anticipation of spring's pending return and the personal liberation and physical restoration that come with it, I've been rereading Andrew Weil's classic *8 Weeks to*

Optimum Health. It's an old text, granted, but like me it's still straight and solid and filled with good advice. Essential to Dr. Weil's "optimum health" strategy for taking charge of your own mental and physical weal is regular walking, the benefits of which he substantiates as multifloral.

For instance, Weil advises us that "walking offers benefits that other forms of activity do not, such as conditioning rhythms in the brain in response to the coordinated motions of the arms and legs." Moreover, says the charismatic physician, while all walking is good, relaxed walking in natural surroundings is better because "connecting with nature is healing. It slows us down, takes us out of our routines and reminds us that we live on a remarkable planet that we share with many other forms of life. Walking or sitting quietly in a natural setting is a simple form of meditation, an antidote for being too much in our heads, too focused on thoughts and emotions."

Too self-absorbed. Too self-centered.

Walking helps to draw us out.

Walking as mobile meditation.

Among my most valued advisers is Dr. Florence Rose Shepard. Although Flo has not read Andy Weil on walking, she backs his views as I've related them based on her own long experience. Last June, she and C and I were strolling together across the rolling sage plains near her Bondurant, Wyoming, summer cabin, watching pregnant pronghorn does and busy birds of prey, when Flo offered an abrupt non sequitur: "Walking draws up ideas for me. It may be that movement, motion, and terrain all interact to reach into the unconscious. That's certainly the way I experience it."

Me too. Nor are we and Andy Weil by any means the first to discover the mental magic of bootstrap meditation. After all,

Jesus wasn't likely reviewing his investments portfolio during those mysterious forty days and nights he spent wandering the Sinai Desert, alone save for occasional visits from angel emeritus Lucifer.

Another well-known wandering prophet was Henry David Thoreau, who went so far as to praise walking as the "noble art." The contrary implication, which he elsewhere makes quite clear, is that sitting and riding are ignoble and artless. Speaking of acquaintances who spent most of their lives indoors and never walked when they could ride, Henry is not entirely joking when he quips, "I think that they deserve some credit for not having all committed suicide long ago."

As exaggerated as that sounds, the sage of Walden Pond is not only dead serious, he's dead-on. Indoor "living" and prolonged lack of exercise are well-known catalysts for emotional as well as physical degeneration, that is, depression.

And depression, in turn, is among suicide's favorite friends.

If you're looking for a tool for battling depression, I can offer personal testimony in praise of walking. Sustained aerobic exertion of any sort—say, struggling up a snow-packed mountain on cross-country skis—temporarily ameliorates the acute symptoms of depression by stimulating the brain to manufacture soothing endorphins and other pain-relieving, mood-elevating, morphine-emulating chemicals, at the best of times facilitating the mythic (as opposed to mythical) runner's high. And indeed, back when I could do it (before I ruined a knee by overdoing it), running was a wonder drug in my marathon struggle against grinding depression resulting from loneliness and an unshakable feeling that I was wasting my life or already had. Although I was barely thirty, it was a midlife crisis. And running helped me beat it.

These days, while I still find physical exertion an effective antidote to melancholia, I rarely let myself get far enough down to need such a lift. These days, rather than waiting until I need an antidote to depression, I keep that old blue devil at bay by taking long, relaxed, spontaneously reflective daily strolls alone in the surrounding woods. Silent aimless ambling in tranquil natural surroundings helps distract if not extract us from the emotionally claustrophobic shell of critical introspection and self-pity; helps place our personal lives in soul-soothing context as miraculous, yes, yet infinitesimal droplets in the great tossing sea of life, death, and rebirth, rolling on and on forever. In this gentle way, reflective walking helps humble us without the searing pain of humiliation; helps put seemingly overwhelming personal problems into a larger, thus diluted and far less overwhelming context. And as Professor Flo suggests, walking also facilitates creative spontaneity.

Through it all, best of all, walking alone in natural surroundings lifts the blinding veil and clutter of culture to reveal the living face of peace and beauty in nature and ourselves. In a human-made world gone horribly out of whack, nature provides the only unimpeachably, unwaveringly reliable source of sanity and hope we have. No faith required, since the living proof is always at foot, encouraging us to touch, see, hear, smell, even taste. Ambling in wild nature—or, lacking that ideal, in the most serene, safe, and natural setting we can find—facilitates a Zen-like state of mental clarity and feelings of personal well-being, in part because, as Dr. Weil points out, the repetitive motion of walking has the effect of "conditioning rhythms" of mind and mood to match those of legs, arms, and lungs. As does Nordic skiing. Yet, because our inner mood tends to absorb and reflect the outer mood surrounding us, the former is relaxing while the latter is invigorating. Though both offer physical benefits, it's hard to find solace in speed. As William Wordsworth poetically puts it, walking alone opens "that inward eye which is the bliss of solitude."

Having long since discovered the wonders of walking, young

Henry David claimed he couldn't stay indoors and inactive for more than a few hours at a stretch "without acquiring some rust." And rust never sleeps. Either we keep at it religiously, flexing and oiling our bodies, minds, and spirits with focused daily physical and intellectual exercise, or the insomniac corrosion of chronic sloth insidiously consumes us, eating us guts-first alive, like the cancerous creature it is.

· 14 ·

Gradually the greater world beyond the cabin windows—the *real* world of nature—reawakens, slipping its blanket of snow to reveal green new life beneath, ready to roll. And like that green new life, after months of far too much time spent indoors, we too are hot to trot. Day by day, as the snow patches dwindle, our walks grow longer, greener, and more exciting.

Just now, as Caroline glides (and Otis gallops) down the two-track drive toward my office, returning from a typical three-hour morning walk, I see in her petite right fist a stem of some leafy herbaceous plant, blue-green and dull. What now? Like a child collecting snakes and frogs, she's forever hauling in some little treasure or other from the wilds.

Two days ago she carted in a shard of whitish eggshell, perhaps mourning dove, remarkable in that the delicate artifact, whatever the species, is a survivor of last summer's hatch.

Yesterday she hauled home the greasy fresh skull of a young raccoon she had found near a known bear denning area at a place we call the Point of Rocks, where I'd rather she didn't venture alone in spring, since if a bear in fact winters there it is due to emerge real soon, at least if it's a male. (Sows with cubs sleep a few weeks longer.) Waking spring bears tend to lounge just outside their winter digs for several days, defecating the plug of forest litter that has bunged their bowels all winter and otherwise getting their digestive act back together before moving on to begin a new season of roaming—so it's a good time and place for a bad encounter. Naturally, given my overt concern and C's covert independence, she made a special point to go there alone, where she found the once and former coon's cranial remains and carted the skull home to show me: a conversation piece, Petersen style.

Several long gray whiskers were still attached to scraps of dried meat on the muzzle, and the top of the skull had been bitten off by some enterprising carnivore to get at the high-fat brains. (Historically and prehistorically, through countless cultures, we humans have done the same.) The condition of this smelly item, preserved all winter by snow and cold and only just now, with the slow unveiling of spring, exposed to light and air, along with the fact there were no other bones nearby, provoked a discussion between us regarding what brand of carnivore had killed or scavenged the little killer.

And raccoons *are* killers, miniature bears, opportunistic predatory omnivores with fanglike canines and crushing-and-grinding molars, munchers of veggies and mast when they must and rippers of flesh when they can get their dexterous paws on it. Common coon chow includes birds' eggs and flightless chicks, bunny babes and occasional adult rabbits, crawdads, fish and other aquatic protein, bugs, carrion, and, just like bears, reachable bird feeders and carelessly stored pet food and garbage.

So it is, with this morning's mystery item in hand, C approaches Angel and me as we stand in the sun out front of my Outhouse office, from whence we've just emerged. My wife smiles coyly, as is her way when preoccupied or scheming, and says simply, "Hi."

I hi her back and ask, "Whatcha got there, darlin'?"

"Not sure," she says. "That's why I brought it home—in order to find out."

My smart-aleck spouse proffers the mystery plant for my

inspection, and I see that it's topped with numerous umbrella clusters of tiny, off-white flowers. Per usual in the rare-flower department, I am clueless. (Like stars, bugs, and little brown birds, there are so *many* of them.)

A few minutes later, with a cup of hot tea in hand (her Limey heritage), our resident amateur botanist begins paging through our library of illustrated field guides, searching for a match. When she finds it, she'll confirm by cross-referencing other books. Once certain, she'll add the name, date, and location of the find to her encyclopedic memory and her written phenology (calendar journal of seasonal biological events) of local life and events.

Today's specimen proves to be *Comandra umbellate*, commonly called pale comandra, a perennial herb native to specific eco-niches throughout the American West. Like politicians, CEOs, CFOs, televangelists, insurance executives, medical-management groups, lawyers, and land developers, this plant gains an unearned living by parasitizing the roots of its fellow plants and is also known, less gently, as bastard toadflax. "Name It If You Can" (plant, bone, hunk of fur, shell shard, turd) is a game we love to play because, as with hunting, it is played primarily outdoors. Suddenly and without premeditation I hear myself asking, "What do you think about when you're out walking alone?"

"Huh?"

Fair question. The poor girl, locked in her flowery concentration, is understandably confused by my abrupt leap of topic. So I back up and try again.

"What do you *think* about when you're out there walking, hours on end, day after day, with no one to talk to but Otis and the trees?"

"Oh," she says, smiling bemusedly, "nothing and everything."

While that sounds like a dodge, I know that it isn't. I grin and nod my concurrence.

"Me too."

Which is to say that when out walking, Caroline and I both practice the antithesis of Zen "mindfulness"; we become mind-*less*. Blissfully *un*aware of our breathing (except when we take a steep pitch too fast), of our footfalls (except to avoid making undue noise or walking on wildflowers), of our*selves*, as much as that can be. Not trying to think of anything. Not trying to *not* think of anything. Simply walking—watching Otis sniff and poop and do his Little Tramp waddle (the legacy of a fractured pelvis suffered as a pup) and, this rebirthing time of year, pondering the secret language of chirping neotropicals just now returning north from their southern wintering grounds, breathing deep the fresh clean smell of erupting spring—our minds wide open to the smallest external cues, unobstructed by internal static. And all the while, without conscious thought or effort, our senses are scanning for anything new, unusual, and thus of special interest: an unfamiliar plant or fresh animal track, a gooey smelly bear plop (been eating meat) or green-black hay-scented bear biscuits (been foraging veggies), feathers (preened and plucked by their owners, or yanked out by a predator?), a shard of bone or eggshell (clean inside suggests that the chick hatched success-fully while dried interior goop speaks of failed incubation, pre-dation, or an accidental fall from nesting grace). Such little clues prompt speculation that leads in turn to such cosmic koans as, Why is an ermine (the winter phase of the short-tailed weasel) perfectly white—*except* for a conspicuously black-tipped tail?

This past December, C and O had just stepped outside one snowy morning when a churning blur of white came hissing out from under the woodpile to thrash furiously around on the snow just a few feet away. When Otis instinctively made a dash at the whirling albino dervish, the ermine let go of its prey—a snow-shoe hare many times the weasel's size and weight, also winter white, which the tiny killer had grasped by the neck with its fangs and was riding like a rodeo cowboy. When Otis inter-rupted, the ermine ran one way, the hare another, while Caroline just stood and watched, awestruck. Later she would allow, "Weasels have to eat, just like everything else. But there are plenty of mice around, and I'm glad the bunny got away."

Fair enough, I reckon, unless you are a hungry weasel.

But no matter what we do or do not see, hear, smell, or collect on a given outing, the result is always the same: when we are walking quietly in the woods alone, the weight and woes of our purely personal and human concerns fall away unnoticed. The walker is transported, expanded into the more-than-human world . . . where we all came from and, in our deepest heart of hearts, continue to belong. Where everything fills a meaningful niche and nothing exists by chance.

Ermines, for example, are themselves attractive prey to larger predators, particularly great horned owls. Were it not for the ermine's black-tipped tail, a winged hunter would have an advantage, since it instinctively leads its target by aiming for the tiny dark dots of nose and eyes at the head of the blurry, snow-camouflaged form. In its conspicuously contrasting tail tip, the ermine has a built-in decoy, tricking its predators, particularly those who hunt at night from the air, into aiming for that highly visible and hard-to-hold inch of expendable hair, thereby greatly increasing the weasel's chance of escape, survival, and continued procreation.

This is natural selection and evolution in action. And thus is the Darwinian phrase "survival of the fittest" tragically misconstrued when taken to mean "survival of the strongest"—or meanest or smartest or richest. Rather, evolutionary fitness is measured by how well a species, plant or animal, adapts itself to fit, not fight, its environment. In the end, long-term survival and prosperity—for humanity as for all species—are products not of force but of finesse.

In sum, we live to walk and walk to live, C and O and I. And occasionally our walks get weird—like that spooky evening a few years back when I ran into Bigbutt.

———

The monsters among us, real and imagined ...

The last known native Colorado grizzly bear was killed in close combat with a bowhunter it attacked in September 1979 in the South San Juan Wilderness Area, some sixty miles from here. Before then, no one had seen a grizzly in Colorado for decades. Since then, reports of grizzly sightings hereabouts have become an annual phenomenon. Most such "grizzlies" turn out to be brown- or blond-phase black bears, and the few sightings that promise potential credibility invariably lack such solid supporting evidence as photographs or track casts. But whether the sightings are real or imagined, one thing is sure: now that the grizzly is (probably) gone from these mountains forever, people want it back—or at least they want the thrilling *idea* of it back: ghost grizzlies.

Another example: while working in rural North Carolina years ago, in the foothills of the Smoky Mountains, I learned that panther (mountain lion, cougar, puma) sightings were an active part of local folklore—no matter that *Felis concolor* had long ago been killed out thereabouts. More curious yet, every single sighting report involved a *black* panther. Why black? Because, it's fair to speculate, black is spookier, more mysterious, and a practical impossibility, thus more befitting a ghostly mythical creature.

It's likewise fair to speculate that this ironic but culturally universal human craving for preternatural beings explains the widespread belief in "crypto" creatures—animal freaks with no antecedents in nature, like Scotland's Loch Ness "monster," South American space aliens, African dinosaurs, the werewolves of London, and, of course, our own North American Bigfoot. Traditionally, this last creature has been reduced in hokey novels and horror flicks to a murderous ape-man, a kidnapper and rapist. (Introducing a new twist on this pulpy old theme, the supermarket tabloid *Weekly World News* once ran a cover photo of a dazed-looking plump fellow with a headline confessing, "I Was Bigfoot's Sex Slave!") But sighting reports that strive for credibility generally characterize Bigfoot as a shy and curious Peeping Tom suffering a permanent bad-hair day. Hardly a monster at all—yet big, mysterious, and undeniably scary. Exactly like the "thing" I once met right here on Spring Mountain.

During archery big-game season each fall, I am out there almost every day for a month or more, often well after dark. On morning hunts, with hours to get myself lost and found again, I'm a hardy explorer and long-haul hiker. But as evening approaches, I'm coming increasingly (with age and the conservative wisdom of experience) to appreciate familiar scenery, preferably within a short walk of one of the grown-over logging trails that scar the mountains hereabouts, remnants of a mule-powered salvage logging operation conducted in the wake of the last major wildfire, a hundred years ago. None are navigable today by anything with wheels, and all provide a blowdown-littered challenge even for horses. But they're perfect for foot-powered sneak hunting and provide fast access up and down steep wooded slopes, especially in the dark. During two decades of quietly coming and going along these old trails, I've enjoyed some excitingly close encounters, including run-ins with countless elk and deer, several bears, and one mountain lion, yellow as summer butter, a ghostly specter that floated silently across just ahead of me, right at the edge of darkness. I love it all—and all of which is by way of saying that I bear no phobic fears of woods or wildlife, day or night. I don't drink or smoke wacky-weed while hunting, and I don't believe in the tooth fairy, Santa Claus, trickle-down economics, Iraqi weapons of mass destruction, or "Your check is in the mail." That said, here is my Bigbutt story.

———

It was late September and I'd sat in evening ambush over Hillside Spring for several quiet hours while the elk were someplace else. When the last good shooting light was gone, I quietly picked up and headed cross-country toward a logging trail that would snake me down the mountain to home. From my hunting spot above the spring to the trail took about fifteen minutes at tiptoe speed. Once on the familiar byway I picked up my pace a bit, having declared the day's hunt done. Even so, I try never to make unnecessary noise in the woods, whether hunting or just hiking; it's a matter of respect, like not using a cell phone in a quiet public place. With my eyes adjusted to the dark, as I walked downhill toward an open starlit sky, the ground and trees provided a silhouette horizon that allowed me to follow the twisting, tunnel-like cut through the old-growth forest without a flashlight, as is my preference. After poking along for a bit, I approached a right-hand bend in the trail and was startled to see, coming around that bend toward me, just twenty yards below, the hulking form of some two-legged shadowy thing. In the same instant, whatever it was saw me. We both stopped short and stared, though I could see no glint of eye in the hairy face.

Studying this eerie stranger in the night, I registered two short legs, two long arms with huge hands or paws, a short thick neck, and big head bushy with hair. The face was rounded and broad and covered with dark hair or a beard. No hat (unless the "hair" was in fact a hat) or clothing, so far as I could tell. Upright posture, bipedal locomotion, just over five feet tall and easily two hundred pounds. From the side, which I'd glimpsed briefly as the creature rounded the bend, its body appeared as thick as it was wide, with no obvious lumps that could be a pack or other load. Likewise, the hands (or paws) looked empty. While I could not see the feet, big or small, I was struck by the protruding mass of the shadow creature's posterior. All things considered, my first impression was "short, big-butted, bearded man." But then it struck me that Bigbutt's legs were too short in proportion to its arms and upper body to be human. Besides, I had never before encountered anyone so far up our mountain after dark (a meeting is rare even in daylight). The idea of someone headed uphill and into the wilds on a chilly, moonless night, without a flashlight or gear of any kind, seemed nonsensical. And if the being was human, why was he acting so . . . strange?

My next thought was "bear." Certainly, an adult bear standing on its hind legs could cast a silhouette similar to what I was seeing. But Bigbutt had no protruding ears, a flattish face rather than an elongated muzzle, and front-set eyes; furthermore, its legs, though too short to be human, looked too long for a bear. And how often do bears stroll around on their hind legs in the dark? I almost called out, "Hello?" But for reasons I can't explain, I held off.

Though I was buzzing on adrenaline, I wasn't really scared. Even so, as the tense frozen seconds passed, it occurred that maybe I should make ready to defend myself, just in case. My recurve bow hung from my left hand, with four arrows in a bow-mounted quiver. I wore a small sheath knife on my belt and had a mini-flashlight in a jacket pocket. Not wanting to startle the creature, I moved slowly to extract an arrow from the quiver and place it on the bow string. But even that was enough to prompt Bigbutt, obviously the nervous sort, to shuffle to the edge of the old road cut—a sudden move that made me jump and set my heart to thumping.

With an arrow strung and the creature now standing at the edge of the woods, swaying slowly back and forth as if trying to get a better sense of me, I reached for my flashlight. This second movement, small as it was, was enough to prompt Bigbutt to lurch into the blackness of the adjacent trees and brush. By the time I got the flashlight out and turned on and pointed down that way, just a couple of fumbling seconds, there was nothing left to see. Incredibly, this beast the size of a bear or a man had made no sound moving into or through the dry woods, an eerie anomaly that set me worrying that it had not gone far and was crouching there, just off the trail . . . waiting.

But waiting for what?

Now I did call out, calmly but in a strong voice: "Hello?"

Silence. Darkness. A wormy squirming in my guts.

My options were but two: backtrack, circle wide, and rejoin the trail farther down (a *lot* farther down), or walk right by where Bigbutt had just been standing and might still be lurking. After waiting a long tense minute or so, listening and shining the light all around, I took a deep breath and edged cautiously down the trail, hugging to the side opposite where Bigbutt had been. As I approached what felt very much like a danger zone, I nosed the air for any unusual scent, animal or otherwise, but found only the piney night. Nor did my torch's yellow beam reveal anything crouching among the brush and trees.

Safely past, I stopped to listen and look some more, fighting a sudden reckless urge to go back and investigate. Finally, I returned the arrow to the quiver, laid my bow on the ground, withdrew my skinning knife from its sheath, took the flashlight in my other hand, and moved cautiously back up to where the thing had stood. But the ground there was hard-packed and rocky and nothing for tracks. Increasingly convinced that whatever it was was gone, I ventured a few nervous steps off the trail for a better look around. Finding nothing, I retreated, retrieved my bow, and hurried down the mountain and home to tell my incredible story to an openly skeptical wife.

The next morning, my courage recharged by the sun, I returned to Bigbutt country, conducted a thorough search, and found . . . nothing.

And there you have it. I've tried and tried to convince myself it was a bear with an unnatural talent and weird preference for walking around upright in the dark or some wacko human with an equally unlikely appearance and behavior (we have several such in town). But neither supposition is any more convincing today than it was at the time.

And the greater mystery yet is how anything that big—bear, man, or spaced-out alien—could simply *disappear*, without so much as a rustle or crunch, into a crunchy woods.

Who knows?

Who cares?

I do, I suppose—still care, that is—insofar as even now, every time I approach that spot alone in the dark, or kill a deer or elk at twilight and get stuck out there alone butchering, late into the night, reeking of blood and guts with my flashlight growing dim, and hear a mysterious crunch, bump, or snap out in the inky void . . . well, you know how it feels.

But no worries no more. These days, and especially these nights, I pack an aerosol can of hot-pepper courage, whether hunting or merely hiking. While most folks call it "bear spray," I think of it as my Bigbutt blaster.

I reiterate that I'm no "believer." I find mystery and awe aplenty in the known and natural world. And should I feel the need to be frightened for my life, I'll visit some big city and walk around at night. But I did see *something* out there—something large and very alive, something sentient and willful and beyond logical comprehension. While I have no doubt that a perfectly pragmatic explanation exists, I doubt I'll ever find it, since I don't intend to look.

· 15 ·

All of the foregoing talk about the physical, emotional, and (in the case of Bigbutt encounters) mystical benefits of walking—well, that's all fine and dandy for such rural dwellers as C and Otis and me. But an easy majority of people today live in concreted, traffic-clogged, cacophonous, and often dangerous urban and suburban settings that offer little opportunity for regular walks in safe and tranquil surrounds, much less anything remotely resembling friendly intercourse with my truly wild (as opposed to park-employee-manicured) nature. Yet urban and suburban living doesn't have to preclude the enjoyment of mobile meditation, even though it mostly does. That this ancient, natural medicine for body, mind, and psyche is so widely unattainable in these overcrowded days points to the ignorance and unresponsiveness of urban planners and suburban developers about the most basic needs of the human spirit—needs that, after all, evolved from within the wildest sort of nature imaginable and, thus, can be satisfied only in nature.

Only when our cities and suburbs come to incorporate extensive natural elements in their design and ambience, including reasonable efforts to provide insulation from blaring traffic noise and glaring artificial lighting, significant areas made off-limits to motorized vehicles, and sternly enforced laws against publicly played private music (that's why God invented Walkmans), will the places where most of us live begin to feel like home. Only then will our children be safe alone outdoors and on the right spiritual path, and our minds and bodies allowed to return, at long last, to their biologically intended state of natural ease.

If I lived in a city or suburb, as I have before and might someday again (who can know the future?), that's what I'd be working for, hard and long: a tranquil, safe, pleasant, and natural place to walk, retreat, reflect, heal, and re-create.

· **16** ·

Our longest walks as a family generally come in summer, under the liberating weight of backpacks, when even the highest passes are briefly snow-free and mountain streams are low enough to be fordable and fishing is prime and no wild place is out of bounds, given grit, will, and time. In the solo realm, my favorite walks begin in late summer and continue through autumn, undertaken while scouting and hunting, when intensity of purpose and the need for stealth enhance perception, reflection, and pleasure. But for both of us, C and me, the most self-evidently joyful walks, year after year, together and alone, always come in spring.

This late March afternoon, after two gorgeous weeks of warm, cloudless days, barely freezing nights, and a rapidly regreening world, I decide to venture up the mountain and partway down the far side, probing for the first time since last fall into the wapiti's secret world: my private heaven here on Earth. They're on the move now, those giant Pleistocene deer, sneaking down in the safety of night to graze on sweet new grass. Last night, a cow or yearling bull (judging by the size of its tracks) strolled boldly into our yard, where it tromped around, nibbled green sprigs, and took a bite from the compressed birdseed block that sat on the ground all winter, just outside our bedroom. Of all our feral neighbors, none brings us more joy, in more ways on more nights and days, than the wapiti.

Hippity-hoppity, here comes the wapiti.

A silly little ditty, you bet, but it's an easy way to remember the correct pronunciation of the proper name of North America's most vocal deer. Not *wa-PEE-tee*, as novices are wont to say, but *WOP-a-tee.* While the word is Shawnee for "white rump," "beige butt" would be more apt. The more familiar common name, *elk*, traces back to a case of mistaken identity, when early European immigrants—farmers and tradesmen, not hunters and naturalists—misidentified the animal, which was new to them, as *elch*, the German name for moose, which, in its turn, enters the English (together with the Swedish and Norwegian) as *elk*.

The wapiti is the second largest of North America's five-member deer (cervid) family. The Cervidae includes, in general descending order of size, the moose, wapiti, caribou, mule deer, and whitetail.

Although not as big as a moose, the North American elk is huge, averaging five hundred pounds for mature cows and seven hundred pounds for mature bulls, with half-ton bulls the rare maximum these days. Nose to rump, the average elk goes eight feet or so (their tails are stumpy and of no great measure). In the transition from woods to freezer, the average wapiti nets about two hundred pounds of choice boneless meat that's notably lighter and less gamey than venison, rather like a cross between deer and beef and the leanest red meat you can eat. Another element of the wapiti's appeal, to hunters and nonconsumptive viewers alike, is its massive, ornate antlers. Those worn by mature bulls, six years and older, commonly have six long tines, or points, per side, with each main beam standing four feet high or higher and with a spread between beams of four feet or more. During the fall breeding season, or rut, the bugled calls of bull elk lend the mountains an inimitably eerie mood. And thanks to the tenacious efforts of the North American hunter-conservationist community, wapiti are once again numerous and widespread, with at least one million of the wild, free-ranging ungulates roaming twenty-six states and every Canadian province. Of that total, Colorado can claim at least a quarter. Happily, my home mountains host a significant percentage of that statewide bounty, and our own Spring Mountain a fair share of that, especially during the spring and fall migration periods.

Although the wapiti is hailed as a native North American, in the long view of geologic time the elk, like its human predators, is a last-minute arrival.

According to the fossil record, about 1.3 million years ago, early in the Pleistocene epoch, elk first appeared as a distinct genus, *Cervus*, in central Asia, having split from the sika deer lineage. From their evolutionary cradle in the foothills of the Himalayas, ancestral elk spread west into Europe, adapting to their new surroundings to become the red deer (*Cervus elaphus elaphus*). At the same time, another branch of the primordial *Cervus* clan drifted east, adjusting to the harder winters, higher mountains, and open grassy steppes of Mongolia and the Siberian Uplands. Descendants of this second, more adventurous group continued to disperse across the Chukchi Peninsula and, eventually, onto the low-lying mammoth steppe of Beringia, also known as the Bering Land Bridge. And there they remained for hundreds of millennia, evolving to fit their new, climatically harsh, half-Asian, half-American habitat and to outwit its deadly predators (human hunters included), in time becoming the wapiti we know today (*Cervus elaphus canadensis*).

As the last Ice Age began to thaw, billions of tons of ice-locked ocean water were released from glaciers. Sea levels consequently rose, and Beringia began to "sink"—a gradual (though geologically rapid) inundation that concluded only about ten thousand years ago. Forced to higher ground, some Beringian wapiti were isolated on the Siberian side while others wound up in Alaska. And so it is, today, that wapiti on both sides of the Bering Strait look the same, sound the same, behave the same, taste the same, even stink the same in rut. They *are* the same. The Eurasian red deer, meanwhile, even though it belongs to the same genus as our wapiti, manifests readily identifiable differences in size, coloration, antler configuration, behavior, and voice.

From Alaska, the ancestral wapiti dispersed to occupy every habitable niche throughout our continent—and then, ironically, went extinct in Alaska. (Although they've recently been successfully reintroduced there as island populations.)

Since little genetic change can take place in mammals as large and complex as the elk in just ten thousand years, true subspeciation of North American wapiti is doubtful. Far more likely is that all four living North American elk "subspecies" (plus two extinct models, the Eastern and Merriam's) are in fact one and the same critter. Their minor morphological (physical) differences are merely short-term regional adaptations. Consequently, such newly popular alternative terms as *geographic variants* and *ecotypes* are more accurate than *subspecies*. But the subspecies concept is so deeply ingrained in the American biological and hunter vernacular that, right or wrong, the four familiar wapiti types—Rocky Mountain (also known as Yellowstone), Roosevelt's (Olympic), Tule (dwarf), and Manitoban—will for now remain in active play.

During the autumn rut each year, mature bulls employ both vocal and visual advertisements to attract females. Those same bugles and antler displays serve secondarily as threats to intimidate competing males. In a balanced population, a rutting hierarchy evolves that allows the fittest mature bulls to enjoy most of the breeding opportunities and pass their superior (time- and survival-tested) genes on to future generations.

In all deer species, antlers are luxury tissues. No matter how genetically blessed a bull or buck may be, only after the animal's primary survival needs are satisfied—bone and muscle growth and the healing of injuries and infections—will surplus nutritional resources be channeled into exceptional antler growth. Since big, symmetrical antlers signal both genetic and individual fitness, estrous cows are instinctively attracted to the best-hung buglers. Meanwhile, in overhunted and otherwise stressed and imbalanced populations, younger, inexperienced males are left to do most of the breeding. They generally do it poorly, greatly enhancing stress for all concerned and leading to late and failed pregnancies, smaller and later-born calves come spring, higher calf mortality the following winter, and, potentially, permanently stunted elk. Consequently, since most elk managers today look only at "recruitment" figures—births minus infant deaths—they are taking a dangerously short-term view. Yes, immature bulls do successfully impregnate cows when older bulls are lacking. And yes, this keeps the numbers up. But what about the long-term welfare of the species itself? Doesn't forcing an animal to repro-duce, generation after generation and potentially forever, within a biological paradigm that's radically different from what evolu-tion decreed raise some bright red flags?

Not so far as I can see among state wildlife commissions and career agency biologists who serve them. But of course I am merely a hunter and wildlife watcher, a lowly nature freak. What do I know?

I know, at least, that most cows begin breeding in their third autumn and produce one calf a year throughout their long reproductive lives. Elk twins are a magnificent rarity. Calving season is mid-May through mid-June, peaking around the first of June. At birth, calves average about thirty-five pounds. Weight gain is rapid, with youngsters adding more than a pound a day throughout the summer. By September, a healthy calf will be big-ger, on average, than an adult deer and on the fend for itself. Cows can live twenty years or longer in the wild, while bulls are lucky to make it past the age of three, when they become legal prey for human hunters in most states, as "raghorns" (three- or four-point subadults). Beyond the security of national parks, pre-cious few bulls in these times of rampant habitat destruction, media-nourished trophy-hunting mania, and insufficient protec-tion attain the prime antler-growing ages of six to twelve years.

And so unfurls another spring, up here on Spring Mountain.

· 17 ·

An ibuprofen kind of day. When Otis wakes me just after daylight with a vigorous head shake and attendant noisy flap-flapping of leathery ears—dogs learn to do this as a nonvocal means of requesting attention—I see that the world outside has changed for the better. Where yesterday all was green and brown with sprouting grass and snowmelt mud, now all is white again. A brief relapse into winter, and not at all uncommon. Eight inches of snow on the ground at dawn and more still falling. Apropos for the season, this is spring snow, or graupel. "Corn snow" in the mountain vernacular. "Popcorn snow" is another apt moniker, but by any name I'll be moving the dense granular stuff today. And to get a jump on the predictable lower-back pain that comes with such repetitive stoop labor as shoveling heavy snow, I've learned to start such days—same as chain-sawing and elk-packing days—by downing a brace of pain pills before the pain begins.

While shoveling snow, roof raking (in fact, roof "rakes" more closely resemble giant hoes with really long handles, but "roof hoeing" lacks alliterate appeal), putting snow chains on the truck and taking them off, and other forms of serious snow play are sometimes major hassles, spring snow makes me smile. Aside from its cleansing beauty, a good March snow melts rapidly to become April wildflowers and May morels, chokecherries blooming to perfume the June breeze, the sound of mountain water all summer long, brim-full reservoirs for farmers and fishers, and groundwater in the well for us. Spring snow is mosquitoes soon to hatch and trout leaping after and chorus frogs peeping from hidden vernal ponds and nighthawks at dusk above. March snow is green grass for spring elk calves and den-starved emerging bears. Snow is the lifeblood of mountains.

Besides, as warm as the days are getting, this dump won't last for long.

Nor did it.

And so, here we are, the usual suspects, on our final evening outing of the month. While snow lingers in places—patchy and shallow on north- and east-facing slopes, deeper and solid down in shaded hollows—most of the mountain is again snow-free, and the wildflowers are having their day. Among the first are the tiny pink claytonias, spring beauties, whose root bulbs taste sweet and nutty. White-rimmed wild candytufts, as big around as quarters, are showing everywhere. So are the first dandelions, which Caroline claims to hate, protesting correctly that they're nonnative, invasive, and "ugly when they die and go to seed." Quite so, I gently counter, but aren't we all? Besides, tender new dandelion leaves add a special zest to salads, while the entire plant is a favored food for countless animals and birds, especially wild turkeys—like the tom I just heard gobble off across the valley, between here and Miss Erica's place.

The first wild gobble of spring! This news will make our local huntress wide-eyed with anticipation, even as it thrills me to the Paleolithic core. Late April and early May is turkey time here, and hunting them, win or lose, is a cherished celebration of renewal, a rite of death in celebration of the rebirth of life. For a broken month of mornings I will rise in the dark, dress hurriedly in camouflage, gulp strong coffee, toss some snacks into a pack, check my bow and arrows (or, in the old days my fifty-year-old shotgun), and step out into the black and cold for a long, bracing walk up the mountain. I'll be out well before the first hint of dawn, the aspens and oaks yet leafless from winter, the temperature at or below freezing, the snow still crusted here and there and more so as I climb.

Only the hunt can move me so.

· 18 ·

"I can't shoot!"

My companion's whisper is quiet as thought and further muffled by the leaf-print gauze of her camouflage face mask. Sitting close beside me, Erica—flight attendant and "gnarly mountain chick" (her own description, and fair enough)—is sighting down the barrel of a shotgun almost as big as her.

"Good," I whisper back, not joking.

Since we've got our backs against the same fat tree to facilitate whispered communication, I notice that Erica is trembling. Notwithstanding the nineteen-degree chill on this April mountain morning, she is shaking not from the cold but from acute excitement. Just a few feet in front of us, two tom turkeys are locked in a cockfight so fierce it will likely end with the death or debilitating mutilation of one or both warriors; in either event, food for coyotes but none for us.

Although I know she heard me, Erica's perpetually tanned cheek (Hispanic and Basque) remains pressed to the stock of her twelve-bore shoulder cannon, her finger poised above the trigger. She's hoping the tangled birds will separate long enough to give her a shot at one or the other.

Frankly, this time, I'm pulling for the birds.

The eastern horizon went rosy at 5:03 A.M. this pre–daylight savings morning, among the earliest sunrises of the year. In order to hike the two miles and one thousand vertical feet up from my cabin and arrive here before the crepuscular rose brightened to yellow, revealing all secrets, I had to abandon the comforts of Caroline and covers just three and a half hours after midnight and scoot out the door a few minutes later with just one cup of coffee and two cookies to run on.

Insane, perhaps.

Meanwhile, half a mile down the valley, in her own cabin, Erica got up even earlier in order to shower, eat a bowl of oatmeal, and still make our four A.M. rendezvous. For a hunting date, Erica is never late.

On our slow, stumbling, snow-crunching walk up the mountain

in the dark (gnarly mountain chicks and macho mountain men don't need flashlights) we heard no gobbles. But from recent scouting hikes I knew that several birds were working the area, as evidenced by an abundance of soft, moist droppings and sharp-edged tracks; circular dusting bowls that hadn't had time to collect pine needles or other blowing debris; preened feathers and the dark dampness of freshly exposed soil in fan-shaped feeding scratches where turkeys had explored for overwintered acorn mast, budding spring greens, and—wishful thinking so high so early—bugs. But sprouting in abundance wherever the hard-packed snow is gone are grasses, wildflowers, and sedges. Dark green grasslike plants with black seed tops, sedges prefer marshy soil and are eagerly sought out by elk and bears as well as turkeys. Among our first wildflowers, claytonia is a favorite among elk, deer, bears, rodents, and wild turkeys. This common mountain member of the herbaceous purslane family is crisp and tasty top to bottom, increasing in sweetness from its delicate pinkish flowers as you nibble down, an inch or two, toward its starchy, peanut-sized root corm.

After finding a good place to sit—on the west side of a Douglas fir, where we'd remain in the cold shade long after warming daylight, uncomfortable but better hidden—we pulled up our face masks and made ready. (The largest and longest-lived tree hereabouts, the Doug fir often stands well over a hundred feet high. The rotting stumps of old-growth Dougs that were logged here a century ago often span more than four feet, evidencing trees that may have lived for a thousand years before being cut to build somebody's barn.) As I laid out my calls on the ground beside me, Erica slipped a No. 5 high-brass shot shell into the maw of her long-barreled pump, gently snicked the chamber closed, and flashed me her "I'm ready!" wink.

While we waited for a bit more light, two Canada geese carved a quick broad circle through the cold pink sky, honking nonstop.

How odd and wonderful to see and hear geese in the mountains in springtime. Twenty years ago, any goose any time of year here was rare. Then the Colorado Division of Wildlife and community volunteers began constructing elevated nesting platforms along the Animas River, where eggs and goslings were safe from raccoons, foxes, house cats, dogs, and other predators, and the geese obligingly returned. These days, this time of year, there's a nested pair of Canadas on every country pond, though many will be run out when mobs of cattle are trucked in for summer pasture. I know embarrassingly little about geese. Yet this vociferous morning flyby is obviously ceremonial, some sort of mating or bonding ritual. I've hunted geese only once, with my cowboy friend T. Mike Murphy, and took my limit of two. But C and I found the dark red meat livery and strong, so these days I merely look, listen, and admire. The first rule of ethical hunting is to kill only what you will eat. Robins, I'm sure, would be yummy, if times got really hard. And a tender young wild turkey, well, tastes just like turkey.

As always here in early spring, the defining sounds of morning are the shrill calls and brassy *ratta-tat-tap-tap*s of red-shafted flickers and other woodpeckers, primarily the downy and its slightly larger cousin, the hairy. The Lewis's—to my eyes the loveliest of our local birds, with its striking hues of iridescent green, red-hot pink, and black—has yet to make a show this high, though Caroline has seen them farther down the mountain. In a month or so, nesting pairs of Lewis's woodpeckers will excavate nursery cavities in dead or diseased—and thus pulp-hearted—aspens, occasionally right outside our door. I've never heard a Lewis's make shrill calls like other 'peckers, though they sometimes churr.

But plenty of the Picidae family have already arrived, while others never left. And with the springtime mating mood hard upon them, the agitated 'peckers can hardly wait for sunrise to redeclare daily their territories. All combined, the constant calling and tapping of woodpeckers often coalesce into a loud, shrill, and at times (when you're straining to hear other sounds) distracting cacophony. I love it.

Yet it's not the woodpeckers we've come here this morning to hear. Nor even the throngs of sweet-voiced pine siskins singing from the treetops all around. And we have not been disappointed. Just a few minutes ago, even as the roaring orb of the sun heaved itself over the eastern horizon, we were treated to an explosive *Gobble-obble-obble!* Not real close, eighty yards I'd say, but plenty close enough. If you've never heard a wild tom yodel, the sound is at once high-pitched, deep-throated, melodic, and maniacal, with emphasis on the last quality. This tom, like all red-blooded gobblers this time of year, this time of morning, was announcing his intent to fly down soon from his night's roost. As Erica stirred beside me—turning slightly to better face the invisible bird, raising one knee, resting her shotgun across that knee, tossing her long black waves of hair over one shoulder, and lowering her left cheek to the stock (she shoots left-handed)—I picked up my cedar box call and scratched out two brief triads of hen-turkey talk.

Yelp-yelp-ark. Ark-ark-yelp.

Before I could complete the second stanza, the tom fired back with an excited double gobble, cutting himself off midstream.

Gobble-obble gob-obble-obble!

For me to yelp again was unnecessary and could be offputting to the tom, as that isn't how it's done between turkeys. He had acknowledged our presence and would come to visit if and when he wished. In nature, the toms gobble and the hens come. The hunter's challenge is not only to reverse this instinctive gender protocol but also to defeat an attitude I've consistently seen demonstrated by strutting spring toms and playfully translate into human terms as macho swagger and inflated pride. Which is to say, many times a tom will come several hundred yards toward a yelping hen, real or faux, only to "hang up" near the end, gobbling impatiently while refusing to close those last few dozen yards—almost as if to complain, "Hey, girl, I've come this far and you're still hiding; now it's *your* move. Take it or leave it." Nor is he kidding. If no hen shows right away, a hung-up tom predictably shuts up and walks away.

Whether this morning's gobbler would hang up, waltz right in, or pay us a visit at all remained to be seen. Meanwhile, we hunkered in the cold shade watching, listening, waiting. So much of hunting is waiting. Not just any old kind of waiting, but strategic waiting. As the great American ecologist, hunter, and sometimes satirist Aldo Leopold phrased it in his essay "The Deer Swath":

> When the deer hunter sits down he sits where he can see ahead, and with his back to something. The duck hunter sits where he can see overhead, and behind something. The non-hunter sits where he is comfortable.

The turkey hunter most closely resembles the deer hunter in this regard, and the warmth generated by our uphill hike had long since been sucked from my bony old bod by cold and inactivity, leaving me to long for the thermos of coffee in my pack. Erica had likely packed substantial snacks, as she always does. Yet this was no time for comfort food. We dared not take the chance. The gobbler could silently appear at any moment, as they tend to do when suspicious yet intrigued—blue-white heads a-bobbing, lipstick-red neck wattles reptilian and swollen, marble-sized eyes bulged and roving, radar ears open wide, nerves honed razor-edgy from millennia of harshly selective evolution, hardwired to flee from the smallest unnatural sound, the slightest flicker of suspicious motion. But more than likely, we knew, things would never get that far; the gobbler we'd heard talking would never get that close to us. Most often, a tom's pre-fly-down gobbles accomplish their intended goal of attracting a group of hens to the base of his roost tree, awaiting his descent. And the ad hoc matriarch of that ad hoc harem, predictably, would lead him and them intentionally away from my foreign calls. But maybe not.

In any event, with the exchange of my hennish yelps and his eager gobbles we had entered active play. Coffee and comfort must wait.

As a boy in Oklahoma, I traveled with adult friends each spring to hunt Rio Grande turkeys in the sparsely inhabited ranching country around Cheyenne, at the western edge of the state, near the Texas border. There, only eighty years before, a flag-waving patriot named Custer, ranting about the threat they posed to white America, had slaughtered Cheyenne Chief Black Kettle's peaceful band of noncombatants in their winter encampment along a cottonwood-sheltered bend of the Washita River. Just twenty years later and a few miles north, my paternal grandparents homesteaded 640 dry sandy acres, one square mile, where my father, a Depression-era Dust Bowl child, would grow up hungry and hard.

Like deer and most other edible wildlife, turkeys were rare nearly everywhere in North America through the middle of the twentieth century, having been almost exterminated by my grandparents' "root, hog, or die" homestead generation—even as passenger pigeons, two of the six varieties of North American elk, the giant plains bison, and numerous other natives were eaten into oblivion. My grandparents, of course, were merely continuing and concluding a tradition of Manifestly Destined habitat and wildlife destruction begun a century before by ambitious sodbusters and desperate market hunters, the first and most colorful of whom we romanticize today as mountain men. Truly heroic last-minute conservation and restoration efforts narrowly saved the dying day—initiated, funded, and politically pursued almost exclusively by farsighted hunter-conservationists as personified by Teddy Roosevelt and a hundred or so influential fellow "gentleman sportsmen" comrades. Motivated by enlightened self-interest, these nabobs certainly were. Ironically, were it not for the efforts of hunter-conservationists yesterday, today those who protest against hunting would have no wildlife left to try to "protect" from our current sorry crop of media- and marketplace-shaped pretend hunters.

So it is now, in the opening decade of the twenty-first century, that wild turkeys once again abound in what remains of suitable turkey habitat throughout North America—an American wildlife tradition reborn. Here in southwest Colorado we have the hardy and wily Merriam's subspecies. But I'm a wily old bird myself, and doggedly persistent. Consequently, by way of reenacting the largely mythical first Thanksgiving, I see to it that a member of the Merriam's tribe provides the centerpiece for our dinner table nearly every Turkey Day.

All of which is by way of leading up to saying that in my years spent hunting and watching wild turkeys, I've witnessed normal behaviors from combat to copulation. I've also been privy to some truly curious anomalies, such as a hen-yelping tom with a six-inch beard and otherwise normal male morphology and a fully developed egg inside "him." But never before have I seen, heard tell, or read of anything like the gladiatorial spectacle Erica and I are currently watching. Whether the combatants are enjoying themselves or not is hard to say. But for now, so long as they keep at it, they are safe from Erica's Annie Oakley instincts.

In the minutes following my fake hen yelps and the roosted gobbler's excited response, he sang several more times and then fell quiet. Once again the woodpeckers reigned. Although we were too far away to hear the heavy drumming of his fly-down wing-beats, the gobbler's sudden silence said he had gone to ground and was in the company of hens. As more quiet minutes passed, our hopes began to fade. Then suddenly, and startlingly close:

Yelp-yelp-ark.

Gobble-obble-obble!

No sooner heard than seen: a swirling wad of hens moving up the hill toward us, pecking and scratching as they came. The much larger and darker gobbler trailed a few yards behind, delayed by his pompous tail-fan displays and a strutting, wing-dragging courtship dance that took him around and around in circles and figures of eight. Perfect. I needn't even call again, which would only serve to alert the birds to our presence and precise location. Ever-ready Erica had a bead on her target, wait-ing only for the tom to move well clear of the hens and extend his neck to gobble, offering an instant-death head shot. His beard—the clutch of long wiry feathers that sprout from a gobbler's breast—hung a full six inches, flagging him as a three-year-old. Average in size, he'd weigh maybe eighteen pounds (an eleven-pound bird in the oven). Notwithstanding the sleep we'd sacri-ficed, our long uphill climb in the dark, and the discomfort we'd endured while sitting motionless in the cold for over an hour, this seemed too fast and easy.

As the flock approached to within twenty yards and Erica's trigger finger began to twitch, a heart-stopping *Yobble-obble-gobble!* exploded from directly behind our backrest tree.

A second tom, boldly challenging the first.

In the instant after the intruder's gobble, the two toms ran at each other, tail feathers fanned like dark half-moons, backs and breasts gleaming in the soft morning light. Both birds spit fiercely as they charged to the attack—*Pffftt! Pffftt!*—war whoops emitted from egg-sized heads pulled tight into their chests. When about three feet apart and smack in front of us, the runners simultaneously folded their tails, extended their necks, leapt into the air, and body-slammed each other with an audible thud. Flapping their wings wildly to defeat gravity, each bird fought to rise above the other, whirring and slashing with long-clawed toes, like feathered dinosaurs. Breast feathers flew—this fight was for keeps.

Even so, I'd seen it all before. It was only when they returned to the ground after several seconds of airborne combat that things got really weird. Somehow, they'd managed to twist their necks together, each a full turn around the other, like serpents making love.

And so they remain even now, several furious minutes later—necks twined tight, battling breast to breast on the ground, one tom pushing the other back a few steps, then the other pushing forth, dancing the Darwin waltz. Suddenly they leap again into the air and hang there briefly, wings thrashing, claws churning—trying to kill each other.

Many or most animal "fights" to establish a breeding hierarchy are far more show than blow, instinctively ritualized performances that allow the opponents to size each other up without anyone getting hurt. At some point the loser simply breaks off and leaves. These two toms, to the contrary in extreme, are out for arterial blood.

And all the while, like movie extras milling in the background, the scattered hens peck, scratch, feed, and purr, feigning a lack of interest in the brutal battle for their affections playing out nearby. Right now, I'm aware, would be a uniquely opportune time for a bobcat, fox, coyote, or one of our recently reintroduced Canada lynx to leap from hiding and nab an off-guard tom. Or maybe even two, though predators are rarely greedy. Such dramas are common in spring. Frequently, from March through May, Caroline and I find the remains of predator-killed turkeys—almost always males. And just as often we find damaged tommy tail feathers (back in Oklahoma, I'd known a Kiowa boy named Tommy Tail-feathers), where something hungry had made a grab and the bird had barely escaped, not quite unscathed.

"Do you think they're *stuck* that way?" whispers Erica, referring to the twisted necks.

Good question, and one that reflects my companion's growing impatience and mounting frustration. Several times the battling toms have flopped near enough for us to clobber them with a broomstick—if we had a broomstick and if we wanted to—yet they remain beyond Erica's ethical reach. In order to kill a turkey with a shotgun, instantly and without spoiling precious breast meat, you shoot it in the head, emulating the farmer's swift axe. No such shot is possible now without killing both birds. While I have a turkey license in my pocket, that's not how I want to get "my" bird.

Ironically, had I brought my bow along, this freak situation that's proving so frustrating to Erica would be a gift to me. Since an archer aims midbody, for the heart and lungs, killing just one of this close-up pair would be cake. Normally, bagging a turkey with a bow—barring such crutches as bait, mechanical decoys, or a blind—is the nearest thing to impossible. With a shotgun, you can unobtrusively track an approaching gobbler with slow movements of the barrel, as Erica is doing now. When your bird is in range—thirty yards will do for a twelve-gauge with full choke and heavy turkey loads—and no other birds are in the line of fire, you wait for Tommy to crane his neck the better to gobble or gawk, and then you lower the boom. If it's done well, your low-fat meaty entrée never hears or feels the shot that kills him. So much more humane than the industrial factory "farm," where the caged inmates are denied even those activities most essential to fowl contentedness: roaming free and scratching in the dirt. Compared to factory farming, ethical hunting is a truly benign and honorable—not to mention healthy—way to get your meat.

Or not.

Ten tense minutes this spectacle now has run (Erica will later estimate fifteen to twenty), and still they waltz and helicopter—necks twined, American-flag heads like color-coded blood-pressure gauges segueing from red to white to blue, long claws (three forward, one back) kicking and slashing, dislodged feathers swirling like snow in a whirlwind. Yet no real harm has been done, so far as I can see. Like Erica, I'm beginning to wonder if maybe they've somehow become "stuck," unable to separate their twisted necks. But even as I pose this silent question the two hissing pugilists pirouette around a low rise and out of sight. Several more flapping wingbeats, a couple more spits and hisses . . . silence.

Simultaneously disappointed and relieved, I lower my face mask, smile, and whisper, "Coffee time!"

"Well," says Miss E, placing her cannon gently on the ground after checking the safety, "*I've* got breakfast burritos! And wasn't that just *way cool?*"

Cool it certainly was. Frequently in hunting, it's the ones you *don't* bring home that carve the deepest memories. After all, they're still out there, somewhere, like an open promise, awaiting your return.

· 19 ·

I've known no better teacher than hunting. And what hunting has taught me is hardly restricted to the ways of wildings and woods.

Much of what I've been able to decipher about the nature of human nature, including my own, is revealed in the attitudes people hold toward hunting: for, against, or disinterested. Among hunters, much is said about ourselves in the way we go about killing and how we view our prey. My own lifelong interest in the workings of wild nature was spawned as a child by hunting. More specifically, most of what I know today about turkeys, elk, deer, other game species, their nongame neighbors, and the ecological community that supports and unites us all, I've learned through exacting and tenacious tracking, patient watching, attentive listening, even picking through fresh poops, all in the course of scouting and hunting. Back home from forest or field, to maximize my enjoyment of the mysteries, questions, and curiosities provoked by direct experience, I turn to reading and pestering biologists.

No matter what you think of hunting as practiced today—and my own feelings run from widespread outrage to narrowly focused respect—it's hardly surprising that the most intimate wildlife knowledge would accrue to those who spend the most time in the woods with the greatest motivation to blend in and pay attention. And most of those are hunters. Concluding the Leopold quote begun above: "The deer hunter habitually watches the next bend; the duck hunter watches the skyline; the bird hunter watches the dog; the non-hunter does not watch."

Today, tragically, hunting has been commercially co-opted and transmogrified into just another product to sell to people in a hurry. As with almost everything else in our "bigger, better, faster, easier" human-constructed world of heightened expectations and computer-enhanced impatience, you can buy catalogs full of "sporting aids" designed to make hunting less demanding and more certain, many of which gadgets are illegal in most states but not in all. These include motorized decoys; electronic game callers; solar-powered automatic "feeders" that can be set to spray out a load of corn or other bait at precise times each day so that turkeys (or deer) become conditioned to appear promptly at, say, eight A.M. and four P.M. and pretend "hunters" (the real turkeys) don't have to learn how to actually hunt. Other recent "improvements" in turkey-killing technology include scope-sighted magnum shotguns that can reach out and kill at sixty yards, remote infrared game-monitoring cameras, portable camouflage blinds, and night-vision optics. To learn more (than you ever wanted to know) along this line, just swallow a protective dose of Pepto-Bismol and tune in to the Outdoor Channel, or page through the latest Cabela's catalog or *Outhouse Life*.

Ethical concerns aside, the obvious nerd factor in high-tech hunting is that anything one buys in an effort to make "success" (as measured by kills) come more quickly, easily, and often—that is, the more we rely on purchased shortcuts to replace personal skill—the less challenge and pride of accomplishment we net in return. Hunting is by nature and tradition a back-to-basics endeavor, a ceremony of process over product, a celebration of our evolved human-animal wildness tempered by respect for all living things, by conscious self-restraint (that's the "sport" part), and founded in personal honor when no one else is watching. Today's high-tech toys and cheater ploys help make dilettante nimrods more efficient at killing without knowledge, effort, dedication, or honor, speeding their return to home, beer, and TV—but what's the point? Why reduce what should be an unpredictable, challenging, and adventurous *hunt*—a character-building and spiritually meaningful *learning* experience—to a ho-hum turkey shoot?

Alas, that's the cage we've built for ourselves . . . and why some people hate hunters.

Having drunk my hot coffee and et Erica's cold scrambled-egg-and-green-chili burritos, still talking in whispers (as always in the woods, whether hunting or not), we stash our trash in our packs, rise, stretch, and go sneaking around the bend toward where we last heard the two hissing, neck-locked gladiator toms. We find only empty woods. Farther on I try a little calling. Nada.

The morning grows late. Where it's legal, turkeys can be hunted all day. You walk and call and hope to incite a gobble. If and when you do, you promptly sit down in the shade, make ready, call some more, and hope the tom will come. Yet this day, both Erica and I have "real world" obligations and so must head for home—moving slowly and quietly, keeping to the shadows, and occasionally calling as we go, just in case—unspeakably thankful for all we've seen, heard, and felt on this unforgettable April morn.

Without the visceral motivation of the hunt, we'd have slept in and missed it all. Without the nutritional, physical, intellectual, anachronistic, and spiritual stimuli of the hunt, I would never have come to know this place, its secretive inhabitants, or myself as I have.

As to the killing: Erica will tend to that chore tomorrow, at a place of her own discovery, hunting alone while I still snore.

· 20 ·

Cinco de Mayo: May 5—Mexican Independence Day and a party-time holiday here in the multicultural American Southwest. Apropos, Erica (Hispanic), George (Turkish and Irish), Nancy (Italian), Caroline (a British cornucopia), and I (Danish, German, and, according to undocumented family legend, one-eighth Cherokee) will celebrate tonight at Erica's place, with margaritas, Mexican food, music, laughter, and as many dogs as people.

But all of that is later, after a good day's work and—you guessed it—a long evening walk.

Half an hour before dark, Otis and I jump a bobcat a quarter mile above the cabin. Not just any wild kitty, this one, but the biggest tom bob I've ever seen, bigger than any of the several Canada lynx I watched exit their cages and casually depart during a local reintroduction last year. This outsized bob sat crouched and unmoving in a low tangle of spring-green oak brush and aspen saplings as Otis and I strolled past, a bare few feet away. But a few paces farther along, while angling across the downstream breeze, O caught a whiff of intrigue, whirled around, and followed the scent back into the jungle of brush, at which point the long-legged cat, almost as tall as the dog, broke and bounded away.

Wisely, the dog did not give chase, opting to wheel about and savor the gone kitty's scent among the new leaves of oak and aspen.

Aspens. I'm not at all sure I could live without them, and I don't intend to try. Long ago, I felt this same mystically magnetic attraction to the ocean; but others felt it too, and too soon it got to where you couldn't see the waves for the people and their high-rise luxury hotels. While the human population here in La Plata County has doubled in the past ten years and is trying to double again and the future looks grim, so far, for now, aspens still outnumber humans. And May is the month of aspens greening.

One of the many qualities that give the quaking aspen its unique beauty and magic is that it grows in clones—colonies of genetically identical trees ranging from a few dozen to hundreds. I find that it simplifies matters to think of an aspen clone as a family group consisting entirely of genetically identical parents and siblings. Every aspen-cloaked vista here in the San Juan Mountains— a region blessed with the largest and healthiest quaking aspen forests in the world—comprises a community of independent family organisms that green in spring and turn to gold in fall according to schedules that differ from clone to clone. Additionally, the colors of autumn vary by clone. While the dominant tint is yellow, scattered family groupings of tangerine and scarlet provide striking minority highlights; a multicultural neighborhood.

The quaking aspen, like its cottonwood cousins, is a member of the Salicaceae, the family that includes willows and poplars. Our aspens—the little grove surrounding our cabin on a sunny southwest slope—are all of a single clone. And that clone, as it happens, is a late bloomer, among the last hereabouts to leaf in spring and go to color each fall. The earliest aspen bloomers in this area belong to a clone growing on a steep, north-facing slope above a series of five big open fingers we call the Elk Meadows, halfway between here and town. (Indeed, in spring and fall these protected, private-land meadows may entertain several hundred grazing wapiti each evening, a risky distraction to rubbernecking drivers on a curvaceous mountain road.) Toward the end of April each year, the western edge of the Elk Meadows quakie grove goes light green overnight. Since I go to town only once a week or so, every commute in early May reveals a remarkable gain in area and intensity of greening. Here on Spring Mountain, by May's end, our yard is once again flickering in the shade of freshly unfurled quakie leaves, giving voice to the warming winds.

But before rebirth comes reconception.

Quakies reproduce after two distinct fashions: through flowering and the consequent production and distribution of seeds, and via clonal suckers that sprout directly from the roots of parent trees. This duality, floral and clonal, helps ensure long-term species survival and expansion in a variety of habitat types under environmentally stressful conditions.

Aspens produce seeds in almost incomprehensible profusion. However, the environmental requirements for the successful germination of aspen seeds are so stringent as to severely limit the effectiveness of this method of reproduction. Even so, each and every year, the aspen folk perform their seeding dance. The ritual is announced as early as late winter, when the naked white groves assume a collective ruddy blush. While the process actually begins shortly after leaf drop each fall, only with prespring swelling and reddening does aspen budding become obvious. By early spring, the aspen buds are swollen and ripe, providing a favored treat for a variety of winter-starved mammals and birds. Only last month, while Erica and I were turkey hunting below a place called Madden Peak, an hour's drive west of here in the La Plata Range, we watched a big gangly jake fly up into a young aspen, where it perched for several minutes, craning its reptilian neck this way and that to nip bud after bud. I have sampled aspen buds, and they're really not so bad, hardly even bitter—at least early in the process, before the chlorophyll rises.

Back in April, our aspen buds sprouted tiny flowers like white fur coats. A given tree and its flowers will normally be either male (staminate) or female (pistillate), with the genders more or less balanced. When the time is ripe, clouds of microscopic pollen are released from the anthers of the male flowers to be distributed by the wind. With favorable conditions, enough of these millions of wandering pollen germs will get where they need to go to facilitate the sperm-egg synthesis by which embryo seeds are conceived. The resulting seed-bearing capsule stringers of the female flowers, called catkins, resemble the fluffy tips of pussy willows. Dangling dense as summer leaves from the ends of new spring twigs, they paint the groves a silvery white. Just last week I stood outside puffing on my pipe and gazing at the late-night sky. Viewed through a screen of aspen catkins backlit by a waxing moon, the effect was not merely lovely, it was viscerally exciting, like fine white lace on a smooth dark thigh.

Aspen seeds are perfectly suited to breezy flight. In addition to their near weightlessness, each seed has wings, as it were: feathery tufts that botanists call dispersal hairs sprout from the stem. Normally, aspen seeds glide no more than a few hundred yards. But given a sustained wind to ride on, they can stay aloft for miles, providing old clones with new footholds in diverse locations. In addition to sailing on the wind, aspen seeds also sail by water. While afloat they often sprout prematurely, in anticipation of being beached on rich soil in a sunny situation felicitous to rooting and growth. (Along with Gambel's oak, aspen is our primary woody colonizer of fire-carved clearings.)

Emulating human physical development, the average quakie will begin flowering by its fifteenth spring, though sexual productivity won't peak until the age of fifty or so (emulating me). Each reproductive stem on a mature aspen—a healthy tree may wear them by the thousands—is capable of manufacturing from two to ten catkins. In turn, each catkin contains a hundred to a thousand seeds. In all, a given tree may produce well over a million seeds. And yet it's not unusual for not a single seed among all those masses to sprout, take root, and grow to maturity. Soil quality and air temperature, soil moisture and drainage, sunlight, protection from being nipped in the bud by hungry browsers, competition from other vegetation—all these variables must cooperate in unison, which they rarely do.

Little wonder aspens have evolved a second and infinitely more reliable means of reproduction, through cloning.

Cloning begins when "starters" develop beneath the parent root's subbark layer. Strip the thin white bark and soft green cambium from a section of aspen root and these starter buds, technically called meristems, appear as a rash of nibs and teats. The next stage in the cloning process is for the buds to elongate into short, hairlike shoots, which typically fall dormant for a few years before reawakening, resuming growth, and eventually breaking the surface as saplings. After an initial period of growth and root development on the tit, as it were, of the parent tree, the cloned saplings become independent.

Why the intervening period of dormancy? To discourage over-population, self-competition, distress, disease, and doom within the clone and grove. When this marvelous system of birth control fails naturally, or (far more often) is disrupted by human meddling, the ugly result is dense clusters of stunted "dog hair" saplings, most of which are doomed to fierce competition, disfigurement, and early death.

Since the auxin, or plant hormone, which acts as a clonal contraceptive in aspens, is manufactured and concentrated in the leafy tops of mature trees, it can be defeated by cutting, burning, girdling, or disease, all of which prompt defoliation and death. In an ecological tragedy certainly not due to ignorance, the U.S. Forest Service does not view its mandate to be long-term management for healthy forests, much less management for thriving forest ecosystems, but mismanagement for the short-term placation of the "forest products" industry. Toward this end, USFS publicity flacks hail the prolific aspen suckering that's induced by clear-cutting as justification for this destructive practice.

Granted, under favorable conditions—including the strict prohibition of livestock grazing during the tender early years of sapling growth—a clear-cut aspen stand *can* regenerate into a mature aspen forest. But not in the remainder of my lifetime, nor even likely yours. Particularly not if cattle are run in to graze shortly after the massacre, as they generally are. Following clear-cutting, never again will you or I see natural, mixed-age groves so magnificently beautiful and ecologically productive as those that were cut.

What, we're left to wonder, would Aldo Leopold think of it all?

Among writers and readers of contemporary nature literature, references to and quotations from the writings of Aldo Leopold

(1886–1948) have been so extensively trotted out for so very long as to be considered clichés. Many of Leopold's epigrams are so familiar to readers in the environmental, wildlife management, and nature genres as to suggest shallow research and derivative thinking on the part of the writers who use them. And that's a damn shame. If I could think and write like Leopold, providing America with a whole fresh set of groundbreaking ecological epigrams to quote from, I surely would. So would countless others. But a distinguishing characteristic of creative genius is rarity, and for now at least, Aldo is the best we have—and plenty good enough.

How many of our current problems—ecological, global, economic, even interpersonal—would not be problems at all today, or significantly smaller problems, if only we had begun to act forcefully on Leopold's vision and advice back when he first extolled it, more than half a century ago? Leopold's greatest contribution to posterity was to have substantiated for the first time *with unimpeachable science and logic* the moral teachings of such prescientific nature mystics as Buddha, American Indian orators, Emerson, and Thoreau, to wit, that *all things are connected* and *all living things have value in and of themselves.* Today, those of us who care about such luxuries as the survival of planet Earth and the spectacularly varied life it supports lump this far-ranging holistic outlook under the umbrella term *deep ecology.*

Writing in *A Sand County Almanac* (published in 1949), Leopold proclaimed his now-famous land ethic: "A thing is right when it tends to preserve the integrity, stability, and beauty of the biotic community. It is wrong when it tends otherwise."

Why "right" and "wrong"? Aren't these moral, thus purely human constructs? Indeed they are, just as humanity is purely a construct of nature. All life on Earth depends utterly on integrity and stability in the biotic community—the air we breathe, the water we drink and bathe our children in, the soil from which we take our food. Moreover, for the human animal at least, a world devoid of natural beauty would be a world devoid of sanity.

"To keep every cog and wheel," Aldo points out, "is the first precaution of intelligent tinkering. Have we learned this first principle of conservation: to preserve all the parts of the land mechanism? No, because even the scientist does not yet recognize all of them."

Today we recognize at least *enough* of them—enough to know without logical doubt that if we don't get our heads out of our investment portfolios and back in the real world real soon, ecological collapse, global war, famine, disease, and anarchy inevitably will reign, as they do already in a growing number of lethally overpopulated "developing" nations. And what are these doomed nations striving to develop into? Rich overconsumers like us, of course. So down and down we go, and too few seem to notice or care.

As Leopold saw and bemoaned right after World War II: "One of the penalties of an ecological education is that one lives alone in a world of wounds. Much of the damage inflicted on land is quite invisible to laymen."

The observable truth regarding forest health is quite the opposite of what the forest products industry, including its federal arm, the USFS, would have us believe. Even the most "decadent" aspen grove, if left largely alone, is constantly regenerating itself via natural processes. Perhaps not with the speed, visual neatness, or profitability our fast-food culture has come to demand, but regenerating nonetheless.

What our forests need, aspen and otherwise, isn't a feeding frenzy of commercial clear-cutting under the political and economic euphemisms of "wildfire prevention" and postfire "salvage" logging, but a scientifically informed and wisely guarded return to the frequent small fires that were common in nature prior to human intervention and are among the many ecologically essential but recently discarded cogs and wheels that would, if allowed, keep the natural mechanism running smoothly. The knowledge, experience, and technical capability to make this happen already exist. The wisdom and will do not.

At this juncture, given the above rant and others perhaps yet to come (how can we know until we get there?), I should point out that while I occasionally hug and talk to trees, I'm not blindly against the timber industry. Our cabin is slapped together almost entirely of rough-sawn local pine and fir, with interior aspen trim milled from local trees. Lumber is an essential and renewable gift of nature. What I am utterly aghast at, and what Aldo Leopold so eloquently warned America against continuing, is the greedy, myopic, red-ink-stained, undemocratic, and ecologically destructive attitudes of federal and state timber-management agencies and their puppet masters, the private for-profit thieves of America's dwindling natural forests.

Compared to clear-cutting, burning is a vastly superior forest "treatment," particularly from a wildlife-habitat point of view. Burning releases nutrients stored in the bodies of trees and spreads those nutrients as ash fertilizer, prompting the speedy regeneration not only of aspens and other trees but of the ecologically symbiotic grasses, forbs, and brush—collectively called understory—so vital as food and shelter for wildlife. The purported ecological benefits of clear-cutting, as touted by the USFS, their industrial partners, and our current rape-and-run political persuasion, are greatly and dishonestly overrated since the trees and their nutrients are carted off by the truckload rather than being recycled into the soil system. Worse yet is the damage—both physical and aesthetic—caused to soil, terrain, and watersheds by the trucks, log skidders, and other heavy equipment necessary to get the job done in what is often referred to as an "efficient and profitable manner."

Clear-cutting not only converts gorgeous living forests into eyesores, it also prompts erosion and the consequent loss or compaction of topsoil (or both) while promoting the invasion of noxious weeds. And in the long-term aftermath of logging, whole new networks of roads and ORV-accessible skidder trails remain, inviting motorized invasion, which further erodes topography, scenery, silence, and aquatic and terrestrial wildlife habitat.

In sum, mowing down a living forest in the name of saving it is the moral, intellectual, and scientific equivalent of tossing out the baby with the bathwater. But, of course, we are living in mean and stupid times—times that we ourselves, in so many self-serving ways, eagerly endorse.

· 21 ·

Beginning in late May, within the cool shade of newly leafed aspens, the elk calves are born. The luckiest of the lot, at least. Across most of the wapiti's range, calving season runs mid-May through mid-June, peaking around the first of June. A few months hence, with the onset of their initial and most dangerous winter, early-born calves will enjoy a distinct survival advantage.

Foremost, early elk calves have a few weeks longer to gain weight. Born at around thirty-five pounds, in their first six months they will grow to around two hundred pounds. Acquiring strength, foraging knowledge, and social skills, all of which take time, also helps to ensure calf survival through the murderous winter gantlet of deep, delaying, calorie-gobbling snow, of numbing cold and slow starvation. As many as half of a summer's crop of calves (and deer fawns) may perish before or during their first winter. Since late-born calves enter the hard months smaller and weaker, with fewer caloric reserves and less survival savvy, they are more likely than their slightly older and hardier peers to die from exposure, starvation, injury, or predation.

The timing of an elk calf's birth is determined, naturally, by the timing of its mother's impregnation the previous fall. Count back eight and a half months from a given birth, and there you have it, more or less. The timing of a cow's fertilization, in turn, is controlled primarily by the timing of her ovulation, which depends on her receiving adequate nutrition to function on schedule. But a cow's ranking in the herd hierarchy also counts for much, with prime, experienced cows bullying to the front of the breeding quay. The bull-to-cow ratio and the average age of sire bulls also figure in. In overhunted and otherwise poorly managed herds, the bull-to-cow ratio is low, prompting social disharmony and delayed fertilizations. An unnatural preponderance of young bulls leads to inefficient and delayed breeding, stresses both sexes, and can extend the rut as much as six weeks, leading to dangerously late births the following summer. In such unbalanced, unhealthy, and altogether unnatural situations, a higher percentage of cows fail to become fertilized the first time around and must wait three weeks for another ovulation and a second go. And sometimes, like turkey hens who've lost their nests, even a third. The unfortunate calves born late to such unfortunate cows have significantly reduced odds of surviving to adulthood and may be permanently stunted if they do.

It's no surprise that human activity is the root cause of most population, social, and reproductive malfunctions in elk. While livestock overgrazing has hugely negative impacts on arid western wildlife habitat, logging is just as bad. Not only does logging destroy and disrupt the natural forest ecology upon which elk

depend for food, water, and cover, but the resulting new roads
provide easier access for larger numbers of lazier, sloppier, less
nature-connected "recreational users," resulting in yet more
damage to fragile ecosystems, increased harassment of wildlife,
and littering and polluting of soil and water. This heyday for slob
road "hunters" and poachers is further compounded by decreased
wildlife hiding cover and the proliferation of nonnative invasive
plants, such as thistles, hound's-tongue, and knapweed, all of
which eagerly displace indigenous wildlife forage.

Our own Spring Mountain is a textbook example of the lower
montane ecosystem. Comprising the middle ground between
lower-lying wintering areas and the higher subalpine summer
range, it provides migrating elk with rich spring and fall habitat. (The five altitude-determined ecological zones for western
Colorado, bottom to top, are: piñon-juniper—below 6,500 feet;
transitional—6,500 to 8,200 feet, defined by Gambel's oak and
ponderosa pine; montane—8,200 to 9,500 feet, with aspen, oak,
ponderosa, spruce, fir, and Douglas fir; subalpine—9,500 to
11,500 feet, mostly spruce and fir; and alpine—above 11,500 feet,
with krummholz at the timberline threshold and dwarf willows
higher up.)

This puts the herds in precisely the right place for calving season, just when and where all the best forage is attaining its nutritional prime. As a parturient cow's time approaches, she leaves
the herd in search of good cover with access to nearby food and
water. Immediately after delivery, the mother does what she can
to eliminate predator-attracting odors by devouring the after-
birth and licking her infant clean. As soon as it can stand and
wobble on its sapling legs, the babe follows its mother to a fresh
hiding spot, always in the shade, where its white-splotched roan
pelage melts it into the foliage.

Since elk calves (like deer fawns) aren't strong enough in their
first days or weeks to escape predators by running, they've

evolved a hider strategy, of which camouflage is but a single element. Infant calves are also nearly odorless. In order to avoid
attracting the attention of predators by their own visibility and
odor, mothers nurse their calves in brief bouts, move them often,
and stand watch from a distance. Another strategy critical to the
success of an infant calf's survival during the hider phase involves
the mother's skill in choosing good cover and her courage in
defending her young. In any event—whether tucked invisibly
into the shade of a clump of brush and grass or left foolishly
exposed next to a fallen tree in the middle of a meadow—the
essence of the hider strategy is catatonia. No matter how threat-
eningly close a predator may approach, the infant instinctively
remains still. With luck, the hungry hunter will overlook the
immobile morsel and pass on by.

Alas, as survival strategies go, hiding and luck are imperfect.
For many years, during the first week of June each spring, Caroline and I camped and hiked in Yellowstone's then blissfully
tourist-neglected Lamar Valley. Here the elk came by the hundreds
to calve, and here the big carnivores came to feast. The primary
attractions for us were the grizzlies. Happily for the elk, calf hunting is a learned skill in bears and in no way universal. While some
grizzlies do nothing but hunt during calving time, most continue
to eat wildflowers. As Caroline and I have observed, only mother
bears who themselves are calf hunters will teach their cubs to hunt
for hiders. It's a family affair, and while emotionally jolting to
watch at first, this annual spectacle of violence, gore, ecological
balance, and continuation through termination has a beauty all its
own, encapsulating the circle-dance of all life on Earth.

A local example of the imperfection of the hider strategy
played out some years ago just up the hill from our place. At the
time, the third member of our family was a black-and-gold
retriever-setter mix of calm disposition. As we do with all of our
dogs, we had trained Amigo not to chase the deer and elk that

frequently appear on our walks, sometimes quite nearby. With easygoing Amigo, whom we adopted in his later years, the teaching had been easy. Yet things went weird one late May evening when a sleek young cow stepped boldly from an oak thicket just ahead and into the open a few yards uphill—then stood stiff-legged and stared.

Given her behavior and the time of year, we knew immediately what was up—or, rather, what was down and hiding. Taking our cue from the cow, C and I stopped in our tracks and focused on the cow, unaware that Amigo had slipped away and was nosing around in the brush from which the cow had come. While the old hound couldn't locate the hider that he somehow seemed to know was lurking there, he must have been getting warm because suddenly the cow, young and inexperienced, lost her cool and barked the doglike elk alarm. Shocked and confused, the calf jumped up and bolted toward its mom—and right toward our dog. Acting on some dim wolfish imperative, the normally gentle old mutt body-slammed the calf, knocking it down. And there they posed, the calf outwardly calm (the silence of the lambs) while Amigo stood proudly astraddle his catch and grinned, his tongue happily lolling.

As the cow stood paralyzed, I sprinted up, grabbed Amigo by the scruff, and jerked him off the calf—at which happy turn the infant bull rose and wobbled to his mother's side. Without looking back at us, the reunited pair walked—did not run but walked—away, apparently little worse for the wear. And, one would hope, a wee bit wiser in hiding strategies when predators are nearby.

In this encounter it was the inexperienced mother, not the calf, who'd buckled under pressure and almost blown the game. Still, the fact that the hider strategy could fail to the extent of allowing a sick old pet (Amigo would die of lymphoma just a few days later) to make a virtual kill suggests that it fails with regularity in the face of a wild world teeming with skillful and ever-hungry predators. Our ancestral hunting-gathering forebears, likewise, knew where to be at ungulate birthing time and made the most of the short-lived bounty. It's almost as if evolution, in shaping such an imperfect defense, intended that a tithe of cervid young become protein for hungry carnivores—who, after all, have their own spring young to feed. The savior of the calves is that this bounty is indeed short-lived. At the most, considering the time spread of annual births, predators have a window of only a few weeks during which to find and munch helpless hiders. By late June, the surviving calves will have doubled in weight and be competent runners. Previously scattered cow-calf pairs will rejoin the protective maternal herds, and the first harsh round of Darwinian culling will be complete.

For Caroline and me, subsisting on the edge as we do—close to nature and never far above the economic bottom line—all births and deaths are viewed as gifts. For we are foragers.

· 22 ·

What was it my female grade-school classmates used to scrunch up their sweet little noses and squeal whenever I walked by? Something like:

"*Eeeew!*" (The same sound elk calves make.) "There's a *fungus* among us!"

And, by golly, they were right. If hunting, eating, and dreaming mushrooms can make a person "go fungal," I am that person, at least each year in May and June. Yet another of Spring Mountain's springtime benedictions is the annual return of *las morchellas*— our exquisite morel mushrooms. We are blessed here with both blacks (*Morella angusticeps*) and blonds (*M. esculenta*), the ultimate and the penultimate of wild fungal fare.

Other edible mushrooms live here too, of course. Shaggy manes

(*Coprinus comatus*, also called inky caps) appear literally overnight and unpredictably, spring through late summer, standing
white and erect along the hard-packed edges of unpaved forest
roads. They are excellent sliced *very fresh* (get 'em young and
cook 'em quick, before they liquefy), dipped in an egg-milk batter, rolled in fresh grated Parmesan cheese, and sautéed in butter
with a clove of freshly crushed garlic.

White king boletes (*Boletus barrowsii*) make sporadic appear-
ances all summer long but in the mature stage are often spoiled by
boring insect larvae. To preclude that bitter end, we watch for tell-
tale pregnancies where the needle duff is humped up, gently scrape
away the overburden, and collect them young, tender, and bug-free.

In late summer and early fall, golden chanterelles (*Cantharellus
cibarius*) cluster on damp, shady, north- and east-facing slopes in
mossy conifer-aspen forests in upper montane and lower subalpine ecosystems. While we rarely go on chanterelle safaris, I
sometimes luck into a community of them in late summer while
hiking or scouting for high-country elk. They are trumpet-shaped,
orangish in color, and smell like apricots.

Yet morels remain not only our personal pick of the crop but
the universal favorites among fungus-heads everywhere, as evidenced by their gold-scale retail value. In the Pacific Northwest,
pickers are paid an average of $10 a fresh (wet) pound, which
works out to about a double handful. At the local supermarket,
one ounce of dried morels—about a dozen smallish specimens—
sells (to whom?) for $7.99. But they come to us as gifts.

In spring, morels begin to appear as soon as the winter snow-
pack is gone and nighttime temperatures rise above freezing and
stay that way; this usually occurs in mid-May. And so long as it
rains (or snows) just enough to keep shaded ground slightly
damp, the little beauties, some as big as turkey eggs, just keep on
keepin' on, in solemn singles or congregated in gregarious covens
of a dozen or more, right on into June. Once the sun grows sum-

mertime hot and the ground goes dusty dry—no matter how much rain may later fall—the feast is over for another year.

Confusing morels with any of the several false morels takes some doing, as all the falsies I'm aware of resemble lumpy, deformed brains, in no way imitating the morel's attractive conical sponge. In flavor as well as texture, morels are prime-cut meaty and the perfect complement for elk or other wild red flesh, sautéed in salted butter—provided, of course, they've been promptly and properly prepared. When we bring in a batch, we rinse them initially in a bowl or bucket of cold, clean water—swish around real good, let sit for a bit, then swish around some more—to dislodge exterior dirt, wee bugs, and spores. After placing the rinsed 'shrooms in a wire sieve to drain, we carry the spore-rich rinse water outside and dump it in likely morel habitats, thinking ahead to the next and next springs. Now we slice the buggers in half lengthwise, or into quarters if they're big enough (like splitting firewood). This exposes the hollow interior and facilitates both drying and eventual cooking. We then perform a second rinse, this time in salted water, to expel any clinging critters that may still be lodged in the exterior crenulations. Then we drain the meaty pieces thoroughly and spread them, not touching, on a clean bath towel and gently blot them dry. They are now ready to cook, or they can be rolled up in the damp blotting towel and stored fresh for a few days in the refrigerator.

For long-term storage, morels must be dried as rapidly as possible after washing—*thoroughly* dried—and stored in the proverbial cool, dry place away from direct sunlight. While some collectors use zip-closed plastic bags, we prefer tightly lidded canning jars. Thus coddled, well-dried morels require no refrigeration and will keep well for at least several months, which is as long as they ever last around here, even when rationed. Rehydrated for an hour or so in hot liquid—water, broth, or red wine, depending on intended use—they emulate the sponges they resemble and plump right back up to full size. While most field guides caution that some people find black morels upsetting to the stomach, especially when consumed with alcohol, Caroline and I wouldn't think of squandering any morel on a meal that didn't include a nice Cab or Merlot. And we've never suffered so much as a burp. On the other hand, since mushrooms are difficult to digest, it's wise not to pig out on too many at a time, or to eat them day after day. All things in moderation; that's my rule and guide (including, of course, moderation itself).

But there is more to the charm of morels than their prime-meat flavor—to wit, the thrill of the hunt.

While fungi don't run away like elk, morels are cleverly camouflaged and expert at hiding. Once you get the feel of it, morel hunting—if undertaken with humility, respect, and appropriate gratitude—is an earthy, deeply rewarding, and subtly mystical experience. Here in the southern Rockies, morels, especially the blacks, much prefer recently burned forest duff—when their spores can find it. In unburned forests, Rocky Mountain morels seek the shade of low-limbed spruces, firs, and Douglas firs, where the abundant rotting needles provide suitable mulch. As the May days warm toward June and the soil dries, the best hunting shifts to aspen groves on shady east-facing slopes, where last year's fallen leaves provide a moisture-holding bed. In rainy northwest Montana, where we hunt mushrooms nearly every June (coincident with watching grizzly bears), morels abound in recently burned lodgepole pine woods, of which, in recent times at least, mountainous Montana always has plenty.

Within these broadly general bounds, shallow, steep-sided depressions in the soil, such as those created by elk and moose tracks, the root craters of fallen trees, or even your own boot prints in mud, trap spores and can provide just enough additional moisture, shade, and shelter to nourish morels when the surrounding terrain will not. For much the same reasons—moisture retention, shade, and shelter—morchellas regularly hide beneath downed logs.

Even so, once you lock on to the proper search image—given good habitat and a good mushroom year—you will see them everywhere. Only by exercising exemplary stubbornness and stupidity did I manage to remain ignorant of the joys of fungi hunting through our first several years here. As the family meat hunter, I arrogantly preferred to leave the gathering chores, which I viewed as mundane, to the womanfolk. But as Caroline continued bringing the buggers in, spring after spring, and my appetite for morels grew and grew, I eventually—or rather quite suddenly—came around.

As it happened, my initiation into the clan of morel hunters took place on Mother's Day (which Caroline and I honor in our childless marriage as Not-Mother's Day). That year I was still hunting turkeys in May, as is often the case when I hunt with a bow. There I was, slouching slowly along an open-timbered ridge, occasionally offering up a chalky chorus of hen yelps on a box or slate call, relaxed, enjoying my time alone in the spring-green woods . . . when suddenly *there they were*, winking darkly up at me, like a pair of big black eyes. In the instant of recognition— with the same delight I might think "Those are *elk!*" or "Those are *turkeys!*" or "Those are naked *ladies!*"—I thought "Those are *morels!*" In the next instant I acknowledged, with considerable self-embarrassment, that I'd been seeing these things for years.

After leaning my bow against a tree and doffing my pack, I dropped to my knees to collect the pair of big button blacks. I admired my catch, thinking how surprised and delighted C would be, then looked around. From the lower angle provided by my kneeling stance, I immediately saw more, and more—dark, crenulated cones of living flesh, masquerading as wet (thus black) fir cones or scattered chunks of charcoal or even old bear turds. In fact, I realized, for years that's precisely what my hunter's tunnel vision had repeatedly mistaken them for.

In the end, I forgot about turkeys and spent the next half hour crawling around on my hands and knees, fingering through the carpet of composting needles . . . all for a handful of turds.

Back home, Caroline, as I'd predicted, was filled with surprise and delight, sensing correctly that I had, at long last, stumbled upon a fungal epiphany.

These days, our annual morel quest has matured to the level of ceremony, complete as all hunting is for me, with rituals and taboos. This confession provides, I must hope, a passable transition into a brief explication of my personal spirituality, which I call neo-animism and which, at its essential heart, is much the same as Edward Abbey's Earthism or farmer-poet Wendell Berry's "I stand for what I stand on"–ism.

Too often in the modern mind, even in university religion and anthropology courses, animism is arrogantly dismissed as primitive, superstition- and taboo-ridden spirit worship.

Wrong, or at best misleading, on at least two counts.

First, for most contemporary scholars the term *animism* conjures primarily or exclusively the ancient tradition's recent agricultural- and Christianity-polluted aberrations. When previously seminomadic, clan-living hunter-gatherers become sedentary hoers of gardens and tenders of goats and pigs even as their traditional nature-based spirituality is relentlessly assaulted by missionaries of foreign religions, the result, inevitably, is a confused and superstitious mess, such as we see in Bali and voodoo and the Native American Church. (Back in college, for a Religions of the World class, I wrote a term paper titled "The Influences of Christianity on Native American Creation Myths." Of the three randomly chosen Plains tribes I researched—Blackfeet, Northern Cheyenne, and Pawnee—all had suffered an infusion of Christian themes into their creation stories to the point where they'd forever lost track of their original and distinct tribal sense of cosmic place and identity. And this was even before they had lost their physical freedom as nomadic bison hunters. Steal their souls and their minds will follow.)

This pious academic inclination to apply the tenets of contemporary bastardized animism to all animism utterly and arrogantly ignores the timeless history of pure, unadulterated nature worship—which, for hundreds of millennia, was the universal and unique spirituality of all humanity. Naturally and logically, people who forage rather than herd domestic beasts and tend crops for a living—that is, people who depend utterly on wild as opposed to agricultural nature for their welfare—inevitably come to view themselves as merely an *element* of it all, one member of an egalitarian community, alternately eating and being eaten.

Thus did animism antedate and underlie Emerson's and Thoreau's transcendentalism, Leopold's land ethic, and contemporary deep ecology by hundreds of thousands of human generations. The sole difference between preagricultural animism and what I've come to embrace in my spiritually searching life as neo-animism is that the original version invests all of nature with an actively reciprocal intelligence and will—an investment we may choose to call superstition. Meanwhile, we neo-animists and deep ecologists and Leopoldian land ethicists and Abbeyesque Earthiests grant the nonhuman world this same power and equality *electively and metaphorically* rather than in a culturally inculcated physical sense. Restated, neo-animism (scientifically informed animism) expands the rule of reciprocity implied in the Golden Rule and the Buddhist concept of karma to include *all* of creation, not merely us.

The second logical flaw in the modern academic dismissal of

animism as superstition and spirit worship arises from these questions: If not spirit worship, what then do we call Christianity's blind devotion (a.k.a. faith) to the physically nonexistent, logically inexplicable, and intellectually incomprehensible Holy Trinity? If not spirit worship, how then do we view Catholicism's litany of saints and its ceremonial devotion to statuary icons (a.k.a. graven images)? And if not superstition, what then do we call the absolute, to-kill-and-die-for belief of every contemporary messianic world religion in a preternatural, inchoate, jealous, vengeful, and otherwise strikingly humanlike male God? If not superstition, how then do we explain the counterintuitive and scientifically impossible acceptance by Christianity of corporeal resurrection from death, of gravity-defying heavenward ascension, of water walking, sexless conception, and a myriad more biblical "miracles"?

And what, if not taboos, are the Ten Commandments?

I could continue at length in this overtly heretical vein, but I'd much rather dwell on the positive. So let's just say that I quite *like* how the day-to-day, down-to-Earth, live-and-die mortal natural world at hand so logically and sensibly functions, all the while brimming with a mystery and magic so powerful as to render by comparison even the most fantastical visions of any disembodied spiritual postdeath "life" bitterly banal at best.

In sum, here's how it seems to me: if you depend on wild nature for your physical and mental well-being (as we all do, whether we know it or not); if you desire a sustainable, workable, and healthy human society and crave a sense of belonging, spiritual permanence, and personal worth; and if you agree with Aldo Leopold that the collective human destiny is tied inextricably to the fate of the natural world, then you naturally become a homespun animist.

No matter by what name you call it.

Nor need we take ourselves overly seriously with all of this, we neo-animistic Earthiests. Humor, after all, is both the spice and a sign of sapient life. As the satirist Ambrose Bierce so aptly quipped, an animist is nothing more than a whimsical human creature "who has the folly to worship something he can actually see and feel."

And that something, of course, is the natural world. The only world we will ever know.

As mushroom hunting has gradually taken on more importance in our lives—an annual ritual to be anticipated and indulged in with physical and spiritual vigor—it has evolved into neo-animistic ceremony, replete with strict taboos. And those proscriptions, emulating the practical nature of traditional tribal taboos, are rooted in pragmatic soil, like so:

Never pick the first morel you find. Rather, politely ask it to speak kindly on your behalf to the rest of its clan, then leave it there in peace. (Practical purposes: "Leaving some for seed" and the karma- and character-building exercise of self-restraint.)

Never pick tiny morels. (Return when they have grown and enjoyed a chance to spore, ensuring next year's crop.)

Never carelessly pluck a morel bodily from the soil. Rather, carry a small, sharp knife and cleanly slice off the stem at ground level, leaving the stump in place. (Thus will you avoid damaging the mycelium, the fibrous subterranean network of filaments, or fungal root system, whose maintenance is essential for morel continuity.)

Never take more than not quite enough. (An overabundance of anything waters down its moral and aesthetic value, increases the likelihood of waste and future supply failure, and teaches us nothing.)

Never pick an area clean, and never pick the same small patch repeatedly. (Overharvesting limits and disrupts spore production and distribution, adversely affecting future crops. Too, a big part of the joy of gathering mushrooms is roaming far and wide in search of newfound patches.)

Never collect edible fungi in plastic bags or buckets. Rather, use a woven basket or a mesh or net bag and carry that bag in hand rather than in a pack. (Such "leaky" containers, as opposed to the solid-bottomed five-gallon plastic buckets commonly used by commercial pickers, allow spores to scatter as you walk. Plastic bags also induce heat retention, sweating, and rapid spoilage.)

Never serve large portions—say, as a full side dish or by over-stuffing an omelet. Mushrooms are rich, difficult to digest, and best enjoyed when savored as a condiment. Scatter rather than pack them into an egg or pasta dish, or serve just enough sautéed to allow for one tiny bite per mouthful of meat. (This avoids waste, enhances your dining pleasure, prolongs your stash, and minimizes the chance of upset stomachs.)

Beyond what you can eat in two or three days, never delay the drying of fresh morels, no matter how great the hassle. If you know you can't properly dry them, leave all but one dinner's worth in the woods. (Waste is ethically wrong, as is gluttony when picking.)

How you go about drying morels isn't nearly as important as how fast and how well. We've tried many methods but found nothing more all-around satisfactory than an electric food dehydrator, artless though it is. As long as the fungi are placed on a wire screen so that heat and air can circulate freely above and beneath, you can effectively dry morels in an oven turned to low. In warm, sunny weather, mushrooms dry beautifully outdoors but must be protected from flies with a cheesecloth or fine-screen covering. One very effective outdoor drying method is to elevate a wire basket an inch or two (on wood blocks or whatever) above an ad hoc solar heat collector, such as a dark metal roof or the hood of a dark-colored car. This presupposes, of course, warm, sunny days. When we're traveling, collecting, and camping and the weather is endlessly damp as it so often is in the Pacific Northwest, we've had good luck drying morels on the dashboard of the truck, parked to face the sun . . . or, when driving, with the defroster turned on high and a couple of windows cracked.

What matters, no matter how, is getting the spongy, wet flesh, which contains as much as 90 percent water, crispy dry as promptly as possible. Allowing precious morels to spoil from neglect or overcollecting represents the same spiritual failure as wasting the flesh of an animal you have killed (either directly as a hunter or farmer, or by proxy as a supermarket or restaurant carnivore). Gathering and eating from nature are ancient sacred acts. To kill and waste is at once sinful, slothful, and staggeringly stupid.

And we, hallowed *Homo saps*, are the only creatures that regularly do so.

· 23 ·

For my birthday this year (May 18) I got a bear. A big, brown, unkempt bruin, a month or so out of den. Just after Otis and I had returned from our evening walk, the animal shambled down off the brushy hillside that defines the northern expanse of our sprawling mountain estate, appearing in a little clearing directly behind my office and twenty yards from the cabin. There the visitor stopped and leaned heavily against a big ponderosa, seeming a bit lethargic. When the bear spotted C and me staring at it through the west wall of windows above the dinner table, it registered no reaction. Perhaps the glare of the afternoon sun, from the bear's point of view, looking east, converted the windows to mirrors. Otis, as always when there's food being eaten and crumbs perchance to fall, was folded up beneath the table, thus missing all the fun. At one point the bear waved its nose around, sniffing vigorously, apparently having scented our grub . . . yet remained admirably unmoving, slouched against its leanin' tree, wisely polite and cautious.

Even so and for all of our sakes, I got up and closed the north porch door, until then guarded only by a wood-framed screen. As we returned to our dinner, the bear continued to stare.

Only several minutes later, as I attacked a big wedge of fresh-baked chocolate birthday cake, did the bruin finally tire of the frustrating show-and-smell and make its move to leave. In a comedic parting gesture, the bruin took one step back from its support tree, sat on its haunches, swiveled 180 degrees around on its shaggy bum (as if scratching or wiping), then stood and shuffled back into the brush.

Gone, but never forgotten.

Like me on rare unavoidable visits to the big scary city, this old bear had ventured down from the mountain to the edge of civilization . . . sniffed around with cautious interest, been tempted by some of what it smelled but put off by all the rest and wisely retreated, back to the sheltering aspens and their canopy of new-born leaves, where the shadow-mottled forest floor is carpeted with green grass and where elk calves, like big Easter eggs, lie hidden here and there.

· 24 ·

Northwestern Montana, the first week of June.

The three bears appear in late afternoon: a monstrously beautiful sow of some four hundred pounds, golden-brown with a broad blond saddle and trailed by two adolescent cubs. I glance at Caroline and she at me, our faces filled with grin, sharers in happy recognition. We *know* these bears, having met them exactly here, exactly a year ago. We are thrilled that both cubs, against harsh odds, have survived and grown so well. Born in midwinter in the den as helpless one-pound rat-balls, the average grizzly cub will balloon to a hundred rollicking pounds of muscle and fur by the end of its first season, at least doubling that in its second year. The cubs we're watching now are roughly the size of adult black bears, if not so long and leggy.

"Must be a terrific mom," says Caroline, her voice a respectful whisper though the bears are a quarter mile away, across a roaring creek and up the facing hill.

"A *big* mother anyhow," I tease.

Through the optical magic of a 45x spotting scope, it's as if the bruins are in our laps. And even through 8x binoculars they're plenty close enough. Lolling amid a lush low sea of spring beauties, momma griz grazes on the delicate pinkish-white flower tops. The girl cub—we are assigning gender based on differences in size and behavior between the two—the smaller, calmer cub, rakes the ground with long amber claws, plowing up the nutty-sweet root corms anchoring those delicate flowers. The boy cub, meanwhile, mauls a wrist-thick aspen sapling, bending, raking, and biting it. I wouldn't want to be that little tree, whose rowdy playmate looks to weigh two hundred pounds, with Terminator arms, T. rex teeth, and *Friday the 13th* claws.

After an hour of browsing, rooting, romping, and resting, the grizzly family drifts to a nearby grassy knoll, where the sow haunch-sits facing us, while her two huge babes crowd in to nurse. Odd, this. Bear cubs are generally weaned by the end of their first summer, and these are second-summer yearlings. But grizzly sows, given the right circumstances, may lactate and nurse for as long as twenty months. In any event, momma griz seems to be in the weaning mode, for after barely a minute of eager suckling she backhands the girl, sending her rolling, then locks her bone-crushing jaws onto the scruff of the boy-brat's neck and flings him aside as well, as if the brute were weightless.

"Can't blame her," whispers Caroline. "Those cubs look to have the teeth and table manners of killer whales."

Quite so.

Soon all three bears are napping, though the sow rouses frequently to poke her muzzle at the big blue orb of sky overarching and uniting us all, head bobbing, nostrils flared, visibly nervous, continually testing the breeze—for what? Behind her, four black-bottomed feet are all we can see of one cub, dozing spread-eagled on its back; the other has utterly vanished.

· 25 ·

It has been said there are no sacred wild places left on Earth and that the civilized human animal has lost its deep-time animistic gift of perceiving the intrinsic sacredness of nature dispersed equally through all living things. Certainly and tragically, we are well along the doomsday path to collective cultural insanity as a result of divorcing ourselves from the wild world that shaped and continues to nourish and sustain us. Consider the following outtake from bio-acoustician Bernie Krause's sensory-expanding book *Wild Soundscapes*. Of our recent losses he writes:

In 1968 it took fifteen recording hours to get one hour's worth of natural sound. . . . Now, due to human noise and disturbed habitats, it takes about two thousand recording hours to get the same result. About 2 percent of our old-growth forests remain standing in the lower forty-eight states, down from 45 percent just thirty years ago. . . . Over 25 percent of the North American natural soundscapes in my archives were recorded in habitats that have since become extinct; many vital natural soundscapes no longer exist—except on tape.

It's true and incalculably tragic that real wilderness is being destroyed or polluted (the latter by man-made noise, smog, acid rain, and artificial light) at a terrifying rate. Rather than more rapine of suffering nature in the quest for more oil and gas to support the continued insane and ultimately suicidal growth of our already obese and wasteful lifestyle, America, in order to remain the world's richest and freest nation, desperately needs legislation that favors the holding together and reassembling of large, ecosystem-sized pieces of wildlands, private as well as public.

To paraphrase old friend Aldo, I'm glad I won't be young again without wild places to grow up in.

Even so and at least for now, places that to most folks still *feel* wild remain relatively abundant. To not take advantage of this rapidly dwindling treasure, imperfect as it increasingly is, is to deny ourselves experiencing what remains of where and how *we are meant to be*. While millions of Americans eagerly get "out there," it is mostly as puppets on strings being pulled by industry and media manipulators determined to put lots of expensive stuff, as much of it as possible with motors, between us and the Earth. Which is to complain that today we go to nature to play rather than to pray, viewing wilderness as sports arena rather than cathedral and sacred grove. Precious few of us today retain the traditional human knowledge of how to relate in deeply satisfying and meaningful ways to the natural wildness within us, as well as without.

Yet hope persists. I firmly believe that our ancient innate

knowledge of how best to live is not irrevocably dead but has been drugged, sedated, and prostituted by modern material culture. It can be revived. The only requirements are focus and desire—minimal investments that nonetheless keep most of us from even thinking about what we've lost in the realm of the wild and natural, much less trying to regain as much as possible of it. There are simply too many other far less demanding and more glamorous, if largely meaningless, distractions to pursue these virtual days, without the teeth, claws, and precipitous cliffs of wild nature. As in any serious venture, in order to sort out the most precious nuggets of life, we must learn to discern them from the dross.

You need only venture beyond the city's edge, climb down out of your climate-controlled, musically insulated cocoon on wheels, and step beyond the invisible cage of pavement to find such sacred places, adventures, learning experiences, and sense of grounding as Caroline and I enjoy on a daily basis at home, and which we take to the limit, if only for a couple of weeks annually, up in wild Montana, camping and hiking among the largest concentration of free-roaming grizzlies remaining in the lower forty-eight. Perhaps as many as a thousand are scattered throughout the expansive northern Continental Divide ecosystem, with several hundred in the Glacier Park region alone, and no other people within miles. While grizzly bears are not essential to reawakening personal wildness and natural spirituality, they unquestionably add an invigoratingly spicy *edge* to the pursuit. As longtime grizzly-country resident Jack Turner points out in *Teewinot,* his gorgeous natural history of Teton National Park and its wild surrounds, the grizzly bear is "a presence that heightens experience. It is as though the oldest and deepest area of our heart/mind—the Pleistocene heart/mind—is nourished."

For C and me, there is no "as though" about it. In the presence of Lord Griz, seen or merely known to be nearby, we can *feel* the heart-mind nourishment flowing in as the bear quietly makes us stronger by highlighting our frailties.

· 26 ·

It's just a boulder on a Montana mountainside—not so very different from thousands of such calendar-photo scenes scattered throughout the Rockies, including our sublime San Juans of home. Yet because we've seen so many grizzlies here—right over there on that gentle slope, just across the way, as many as four at once and up to nine individuals in a single day, with the nearest paved road fifty miles distant—this place has become our sanctum sanctorum of sanity and grace in an insanely ungraceful world, luring us to drive the thousand miles each way each year to get here, drawn like moths to campfire flame. Since we always camp and never at developed (pay-to-play) sites, gasoline is our only real expense, rendering this trip, our only vacation most years, almost affordable. We have to eat even at home, so as long as I have some paying work in tow, once we're here we can stay for as long as we wish at little additional cost.

Well, not quite *that* long, which would be at least until winter. Although I struggle harder than most to keep them in their place, I, like every other working stiff, have certain sea-anchor "responsibilities."

· 27 ·

Every morning and afternoon in this place—our courage stiffened by a reassuring sun and two big canisters of hot-pepper bear spray—Caroline and I explore, with boots and binoculars, every hidden corner of this dripping Pacific Northwest forest. We search for morels and bears while pondering the magical natures of both, the bears in particular—their daily lives, their survival prospects, and how *their* welfare bears on our own, individually, culturally, morally, and as fellow mammals who must cooperate in order to cohabitate.

Between these twice-daily adventures of discovery, we idle in the scenic comfort of a camp we've dubbed Grizzlyville II, set tight in the elbow of a musical snowmelt creek. Here, in addition to bears at a polite and comfortable distance, we're entertained occasionally by passing moose and constantly by a gregarious family of dippers nested nearby, where they can feel the whitewater spray. Subaquatic predators, they walk the bottoms of whitewater streams in search of nymphs and other prey. Another feathered regular here, though it's never seen and its voice is a total stranger to our outsiders' ears, sings its ringing metallic song dawn to dusk. We call it the telephone bird and have asked several locals its true name, but to no avail, perhaps owing to my poor imitation of a ringing telephone and our inability to offer a physical description of the invisible vocalist.

Through each lazy midday in camp, I alternately read, scribble notes on a legal pad, and glass for bears. Last year, my mobile library included Terry Tempest Williams's artful *Leap* and Henry Beston's 1928 Cape Cod classic, *The Outermost House*. This year I'm reviewing Paul Shepard's *Coming Home to the Pleistocene* (among the most important books ever written, if not the easiest to read), Doug Peacock's hairy-chested memoir *Grizzly Years*, and Yale sociobiologist Stephen Kellert's *The Value of Life: Biological Diversity and Human Society*. Fat squashed mosquitoes, many bloated with fresh human blood, serve as sanguine bookmarks as I rotate among the three meaty volumes while grizzlies come and go across the way—animating, dignifying, sanctifying that otherwise nondescript mountain slope, that otherwise wholly typical boulder, the otherwise unexceptional congregation of brush, wildflowers, and trees over yonder, snuffling and feeding, pooping and playing, napping, nursing, and, the occasional mature male among them, cruising for love.

June is the springtime of bear romance, and doubtless the reason our old friend the blond-saddled sow is so watchfully nervous. Were a boar to catch her unawares, he would try to kill her cubs and eat them—a brutally instinctive strategy to rush her back into estrus. Since bears practice free love, a cub-killing male increases his chances of breeding the same sow he has rendered cubless, thereby increasing his personal stake in the local gene pool. Smaller, first-year cubs, of course, are at far greater risk of such sex-driven instinctive predation. Yet big as they are, that brother and sister over yonder remain vulnerable to attack by a mature male several times their size, thus prompting their mother to remain alert, edgy, fiercely defensive. This is *not* the season to cross close paths with a grizzly sow and cubs. But we've been at this game for many years, Caroline and I, and we play it with the utmost care. Which is to say, we care about the bears' fates as well as our own.

So go our days here: at once relaxed and stimulating. We feel comfortable and secure in our personal safety.

But with every setting sun, anxiety creeps darkly down the mountainside opposite, leaps the creek, and settles over camp like an ominous fog, a shadowy ambience bearing the flavor of fear. Tonight, like last night and tomorrow night, for as many nights as we are here, I'll lie wild-eyed awake in a black hole of angst where bear spray is no use, fretfully anticipating the heavy hungry bumps in the dark nearby that I so hope never to hear. Caroline feels much the same, but reassured by my vigilant insomnia and burdened with a woefully inflated faith in my ability to protect her from all harm, she gets at least some sleep.

How different, this, from home safe home in Colorado. So different—and yet so welcome. We don't deny our dread of the night here, which is frightfully exhausting and deeply humbling. Yet we return—can hardly wait through each long winter just to be here now, again and again for as long as we are able and as long as grizzlies define this place: confronting the monster of fear within, as well as the beast without. Nor are we alone in this love/fear, day/night approach/avoidance maze of feelings for the scarier aspects of nature. Even after ten thousand years of humankind's struggles to beat wildness down to our size, to dominate, exterminate, pacify, and "put nature in its place," such humbling fears remain with all of us. And for that, for those very fears, we should be thankful.

Ecophilosopher Paul Shepard muses metaphorically that nature's scary creatures—from grizzly bears to spiders—"were invented to remind us of something we want to forget but cannot remember either." That persistently perplexing "something," of course, is our own wild-animal nature and evolutionary ancestry, not only as fierce predators but as screaming prey as well. "Our fear of monsters in the night," Shepard continues, "has its origins far back in the evolution of our primate ancestors, whose tribes were pruned by horrors whose shadows continue to elicit our monkey screams in dark theaters."

And in dark woods as well.

Fear and loving. The beauty in the beast. A grizzly conundrum. Beautiful monsters.

Frankly, Caroline and I are at ease with our nocturnal dis-ease with *Ursus arctos horribilis*, literally "the horrible bear of the north," reassured in this regard by Professor Shepard, who notes that such sharply mixed emotions are "phylogenetically felicitous"—that is, faithful to our species' evolutionary design (phylogeny) and thus a good thing. Anyone whose innate human nature, imagination, and intellect have not been utterly anesthetized by modern concrete culture and virtual reality must at least subconsciously respect, if not consciously admire, the grizzly on its own turf, must be forced to acknowledge its awesome beauty and power, keen intelligence, eerily humanlike mannerisms, symbolic sacredness, and patient grace in the face of relentless malevolent harassment at the clumsy hands of our wayward kind.

At the same time, of course, anyone with a thimbleful of survival instinct is wired like a Las Vegas casino when hiking and camping in what little is left of the grizzly's wild domain, especially at night. As Doug Peacock—a gonzo bear addict who's infinitely more courageous and grizzly wise than myself—frankly admits, "You don't get much sleep when camping in grizzly country."

Tracking this same trail of thought—ruminating on the grizzly conundrum—Yale's Stephen Kellert reminds us that people, like bears, are omnivorous not only in appetite but in mood and psyche as well. "As a predator," Kellert points out, "we display a certain aggressiveness and inclination to master and control. As an herbivore, we seek to avoid conflict, to find shelter and security, to remain elusive and out of harm's way. . . . We are a divided creature—one moment dominating and controlling; the next, avoiding conflict and strife."

And so likewise is the great bear a "divided creature," predictably running away at the first hint of human approach, yet unpredictably inclined to rip out and devour your steaming guts. Biophobia is the darker underside of that same adaptive evolutionary coin, as reflected in our species' ubiquitous unease with snakes, spiders, high cliffs, sharks, cavernous darkness, the unknown and utterly unknowable awaiting us *out there* in the

shrouded night—including quarter-ton bears with short tempers
and long claws.

Each of these counterbalancing bio-feelings, philia and pho-
bia, is natural and healthy, within logical limits. An unnatural,
illogical extreme of biophobia is called theriophobia, defined by
writer Barry Lopez in *Of Wolves and Men* as "fear of the beast as
an irrational, violent, insatiable creature." After two decades of
living among and crossing close paths with Colorado black
bears, and an even longer span of time spent periodically camping, backpacking, and otherwise haunting grizzly country (in
Yellowstone and Teton, Glacier, Canada, and Alaska), I've never
encountered a bear of any species that seemed irrational, gratu-
itously violent, or insatiable. Humans with those pathologies,
however, are commonplace.

I'll take my chances with the bears.

· 28 ·

Three years ago, Erica joined us for a week's vacation at a camp
we call Grizzlyville I, a few miles down-creek from here. On a
cold and drizzly June morning that drove Erica and me to shelter while washing the breakfast dishes, a huge dark shadow
floated silently by the open door of our tent-topped pickup
camper. *"Grizzly!"* croaked Erica in a raspy choking whisper, the
adrenaline thick in her voice.

The task at hand was instantly forgotten. Caroline was out
there, somewhere, alone. Only now noticing that C had left her
bear spray behind, I snatched it up and bolted out. Just then, my
wife came walking down the hill, from the same direction the
ghostly bear had appeared only seconds before. Her face was as
pale as ever I've seen it, and before I could speak she pointed

back up the hill and said shakily, "I want to show you something."

I followed without question.

In a shadowy copse of adolescent conifers sixty yards from camp, Caroline stopped, looked down at the mossy ground at our feet, and pointed an incriminating finger at a stone the size of a football and the dent in the forest floor from which it had recently been extracted; a few feet away, a quart of grass-green bear plop steamed warmly in the cold, damp air. And then her story came gushing out.

"An hour ago I came up here, pulled that rock out of the ground, used the hole as a latrine, burned the paper, and rolled the rock back in place. When I felt sick again and came back up here just minutes ago, this is what I found—the rock pulled out, my own mess gone, and *this* in its place"—she fanned a hand at the grizzly scat as if shooing away a fly—"just like a pack rat making a trade. Do you think the bear was trying to *tell* us something?"

Indeed I think it was—and notwithstanding its rude manners, it had done so quite creatively, even metaphorically. Caroline and the bear must have come within a few yards of meeting as she walked up from camp that second time, just as it was ambling down.

Quick to pick up on such a sledgehammer hint, within the hour we'd broken camp and run away—only to discover this new and better camp, Grizzlyville II. A few miles farther up-valley, upstream, tucked discreetly within the woods' shady edge, it offers a panoramic view of a busy bear crossroads at a seemingly safe remove—that shrine of rock, brush, and wildflowers on the hillside across the way. From this distance, I reassured the womenfolk, we shouldn't crowd any bears, and with good karma and good luck, vice versa.

Or so we eagerly hoped. That same evening, as the campfire

flickered low and our world went blindingly black and the spring-flooded creek roared distractingly, punctuated by random, inexplicable splashes—"like some big animal charging across," C said—I began to entertain doubts. My primary concern was the huge boar grizzly we'd watched all afternoon and evening, until he'd dissolved into the thickening gloom while headed downhill our way, lumbering bemusedly along a well-worn game trail leading to the creek. And likely the same game trail, I now worried, that ran smack through our camp, up the hill behind us, and into the forest beyond.

Suddenly obsessed by this threatening possibility, I excused myself, saying I had to go take a leak. With flashlight in one hand and bear spray in the other (safety off), I slipped through the wall of darkness, tracing the moose-tracked trail to where it crossed the creek and disappeared into an alder jungle on the opposite, grizzly-inhabited side. Near as I could tell, it was, as feared, the selfsame trail the boar had been descending, a bit farther up, when the lights went out for the night. Would the raging but narrow creek be enough to stop a six-hundred-pound bear, should he try to cross it?

Right . . .

Scurrying back to camp, I put on my best Mr. Cool act and asked the supposedly weaker sex if, given the uneasy circumstances, they were nervous about sleeping here. "If either of you would feel better about it," I politely offered, "we can pull camp right now and move to a safer place."

"I'm fine," said C.

"No problem here either," echoed E.

My bluff thus called, I was reduced to confessing my deep concern regarding the possibility of that Really Big Grizzly winding up in camp any minute now and firmly suggested that we "go find a safer place so that I can get some sleep tonight."

And so it came to pass, for the second time in a single day, we broke camp and ran away. This time in the midnight dark.

———

One year almost to the day after that heady excitement, Caroline and I are back, with me feeling like Hemingway's Francis Macomber of "Short Happy Life" infamy, shamed by last year's timid retreats, or at least the second one (the first I believe even Hemingway would have agreed was justified), and determined this time to stick it out no matter what. (Within reason, of course.) It's a challenge made easier by a markedly reduced grizzly presence owing to the past winter's drought and a consequent scarceness of green spring forage at this altitude. We've seen no more than four bears a day, all at a comfortable remove, and the nearest fresh tracks a couple of miles upslope—two perfect front prints in compacted snow, like dinner plates with four-inch claws. And only one fresh grizzly pie, piled high as a sheepherder's cairn along a game trail a quarter mile from camp. Too, the creek this year is lower, slower, and quieter, so that maybe we can hear approaching bears and, more important, they can hear us (talking louder than normal) and choose to go elsewhere. Maybe.

Even so, I find my timid nocturnal self demanding of my adventurous diurnal self: What the *hell* do you think you're doing here? And placing Caroline at risk to boot, though she'd not have it otherwise.

What we are doing here, according to Professor Kellert, is voluntarily exposing ourselves to a heady dose of biophobia in order to enhance our "capacity to be humbled."

And that, I remind myself as bedtime nears, is a good and precious thing.

Doug Peacock echoes this same appreciation for nature-induced humility when he writes of tracking the suspected killer and consumer of a European backpacker in the backcountry of Yellowstone National Park: "One last time, I look back at the sign of the huge grizzly whose crooked print etched in crusted mud quietly refutes three thousand years of human dominion."

· 29 ·

Bedtime and then some.

I'm relatively relaxed tonight, having no good reason not to be, yet still unable to sleep. Moving quietly, hoping not to awaken Caroline snoozing peacefully beside me, I grope in the dark for my headlamp, flick it on, sit upright in our double sleeping bag, cross my legs like a skinny bearded Buddha, open a well-worn book, and retreat, once again, into the philosophical refuge of Paul Shepard, who eloquently and disturbingly muses:

> As surely as we hear the blood in our ears, the echoes of a million midnight shrieks of monkeys have their traces in our nervous systems. Modern fiction is rich in allusions to the terror of "victims" in the jaws of raging brutes. But the teeth of a predator may be painless for the prey because of brain-made endorphins, so that such a death may be euphoric, even a kind of epiphany. To understand this, we must stand outside the stereotypes of raw gore, of good and evil among eaters, of innocent victims and bloody demons.

Certainly, I'd prefer never to explore the possibility of euphoric death by tooth and claw, much less the epiphany of personal mastication. Yet without its fearsome creatures, this wild and sacred place would be just another lovely landscape, an ornate stage without star players—like so many people we all have known, superficially stunning but devoid of deeper meaning.

The good news is that in spite of all our fears, nightmares, and rare harsh instances of brutal reality, the great bear is by no means a "bloody demon." Nor are humans often its "innocent victims." Bears, both black and grizzly, are naturally shy, overwhelmingly vegetarian, and very rarely predaceous on humans. Most bear attacks, in fact, are directly attributable to the purported "victim" having done something transparently stupid. Moreover, it's precisely *because* the bear demands thoughtful attention, respect, and compromise from uncompromising, disrespectful, inattentive humanity that—as veteran grizzly biologist Charles Jonkel so perfectly caps the essence of the beast—"a free-roaming grizzly is a symbol of what is right with the world."

Restated by way of paraphrasing something Peacock once remarked in backyard conversation: if we, as the dominant creatures on Earth, can't find within ourselves the generosity to make room for the last surviving remnants of the most impressive creature to have survived the Pleistocene alongside us, how can we expect to manage a sane and peaceful future for ourselves? The grizzly is a survival test for humanity, and so far we are failing.

Some years ago, the Canadian biologist and writer Kevin Van Tighem suffered the trauma of having his sister horribly mauled in a chance trail encounter with a mother grizzly that had attacked instinctively, in protection of her cubs. Who could be more "justified" in hating the bear? Yet Kevin, a wise man, proclaims that "fear, prejudice, human ignorance, macho fantasy and sheer greed—not the nature of the bear itself—account for the fact that grizzlies no longer survive in most of their historical range. We could live with grizzly bears if we were prepared to know them for what they are—not what we imagine them to be—and adjust our own behavior accordingly."

Yes we could. If only we would—as a few exceptional people, living and working in a few last good places, in fact are doing.

My own behavioral adjustment at the moment is the usual edgy insomnia. Even so, a few nights hence, back home in comparatively gentle Colorado, where there are likely no grizzlies left and backcountry sleep comes easy, I'll wish I were here again, confronting the beautiful beast.

Close beside me, Caroline stirs and moans, "Please turn off that light."

Obediently, I close my book, douse my headlamp, lie back, shut my bloodshot eyes—and sleep the sleep of the grateful undead.

· 30 ·

Three days of driving and a thousand miles down the road, we are safely back home. A bit too safely, perhaps, as I find myself suffering from grizzly withdrawal. In the depths of my throes, I fall to contemplating how the insidious loss of natural wildness bears on the human spirit.

Wildness, from a biological point of view, is not a place but a state of being; it is a condition of unfettered ecological self-determination, free of human manipulation. Wilderness is the place where wildness lives. Neither can exist without the other. Wildness and wilderness are not merely a symbiosis—a mutually beneficial relationship—but a synergy: infinitely greater than the sum of their parts. How best, then, to gauge wildness in a would-be wilderness place?

Answer: By the presence or absence of beings that cannot continue to survive, much less prosper, under the pressure of unrestrained human interference.

Here in the lower forty-eight, the primary miner's canaries of natural wildness are grizzly bears and wolves, the definitive North American alpha predators, both of whom the northern Rockies still support, if too often only barely. Meanwhile, my home mountains farther south have allowed these treasures to be stolen away and sold down the river of so-called progress. Neither of these fiercely independent creatures, grizzly or wolf, can survive surrounded by human culture unless we learn to grant them more notable and noble concessions than we so far have. And by way of that granting, we will greatly expand our hearts, spirits, and collective hope—our very humanity.

The grizzly in particular, since it can and occasionally does kill and eat us, is the ultimate icon of wildness. Motivated by these thoughts and a deeply troubling sense of spiritual loss, during the first half of the 1990s I undertook a marathon exploration of what went wrong here in Colorado, beginning more than a century ago and ending, if indeed it has ended, only recently. I also studied how similar forces are working against grizzly-quality wildness elsewhere today.

The San Juan Mountains of southwest Colorado comprise some of the richest grizzly habitat in all of North America. In prehistoric times, the largest omnivore our continent has ever known and the largest predator to have survived the final faunal meltdown of the icy Pleistocene was abundant throughout what is now Colorado. Because the region's pre-Columbian native inhabitants—the Utes, Apaches, Cheyenne, Arapaho, Anasazi, Fremont, and others—embraced an animistic worldview that envisioned a zoomorphic, or animal-centered, rather than anthropomorphic, or human-centered, cosmos, these early southwesterners were compelled spiritually as well as practically to *accommodate* physical forces beyond their control. In the end, most native cultures came to revere the grizzly as a demigod. To our neighboring Southern Utes, the grizzly was the mother of all creation, a powerful spirit that is honored still today in the annual Bear Dance ceremony, which is both a celebration of spring renewal and a matchmaking occasion for young Ute women and men.

White explorers and settlers felt no such spiritual connections to nature; rather, they viewed nature as an adversary. Consequently, by early in the twentieth century, ranchers, sport hunters, and federal trappers had reduced Colorado's grizzlies to a few shy survivors, more like black bears than griz in behavior. In a majority of local and bureaucratic minds, the grizzly was dead and gone; the wilderness had been rendered safe for human occupation and commercial exploitation. Then, in September 1951, a federal trapper used a cyanide set gun to end the brief career of a sheep-killing young male grizzly north of Pagosa Springs, up along the Continental Divide within today's Weminuche Wilderness Area, in a grassy subalpine park called Starvation Gulch. The trapper was a local character named Ernie Wilkinson, today in his seventies. Last I heard, and not that long ago, Ernie was still leading backpacking trips into the backcountry and practicing taxidermy in the high San Luis Valley village of Monte Vista.

Recalling the event for me in 1994, Wilkinson said he had been as surprised as everyone else to learn that his victim was a grizzly. One bright July morn forty-three years since he last had been there, Ernie guided me to the place where the drama had played out. Evidencing no guilt, this soft-spoken, gentle-mannered man explained, "Back then, nobody even thought about there still being grizzlies around. America was busy recovering from World War II, and the livestock industry was important. It was my job to help protect that industry."

In an irony of synchronicity, just a month before Ernie killed his accidental griz, a near twin was shot by a sheepherder near Blue Lake, eighty miles to the south of Starvation Gulch, within what today is the South San Juan Wilderness Area. Ernie the part-time taxidermist, coincidentally, was in the process of mounting that bear's head and claws when his own grizzly came and went. Tragedies seem to come in threes, and precisely one year later, in September 1952, in the same general vicinity, yet a third sheep-killing bear—this time an adult female with two subadult cubs—was eliminated by another federal trapper. Even though both big cubs got away clean, Colorado wildlife officials inexplicably chose that moment to declare the grizzly extinct statewide—even as they quietly hired a researcher to comb the San Juans for evidence of more of the species. Over the next twenty-eight years, many credible grizzly sightings were reported, in the San Juans and the adjacent South San Juans. Yet the official word remained: gone.

And so it went, so it was assumed to be, until September 23, 1979, when the latest so-called last Colorado grizzly turned up . . . again in the South San Juans, and again good and dead. But not, this time, without a heroic struggle.

On that star-crossed autumn day, a local hunting outfitter named Ed Wiseman was guiding a Kansas bowhunter, seeking elk, when the two men separated and Wiseman surprised a supposedly extinct grizzly above the headwater canyon of the upper Navajo River. The bear immediately charged. Wiseman was knocked to the ground and severely mauled, but he managed to stab and kill the bear with a hand-held arrow. Although federal investigators suspected the man had shot the bear first, thus provoking the attack, the U.S. Fish and Wildlife Service dropped the case after Wiseman passed a lie-detector test and no credible evidence could be mounted against him. The bear, a very old female with broken and worn-down teeth with massive abscesses and extensive arthritis, was estimated to weigh 350 to 400 pounds—not large by grizzly standards, but hardly stunted either. As I had done with Ernie Wilkinson, the old trapper, I cajoled Ed Wiseman to lead me to the spot where his fight had occurred. And there, in what for him remains a spooky place, while I sat on the very spot where his bear had died, Ed retold his story.

As an upshot of the Wiseman incident, through the summers of 1981 and '82, the Colorado Division of Wildlife assigned black bear biologist Tom Beck to conduct an extensive baiting and leg-snaring study in hopes of capturing, radio-collaring, releasing, and radio-tracking any remaining San Juan grizzlies. To compensate for his lack of grizzly experience, Beck "high-graded" four expert field hands from the Montana and Wyoming grizzly research teams of Charles Jonkel and Richard Knight. While the searchers failed to catch a grizzly, they did turn up several bits of intriguing evidence—including a confirmed grizzly den that likely was dug by the Wiseman bear, along with several confirmed grizzly digs of indeterminate ages. These artifacts suggested but did not confirm the possibility of surviving post-Wiseman bears. Accordingly, as Tom Beck stated in his final report, "Failure to catch a grizzly does not mean a definite absence of bears." Beck concluded that the wisest official stance would be to assume that a few bears remained and to reduce the primary threats to them—sheep grazing and black bear hunting—in a relatively small area of likely core habitat. Ignoring its own expert's advice, the state reverted again to its traditional public stance that Colorado grizzlies were extinct—though this time the prefix "probably" was inserted before "extinct" and advisories reminded hunters and predator-phobic ranchers that killing a grizzly in Colorado is a federal felony.

Enter writer (*Grizzly Years*), filmmaker (*Peacock's War*), and controversial grizzly champion Doug Peacock. In 1990, responding to continued reports of grizzly sightings in the South San Juans, and after conducting a two-week backpacking wilderness survey of his own, Peacock vowed to do what the federal and state wildlife agencies could or would not do: prove the existence of a remnant population of native Colorado grizzly bears and thus, via the Endangered Species Act, ensure their protection. It was Peacock, a friend of mine by way of Edward Abbey, who drew me into the drama. At first, I was reluctant.

"The importance of this search," Doug argued at the time, "has as much to do with the future and quality of Colorado wilderness as it does with trying to prove the existence of a few grizzly bears in the San Juans. At the heart of this project lies an insistence that Colorado's wildness should command greater respect from those who manage her lands and natural resources."

Yet Peacock too—after enlisting the aid of biologists, ecologists, a come-and-go entourage of journalists including myself, plus dozens of enthusiastic college-student field hands collectively searching for nearly five years—failed to find conclusive proof of living grizzlies in Colorado. By 1995, the San Juan Grizzly Project that Doug had spawned was forced to toss in the towel while echoing Tom Beck's sentiment that "no proof does not mean no bears."

So it is that still today, a quarter century and more since the last confirmed Colorado grizzly died, the question remains frustratingly unanswered. Are there or are there not a last few grizzlies left in southwest Colorado? If you wish to believe that a few ghostly griz still haunt hidden refuges high in the sprawling San Juan Mountains—or, more likely, in the less mined, less logged, less overgrazed, less spectacular, less advertised, and thus less trampled South San Juans—there's plenty of suggestive evidence to uphold your faith. But faith is belief in something you cannot prove and evidence is not proof and should you choose to believe that the 1979 Wiseman grizzly was the dead last of its breed in Colorado, the end of a Pleistocene legacy—the end, that is, of true wildness in these ancient, lovely mountains—there is no way, to date, that you can be proved wrong.

Believers maintain that the existence of a remnant Colorado grizzly population has been demonstrated beyond reasonable doubt. They cite hair samples collected by Peacock's searchers and identified by an independent forensics laboratory in Wyoming as grizzly (doubters say the hairs could have been planted); several finds of huge, grizzly-like tracks (though none have been cast or convincingly photographed); and two seemingly credible sightings, including a female with three subadult cubs observed for half an hour from just eighty yards with binoculars by a highly respected local ranchman named Dennis Schutz, back in

1990. "I've seen hundreds of bears," Dennis told me when we revisited the scene, "and these were definitely grizzlies." Most recently, a large adult bear bluff-charged an experienced and highly credible wildlife photographer in 1995. He swore it was a grizzly, and the location was perfect. Other intriguing, albeit inconclusive evidence includes a hot-fresh bear dig, definitively grizzly in conformation, that Dennis Schutz and I found and photographed in 1993 in a remote subalpine bowl near where the Wiseman bear had lived and died.

Thus, say champions of Colorado grizzlies and grizzly-quality wilderness, pointing to the Endangered Species Act (which itself is now endangered), the time has long since come for the responsible management agencies—the U.S. Fish and Wildlife Service, the Colorado Division of Wildlife, and the U.S. Forest Service— to quit hiding behind the spineless and morally suspect curtain of "no conclusive proof" and take proactive steps to protect Colorado's last few grizzlies and their besieged enclaves of public-lands habitat. Meanwhile, doubters both within and without the responsible agencies counter that it would be a waste of precious manpower and money to take any such action prior to proving conclusively that Colorado has any grizzlies left to protect. Similarly, there's no money or manpower to spare—and precious little motivation—to go yet again in search of ghost grizzlies.

In the biological arena, the question most often asked is this: Even if a handful of native Colorado grizzlies were proved to exist, what about inbreeding? Aren't the survivors so few as to be genetically doomed?

Eventually, yes, though not necessarily soon.

No one really knows at what point an island population of grizzlies will collapse from inbreeding, though observable evidence, in Europe and elsewhere, suggests that brown bears are remarkably, perhaps uniquely, resistant to genetic starvation. This theory is reinforced by the fact that by 1979 there had been so few grizzlies in Colorado for so long, the Wiseman bear must have been the product of multiple generations of increasingly narrow inbreeding. Yet her physical remains are normal in every way, save the skeletal ravages of age. The Wiseman sow also had nursed cubs, offspring that, if they lived to their full potential of thirty or so years, hiding as successfully as had their mother, could still be around today.

On our evening walk today, Otis and I got barked at—a piercingly loud, remarkably doglike sound—by an elk cow near the twin pools we call Bear Springs, a mile and a half northeast of here. While I could not see the animal for the trees, the fact that she was standing in place and barking repeatedly—rather than fleeing without comment, as is the norm—testified that she had a hidden calf nearby. And so we promptly left.

A few minutes later and a quarter mile away, I almost stepped on a spotted elk calf lying motionless in a thicket of native grass, snowberry, and oak brush. This time there was no barking and no momma elk in sight. We left anyway, pretending we hadn't seen.

· **31** ·

"There's a moose in the yard," I say matter-of-factly.

No reaction from the girls, who apparently find my statement so far-fetched that it doesn't even prompt them to look up from their dinners.

It's seven P.M. on July 2 and the giant black deer is striding toward the cabin, seemingly with purpose, weaving his way through a cluster of aspen saplings. After approaching to just three feet, the bull peers curiously in through the west windows as Caroline and Erica continue eating dinner, giggling at what C dismisses as my "silly attempt at humor." But when the huge shadow essentially blocks out the low sun, the giggling abruptly stops. I stand, grab the camera from a nearby shelf, and start firing off shots, thinking how neat the scene will be, with gals and food in the foreground and the peeping moose framed in a window just behind.

But good times rarely last long, and soon the young male—typical of an age and antler size known in moose jargon as a Bullwinkle—loses interest in us and turns and strolls out past my office and on up the hill, where he soon is swallowed by the jungle of oak brush there.

Yesterday, our photographer friend Branson Reynolds, who lives just down the way, saw what must have been this same Bullwinkle trotting along the county road southwest of here, apparently headed for town. And earlier this very morning Erica commented that something huge had bedded in the tall grass between her cabin and the creek. "Way too big," she reckoned, "to be an elk."

Since moose are not native to Colorado, this is likely the first time in the history of the universe that *Alces* has ever set foot on Spring Mountain, having wandered down from a transplanted population now thriving along the Continental Divide between Creede and Lake City, a hundred miles from here. This is a big event for us—to be celebrated, we unanimously agree, by the uncorking of a bottle of Merlot.

Only later do I discover that my camera had no film.

· 32 ·

It's early evening, the third week of July, and I'm vegged out in my twenty-dollar duct-tape-reupholstered recliner, contemplating *Nature and Madness*, Paul Shepard's most difficult and prophetic book, when Caroline, sitting nearby in her own comfy chair, looks up from her own book and says calmly (getting even with me, perhaps, for her recent Bullwinkle embarrassment):

"David, there's a bear at the door. Should we invite him in?"

My chair faces the portal in question, just eight feet away and open to the summer breeze save for a flimsy screen. Otis is snoozing on the floor between the door and me, and in the instant it takes me to digest what Caroline has said and look up and echo, "By golly, there *is* a bear at the door!" the Oatster is up, long tail flagging his sudden excitement, glancing alternately from the bear to me, as if to ask, "Whatcha want me to *do* about this, Dad?" Through the screen we can see our visitor clearly. It has long, brown, disheveled fur and is not large, only a hundred pounds or so—a youngster just recently out on its own, I'd guess, evicted by its mother so that she can mate and begin the reproductive cycle anew. But Otis is impatient and I am momentarily stunned, and before I can say or do anything our self-designated protector is at the door, mistaking the little bear, it seems, for another big dog. Likewise, perhaps, the bear takes Otis for one of its own kind, since they both seem more curious than alarmed.

Ursid and canid touch noses through the screen.

Both animals sniff, sneeze in mutual surprise, and leap comically back.

While Otis stares, hackles erect, head and tail held low in concerned concentration, he does not bark or growl, apparently rendered speechless by confusion. The little bear, meanwhile, bounds off the porch and scampers away, dodging around the Outhouse and disappearing into the oaken jungle of the steep hillside beyond . . . just as had the moose.

Exciting times, you bet. But hardly extraordinary hereabouts, summer through fall. Even as our Montana grizzly friends are working their way ever higher, following the snowmelt and seasonal green-up from grassy lower slopes to alpine wildflower meadows, Colorado black bears are doing the reverse: coming down from the drought-withered mountains, venturing recklessly in among us flat-faced bears in a desperate search for food. And in their searching, several times each recent summer—this is our fifth drought year in a row—local bears have invaded human homes, entering through doors or windows left open or guarded only by screens, following their noses to the tempting promise of a people-food feast. If no one is home to complicate matters, the intruder typically eats everything edible within reach, often opening refrigerators and devouring the contents, demonstrating a special affection for canned beer. (A woman living west of town recently called the sheriff's office at two A.M. to report that a bear was in her kitchen and had gotten into the refrigerator and was eating tamales and drinking light beer. "It must be an adolescent male," she logically deduced.) As soon as the goodies are gone, so is the bear, with the damage generally confined to the kitchen. But should a bruin be surprised inside a house by human or dog, the destruction that often ensues as the panicked beast tries to find or fashion a fast way out renders the image of a bull in a china shop benign.

Here on Spring Mountain, to keep the bears and bugs outside, where they belong, we use the screen door when we're home on hot summer days and close the main door at night and when we're gone—a sturdy bearicade I built from two-by-four tongue-and-groove pine reinforced with one-by-four laterals.

We've never had a problem.

Black bears are by nature solitary animals who, like C and me, prefer the peace and solitude of nature over the headachy claptrap of towns, traffic, and people. Likewise, bears are generally content with the wide variety of wild foods they've evolved to eat; both blacks and grizzlies are dominantly vegetarian but do love meat when they can get it. Trouble is, millions of cattle and sheep are out there in the "wilds" each summer as well, greedily harvesting wildlife chow like bovine combines, leaving tons of gooey crap and swarms of flies in their flatulent wake. Some years in some areas, there simply isn't enough chow to satisfy all the hungry mouths, domestic and wild. *Cow-burned* is the term for such overgrazed places, and it isn't pretty.

In recent years here, this unnatural diminution of wild forage for private profit has been compounded by such natural catastrophes as drought and late spring frosts. The latter nips the production of survival-essential berries and Gambel's oak acorns literally in the bud. And so it is that starving bears have little choice but to search far and wide, uphill and down, in wild areas and settled, in an exhaustive struggle to survive. That search, as the summer progresses, inevitably leads some bears into rural subdivisions, onto the manicured lawns of trophy homes, and, increasingly often of late, into residential neighborhoods in small mountain towns such as Durango, where garbage containers, bird feeders, pet food, small tasty pets, fruit trees, and fallen fruit abound.

What I'm getting at is that so-called garbage and problem bears are by nature neither. It's never a bear's *preference* to be among us, getting harried and harassed at every turn. Rather, it's an unfortunate fate forced upon the opportunistic foragers by both natural and human diminishment of their normal foods and habitats and the irresistible baits we make so readily available around our homes and businesses. Other unintentional baits commonly found in rural neighborhoods include small livestock kept penned or tied outside, compost piles containing meat and vegetable scraps, and, incredibly, *intentional* feeding of bears.

Caroline and I, like others we know, are happy to compromise—to keep the small amount of garbage we generate inside until we can haul it off for appropriate disposal. To feed our mutts only indoors. To use pulleys to hang the bird feeders beyond the biggest bear's reach. To let the charcoal grill burn hot for a few minutes after cooking, thereby cremating any smelly grease and meat scraps to scentless ash, and to store the grill in a sturdy shed when we are gone. In return, when we do have a bear in the yard, or even on the porch, we know it's only a curious visitor. Finding nothing here to eat, it has no reason to hang around or return. We rarely see the same bear twice unless it's using our property as a runway from forest to someone else's garbage.

Tragically, a lot of folks don't share such a neighborly view of bears, figuring it's up to the animals to stay out of trouble, no matter their nutritional needs or the human-made temptations. So each time we see a bear passing through our yard, or meet one in the woods near a human settlement, we worry that it won't be long before some courageous home owner kills the "marauding beast," pleading defense of property or concern for human safety. The scruffy little fellow who touched noses with Otis, to finish the opening bear-at-the-door story, survived less than a week after our brief encounter, shot on first sight by a trigger-happy "garbage human" down yonder in the valley.

As thrilling as such yard and porch bear encounters are, far more exciting for me and less risky for the bears are the run-ins I enjoy a little later most years, on the cusp of fall, out in the wild surrounds.

· **33** ·

I'm bowhunting for elk on public land across the river valley from home, where the dominant slope faces north and consequently is wetter, cooler, and richer in lush vegetation, providing prime summer habitat for elk, mule deer, bears, cougars, pine martens, and other beasts large and small. And gray jays and Clark's nutcrackers too, which we rarely see here on the drier side of the valley. I've chugged two steep miles uphill to a big spring pool in an aspen-filled *rincon,* or secluded mountain bowl, which I discovered recently while on a summer hike. Camouflaged and moving as quietly as an impatient, two-legged, slightly arthritic human predator can manage, I cautiously close the last hundred yards to the spring, going from feet to knees to belly in order to sneak a peek over the final rise.

Nothing.

The spring is still there, of course. No loggers, livestock, ATV cowboys, or other "wise users" having come rampaging through to destroy it. And it has been recently visited by elk. The water is clouded with stirred-up bottom silt, and big cloven prints pock the pool's perimeter. More exciting yet, the sweet, funky stench of rutting bull perfumes the quiet air. But no elk steaks in sight.

Hopeful the wapiti will return, sooner or later, I'm nosing around for an evening ambush setup when I spot a hunter's tree stand, which I failed to note the first time here—a simple plywood platform chained fifteen feet up a sturdy Douglas fir. Whoever built that perch picked the perfect tree, rooted just twenty yards from the spring and overhanging the primary game trail leading in and out. The plywood's weathered appearance speaks of the stand's long-ago abandonment. An urge for upward mobility strikes, and skyward I go, hand over hand, climbing a ladder of big rusty nails spiked into the ancient trunk. After testing the strength of the platform, I step aboard, hang my bow from a handy limb stub, and peel off my day pack. Before hanging the pack from another stub, I retrieve a length of nylon rope, wrap it two turns around the tree—the trunk is so fat I can barely reach around, even up this high—and two turns around my waist, then secure the improvised safety harness with a bowline (an essential survival knot I learned in the Boy Scouts).

I've just taken a seat on the splintery shelf, legs dangling over the edge, and am enjoying the view and mentally surveying the various lunch snacks in my pack when my peripheral vision registers a flicker of movement fifty yards uphill, along the main game trail. Whatever it is will round a bend and come eye level with me at any moment. No time to retrieve my bow, snap an arrow to the string, and prepare for a shot. I climbed up here on a lark, with no expectation of staying long or seeing game—not hunting, just playing—so I am utterly unprepared. Nothing for it but to sit quietly and see what transpires.

But this is no wapiti. It's a bear: medium-sized, 250 pounds or so, a young adult male judging by the big-headed, big-footed, gangly looks of him. And typically, as with most black bears you'll meet here in the southern Rockies, the only black bits on this bruin are his nose and the pads of his feet. His body is sandy brown with chocolate legs and head and, most unusual, a wide blond stripe running the full length of his back. With every padded step the approaching beast utters a soft, guttural grunt, as if it hurts to walk, or maybe feels real good.

Within spitting range uphill from my tree, another big fir has fallen across the game trail, its bottom edge wedged three feet off the ground. When the bear reaches this obstacle he pauses to taste the air with his nose. Instantly his head jerks up and his ears stand erect. I haven't set foot anywhere near that log and there isn't a breath of breeze, yet the bear has obviously caught a whiff of something he does not like, and he's staring straight at me.

After a long, tense minute of alert indecision, the overgrown raccoon relaxes and squeezes beneath the log and continues toward the spring. But at the base of my tree he stops short again.

As usual, I am hunting in rubber-bottomed boots because they are light, quiet, waterproof, comfortable, and seal in my human scent. I wash myself, my clothing, and even my gear in scentless soap and try to avoid touching anything with my hands as I creep through the woods. Even so, that supernose down there has caught a whiff of my stench. The alerted animal looks up and our eyes lock—his are tiny, incomprehensible, lustrous amber ingots set in a head like a basketball with ears. His hind paws are as long as my size eleven boots, with claws in need of trimming. I dare not sneeze, fart, or blink.

I love it!

I don't hunt bears. They are my fellow predatory omnivores, loners like me, and they strike me as half human, half dog. Bears, more than any other mammal, embody the magic of nature born. ("A world of made," the poet e. e. cummings cautioned the civilized world, "is not a world of born.") So I don't hunt bears. But what if that huge skunk down there should decide to hunt *me*? I'm acutely aware of the speed and aggression with which a black bear can come up a tree after you, should it take a notion to. And I'm sitting here literally tied in place, my bow beyond reach, my small skinning knife lost somewhere in the mess of my pack, and neither weapon promising much hope even were it handy.

The bear, still directly below me, sways like an elephant while glancing alternately up at me and down at the tempting spring pool. Since it's a warm afternoon with no other water nearby, he doubtless is thirsty and in want of a dip as well. (Bears love to swim on hot summer days.) Yet he strongly suspects that trouble lurks close at hand, and he seems to have a real good idea of what and where that trouble is. Again he looks up, straight at me. I return his stare through squinted eyes, not moving, barely breathing.

After what feels like a long time the bear reaches a reluctant decision, shoots me one last resentful glance emphasized by a soft *Whoof!*, and spins around. He squeezes back under the blowdown log and shuffles back up the trail he so recently shuffled down. With a mixture of relief and sadness I watch him go—a wise, cautious fellow, a "good bear," it turns out. As almost all of them are.

After waiting and watching for several more minutes, just to be safe, I unlash myself from the tree, gather my junk, scramble down, and scurry away to safety, feeling keenly alive. My quiet life has been touched by magic. For a while there, just like up in grizzly country, the predator in me was made to feel like prey, and life on Earth was in balance.

In other close bear encounters I've experienced such thrills as having three wee coys sniffing my boots while their mother, unseeing and blessedly upwind, fed just yards away. Once she had browsed far enough downwind to scent me, she bellowed an urgent moan and her cubs went bounding after.

Another time, a tiny cub with no siblings or sow in sight, lost or lonely or both, came wobbling up and tried to crawl into my lap as I sat cross-legged on the ground in a dense aspen grove, eating an orange and smoking my pipe. For the cub's sake and my own, I quietly shooed it away, though it took a couple of tries.

On yet another occasion a well-groomed brownish biggie, about three hundred pounds, appeared silently from the woods on the far side of a place we know as Killing Spring one evening just at sunset. It circled the pool while sniffing the ground, then suddenly lifted its head and came straight for me at a run. I just sat there, with no time to act and nothing much to do in any event (this was in the days before bear spray) except to hope for the best. At the last instant and only a body length away, the "charging" animal swerved aside and went crashing away through the darkening woods. Your guess is as good as mine.

I've enjoyed many more such thrilling ursine episodes, including my most recent encounter with a bear in the woods, which, I hope you will agree, merits a full tell.

· 34 ·

Once again I'm haunting the wilds not far from home, hunting for elk and adventure. A quarter mile upslope and ahead of me a bull has just risen from his daybed and occasionally bugles lazily, trying to wake up. I know this routine, can clearly envision it, having seen it several times; such is common bull behavior on rutty afternoons. So I'm sitting and listening, attempting to visualize the wapiti's most likely travel route from bed to feed or water so that I can circle ahead to intercept him and the cow-and-calf entourage he should be tending, when suddenly (they always come suddenly, rarely with any warning) a bear appears: big and black as a midnight cave (as I've noted previously, a rarity around here), but lanky, looking seriously underfed.

And no wonder. The prolonged drought I keep moaning about, abetted this year by a late spring frost, has thrown the local ecology woefully out of whack, rendering natural bear chow scarce. No chokecherries or serviceberries. No acorns. Even the grasses, sedges, forbs, and deciduous leaves have dried and died weeks early. Consequently these mountains are crawling with bony bruins, reduced to ripping apart rotten logs and rolling over rocks in search of ants and other snacks. And down in the valley, where far too many people now live in far too careless a manner, every Dumpster and trash can is tended by its own private bear.

Unaware of my presence, Blackie sniffs the ground, then flops down and rolls with apparent joy, like a horse relieved of its saddle, or a dog in a pile of horse poop. Done with that he stands, shakes like a wet dog, then sits on his haunches just fifteen yards away. As the uncharacteristically black black bear gazes thoughtfully toward the distant bugling bull, it strikes me that he too may be hunting, with a strategy that mirrors my own.

Soon enough and inevitably, the breeze wanders in preparation for its evening shift from upslope to down. Immediately the best nose in the woods perks up and Blackie rises to check me out, his narrow head bobbing, nostrils twitching.

Wanting no confusion or trouble, I stand too, slowly wave my arms, and quietly say, "Go away, bear. I was here first."

But the bear does not go away.

I shake my bow menacingly and growl, trying to appear mean.

Blackie only stares, perhaps perceiving the benign reality behind my fearsome guise. And it's true. Among the greatest pleasures in my life is meeting bears in natural surrounds like this. So no, unless it came to last-ditch self-defense, I could never kill a bear. To the contrary, I view myself as a bear benefactor. Should I find the luck to kill an elk this year (as I do almost every year), Blackie or another of his hard-pressed tribe will benefit mightily from the viscera, bone marrow, meat scraps, and whatever else they can gobble down before the coyotes and winged scavengers arrive. It's an ancient, traditional, and wholly appropriate hunter's tithe to nature. In hard years such as this, a single gut pile can provide enough calories to see even a lean bear through its winter den to greet another spring.

Yet, for his own good—to remind him that people are dangerous—I figure this fearless fellow is due a shot of aversive conditioning. So I take a blunt (rubber-tipped) grouse arrow from my quiver and snap it to the bowstring, come to full draw, and aim for the scruffy black butt. But before I can let fly my harmless missile, Blackie suddenly turns and shuffles away—only a few yards—then sits again and resumes his stare. I hold my shot and return the bear's stare. Moments later, when the bull elk bugles again, I remember what I'm here for and slowly back away.

Unmoving, unmoved, Blackie watches me go.

The remainder of the evening's hunt ends abruptly when the bull quits singing and the whole herd ghosts away.

Come morning I decide to sneak bright and early into the elk bedding area while the herd is still out on its overnight rounds, then surprise them when they return. Toward that end, I'm following a freshly hoof-churned game trail down through a brushy draw when I feel my skin prickle with that ancient sixth-sense awareness—you just *know* that something or someone is watching, and not so far away. I whirl around, and there sits Blackie, haunched down right beside the trail I've just come along. At our closest, we were five feet apart. Again it strikes me that Blackie is elk hunting, in this case apparently waiting in ambush for a bedbound wapiti calf. (Few black bears will tackle a healthy, full-grown elk.) Had he wanted, the bear could have lurched forward, reached out a long-clawed paw, and ripped my face off as I slouched carelessly by. He apparently did not want.

Indeed, by all indications Blackie means me no harm. Yet he *is* a bear. A big, emaciated, desperately hungry bear. So I ask him again to leave.

Again he refuses to budge.

Again I string a blunt-tipped arrow, draw, and aim.

This time my psychological sparring partner hesitates but finally hauls himself up and moseys away. All of a dozen yards farther on, he stops, sits back down . . . and yawns.

Again I opt not to shoot.

Blackie watches impassively as I back away.

Wow! Certainly, the sharp scent of danger provides some of the voltage that so jangles me at such wildly tense times as these, giving me the original and still best version of what other modern folk seek in action books and suspense films, in high-risk sports and speed, trying to feel alive. But there's more to danger than a short-term adrenaline rush, something tantalizingly ineffable, like a dream that leaves you disturbed for days, long after its details have faded. Part of me wants more. Another part is uneasy. It's that internal friction that generates the juice. And you can't get that from fiction.

Later, back at the Doghouse, I phone Tom "Black Bear" Beck

and recount for him my two most recent encounters. Tom agrees with my supposition that Blackie is, or recently has been, a garbage bear, like so many others this starving summer, having lost his instinctive fear of people through repeated nonviolent encounters reinforced by food rewards. Even so, Tom cautions, "Habituated doesn't mean harmless."

Quite the opposite, in fact. Tom allows as how it's probably a good thing I didn't blunt the bruin, as that could have provoked a defensive attack. Furthermore, he warns, Blackie's nonchalance could change to fierceness fast, should elk meat hit the ground.

"Try not to kill late in the evening," Tom advises. "But if you do, stay alert, work fast, bag the meat, and move it a good ways upwind from the gut pile. Try to get out before dark, and be extra watchful when you return the next morning."

But until such a time, says Tom, he agrees with my sense that Blackie is no great threat.

Reassured, I propose that the next time this bear and I should meet, instead of trying to scare him away, I'll engage him in relaxed conversation. See what comes of that.

"Carry bear spray," Tom cautions. And of course I always do.

Alas, the remaining days of archery elk season come and go and my anticipated next meeting with Blackie never material-izes. Not even when elk meat hits the ground.

Only several weeks later, while talking with a game warden friend, do I find out why.

Shortly after my two encounters with the skinny black bear, a bruin perfectly fitting his description—same size and sex, bony and black save for a small white chest blaze—appeared just a few miles from where we had crossed paths and was killed by a bowhunter who found him snoozing beside a forest trail. As the archer strung an arrow the bear awoke, stared, yawned . . . and died.

I don't fault the shooter, who was hunting legally and ethically (that is, in season, with the proper license and without the crutches of bait or hounds, both of which are immoral as well as illegal in Colorado). Even so, I sure wish now that I'd blunted that bear, who put too much trust in people.

· 35 ·

Bears, bears. They're everywhere. And my wife is Goldilocks.

Earlier this morning, trying to beat the late-summer heat, Caroline and Otis were climbing the hogback ridge that separates Bigbutt Trail from Pond Spring bench, which lies below and west, and just as they reached the crest, near what we call Caroline's Rocks, my little family met head-on with a big black-and-brown bear who had just climbed up from the Pond Spring side. They spotted each other in the same frozen instant, just a bare few feet apart. Otis went stiff-legged. Caroline screamed (not from fear but from surprise). The bear said, *Whoof!* Everyone ran in opposite directions.

That Pond Spring area, with its thick aspen canopy, fecund understory rich in ferns, and excellent hiding cover, is the beariest place on the mountain, and we should be more careful when roaming there. Pond Spring, always deep in shadow and spooky in a weird, primeval sort of way, is also the only place on the mountain where Caroline and I (on separate occasions) have found lion tracks. But then, except after rains, it's the only reliable mud on the mountain, since Pond Spring is exactly that: a spring-fed vernal pond, never more than knee-deep and prone to going dry. Muddy, remote, infested with bugs and bears and big cats that creep in the night. A truly magical place.

The sleek and lethal mountain lion, *Felis concolor*—also known as puma, cougar, and panther—is scary by any name. While bears can be furtive, they're far more often oafs, like the one that almost walked over Caroline. Cats, as specialist carnivores rather than generalist omnivores, have to work a lot harder than bears for a living. Their work is death, and they're built to glide like ghosts and sprint like cheetahs. They're seldom seen but often watching; it's their invisibility that makes them spooks.

And rightly by-God so.

The first week of September a year ago—the opening of archery elk season—Tom Beck and I packed a camp into the Lizard Head Wilderness, between Rico and Telluride, a hundred miles northwest of here. On the second day there, Tom returned from his morning hunt in a cold, steady rain and asked if I'd seen the elk carcass along the creek, just a long arrow shot from camp. "Big bull," he said in the characteristically clipped way in which he discusses serious matters. "Nice antlers. You might want to pack 'em out."

After breakfast beneath a plastic tarp strung between trees to keep the worst of the rain off, we grabbed our cameras and walked the short way there. Tom himself had gotten only a shadowy glimpse of the remains in the half-light of dawn as he'd hiked past, headed out to hunt and with no time to fool around. He'd returned by a different route and now was eager to revisit the scene to see what we could learn.

The wapiti's remains lay in a small, dark hollow near where a game trail crossed a wildlife watering hole in the rushing creek. Most striking were the antlers, a heavy six-by-six rack still attached to the skull. Tattered velvet covered the rack, and the tip few inches of the four upper tines were broken off and lying nearby. The skull, like the rest of the big corpse, had been picked and gnawed quite clean; bones were scattered everywhere, many of them stained bright red with rain-freshened blood; others were partially covered with dirt and leaf debris. Elk hair lay here and there in clumps, but no hide, not a shred.

What had happened here? What had killed and eaten this huge beast?

For the next several minutes I poked around, playing wildlife detective. Tom, who *is* a wildlife detective (or was until his recent retirement), did the same. We worked largely in silence, thinking our private wild thoughts. For my part, the exceptional size and symmetry of the antlers—whose opulence, as luxury organs, suggested a healthy, well-fed animal—made starvation or disease seem unlikely culprits. Strengthening that assessment, the forage in that high, wet place, at eleven thousand feet, was magnificently rich and varied, thanks to the blessing that no sheep or cattle had come blasting through to eat it down to dirt.

When had the animal died? Because the antlers were fully developed but not yet fully hardened (as evidenced by the broken tips) and remained sheathed in velvet, the bull's death could be timed to early August, just three weeks ago, since elk antlers at this latitude uniformly harden to the consistency of bone and shed their velvet by midmonth.

So it had been a big, healthy animal in the prime of its life and the fattest time of the year. No hunting seasons had been open when it had died, and given the seclusion of the place and the fact that the antlers had not been taken nor the carcass apparently butchered, poaching could be ruled out.

And that's about all I could surmise, particularly since a series of hungry mouths had come and gone, diminishing, scattering, and confusing the evidence while covering and otherwise confusing one another's tracks. Clearly, the visitors had included coyotes, which eat small bones and hide, hair and all. While I would normally expect a bear or bears to find and feast on such a treasure, a lack of bear scat (they almost always crap near where they eat) cast doubt in this instance. The usual array of scavenging birds had fed here, including magpies, ravens, vultures, and eagles, any and most likely all.

Neither starvation nor disease, nor likely killed by humans. Predation, of course, is always a possibility in the wild, but it didn't strike me as likely in this instance, since bears have an abundance of vegetation to graze on in this season and are inept hunters; it's the rare black bear who would be big and confident enough to take on a mature bull elk of some seven hundred pounds. Even less likely, it seemed to me, was the possibility of a 150-pound lion tackling a well-armed beast more than four times its own weight. While lions do take disadvantaged elk in winter, deer are their primary year-round prey.

How *had* this animal died?

All of this I laid out for Tom, who confirmed my guesses right down the line . . . until I ruled out lion.

"Okay," he began, pointing back up the hill, away from the creek, to where the well-worn game trail entered the cloistered hollow. "Your elk came down this trail to water. Your lion was waiting in ambush. *Big* fight."

My mentor in the ways of wild death made a sweeping motion with one arm, pointing in turn—*tap, tap, tap*—to the hoof-churned ground, broken tree limbs, smashed and flattened brush.

"Big fight. Lion kills elk. Eats his fill. Buries the remains for later."

Tom then turned and walked a few steps and stopped and looked down at the ground at his boots, where lay what suddenly seemed an obviously raked-up pile of dirt and forest debris, though I had missed it before.

"Elk died, got eaten on, and then was buried here. Scavengers came along later and uncovered the remains, fed, and scattered the bones around."

At this juncture I returned to the skull, which remained attached to the upper section of spinal column, with its heavy vertebrae. Lions typically attack deer from above, seizing the victim by the scruff of its neck or biting into the base of the skull, riding the deer like a rodeo cowboy, working to crush the spine for instant paralysis while slashing at the throat with big, deadly, scimitar-curved dewclaws. Knowing this, I searched for tooth marks along the top of the spine or at the base of the skull. But there were none.

Reading my mind, or at least my actions, Tom responded: "That's how lions kill deer, but not elk, whose backs are too high to leap on. And especially not bull elk, with antlers they can sweep behind them to knock an attacker off. To bring down an animal this size, the cat would seize it from below, by the throat, either biting into the jugular or clamping down on the windpipe. The elk would have bucked and whirled, trying to shake the lion loose. Hanging by its teeth and claws, dangling between the elk's front legs, the cat would be safe from the antlers and, if it was agile and lucky, could dodge the front hooves as well, which are an elk's primary defense against predators. Sooner or later, if the prey can't shake its attacker loose, it will lose enough blood, or have gone long enough without being able to breathe, to black out and go down, making it easy for the lion to finish it off. It's the same technique smaller cats like leopards and cheetahs use in Africa to bring down their bigger prey."

"How do you know all of this?" I heard myself asking, revealing my skepticism.

"The research literature," Tom replied. "Eyewitness reports. Necropsies of known lion-killed elk carcasses. And one more thing . . ."

Wearing a satisfied smile, detective Beck walked over and touched each of the four broken-off antler tips: *tap-tap, tap-tap.* "If this animal had just laid down to die, say from starvation or disease, these tips wouldn't be broken off. If it had been shot or forced down by a weight on its back, say a lion or bear, it would have fallen to one side, breaking the tines on the down side, if any. The fact that all the broken tines are at the top of the antlers and on both sides suggests that the head went down hard while the animal was running, the tops of the antlers dug in, and inertia caused the victim to flip ass over teacup, breaking the tines and possibly the neck as well. That's consistent with a heavy weight hanging on from below.

"Of course," Beck concluded, "I could be wrong."

For the remainder of our week in that wild place, which had suddenly gotten a little bit wilder, my walks to and from camp, morning and evening, coming and going, alone in the dark and twilight, felt like real adventures.

· 36 ·

August here is the hottest and driest month of the year. But seasons change fast up in the mountains and weather even faster, and before month's end the first signs of fall will predictably appear, disregarding the weather: a pleasant coolness in the nights, an equally pleasant decrease in mosquitoes, the first golden waves cresting in what for months has been a purely green sea of aspen, and most exciting for me, the first tentative bugles of restless wapiti bulls teetering nervously on the leading edge of their annual mating frenzy.

And so it is that even now, early August and hot as a blister, my thoughts are drifting ahead to winter. When your only source of heat is wood, and you alone must cut, haul, split, and stack thousands of sticks of it, and when vehicle access to the cabin is denied by snow from November at the latest through March at the earliest, getting in your wood must be dealt with well ahead. Other time-consuming, labor-intensive, utterly essential prewinter chores come to the fore as well. In the mountains, when you can't afford to hire other people to come pull you out of a snowy pinch, you think ahead, you work ahead—or you'll have months to wish you had.

Today, with the firewood mountain looking pretty good, I am thinking ahead to our winter's meat. Any day now, those bully boys out there will begin rubbing the soft velvety overskin from their newly regenerated antlers—those towering ivory advertisements of fitness and rank and, should the competition get intense, those fearsome weapons for combat with rivals. In the rut, the wisdom of wild nature expresses itself through a system that allows the fittest adults to maximize their breeding opportunities through the herd's hierarchy strategy, matching the fewest best bulls with the most best cows to collectively pass along their time-tested genes to future generations.

Also-ran bulls, meanwhile—the young and otherwise inferior or insufficiently tested—orbit impatiently around the herd, anxious to take fast advantage of any opportunity to sneak a little love without getting caught by the boss bull, who would whip them like rude children. But with each passing rut the surviving satellite bulls grow stronger and wiser, increasing their chances to displace the king and confiscate his harem. It's an exciting time for elk, and I can't wait to join them.

For Colorado bowhunters, elk season opens near the end of August and runs for a full month. While only one elk can be taken, either sex is game. Too long and liberal? For most bowhunters, including me some years, it's not nearly long or liberal enough, as evidenced in a success rate averaging less than 15 percent. And even that is misleading, since a minority of serious and talented hunters—my game-warden friends call us "predators"—account for a majority of the kill each year.

Blessed with a great place to hunt, twenty years of hard experience, and the time and passion to keep after it until the job is done, my "luck" runs better than most. I am indeed a predator. And if I am to have good luck again this year, next month, I must start manufacturing it right now—by practicing daily with my "stick" bow (no cables or pulleys or cams or wheels, no sights or stabilizers or overdraw or mechanical release, just a stick and a string), shooting arrow after arrow from every conceivable angle and every reasonable range until I can keep every last one in a six-inch circle or better at twenty yards; by fine-tuning gear, body, and senses, sweating myself back into hunting form through long scouting hikes in country where every way is up.

After lunch, looking at another day of cloudless skies and throat-parching heat, I pull on a pair of hiking shorts and a short-sleeved T-shirt, lace up my lightest hiking boots, slap a cotton cap on my naked sun-shy skull, grab the fanny pack I keep loaded with day-hike essentials—emergency rain gear, mini-binoculars, waterproof matches, a bit of string, a tiny flashlight, a bag of hard candy, and a compass—and fill a water bottle for myself (Otis can drink straight from nature, as do I in times of need). And off we go to find out.

Find out, that is, if the scattering of secluded springs that name this mountain and define my personal elk heaven still hold water here at the end of yet another drought summer, and if so, to what extent which animals are using them. For most of the year, out of gratitude and respect, these fragile refuges are avoided by Caroline, the dogs, and me, allowing the wild things to drink and bathe undisturbed. But with hunting season less than three weeks away, I need to know what is happening up there, and what is not. As always, we'll come and go as politely as possible. For instance, since the most concentrated and lingering human scent is spread by hand as we mindlessly touch trees and push aside brush in passing, I've trained myself to walk with hands in pockets or, when wearing a pack, with thumbs hooked under the shoulder straps. While elk don't seem to fear the smell of dogs—no more than they fear coyotes—the stench of humanity, apropos, fills them with dread and caution.

Our first destination is our old favorite Hillside Spring. It was just above there, perhaps you recall, where I had the too close standoff with the huge mother bear and her two tiny cubs. Directly below where the bear and I met, at the base of a densely forested, east-facing slope, a shallow pool of spring-clear water sits hidden and cool in the afternoon shade. This bathtub-sized basin represents a third of all the wildlife-accessible water on Spring Mountain. (The fourth and lowest spring, on private land, was co-opted a few years back to supply a new trophy home.) Consequently, Hillside Spring attracts elk, deer, bears, turkeys, squirrels, and more, plus their predators big and small, including sometimes me.

When groundwater is abundant and the pool's capacity is breached, the overflow trickles the length of a football field down a narrow, tunnel-like lane of green beneath bear-scarred aspens, ponderosa pine, and fir before sinking back into the ground only to reemerge half a mile farther along at Bear Springs. At the terminus of the Hillside seep is a shallow depression that rutting bulls use for a mud bath. I call it Big Wallow, and it marks the center of my wapiti world. In the fullness of my time here I've been blessed to repeatedly observe bulls taking their foul pleasure at Big Wallow and smaller puddles nearby.

In September 1983, I killed my first elk with a bow while hunting the Hillside arena. That was several years before unseen bulls had pawed Big Wallow into existence. Prior to that, for my first two elk hunts ever, in October 1981 and again in '82, I carried a rifle, not a bow. In the dark on opening mornings both those years, I hiked five miles up the mountain from my bivouac camp on our property (our cabin, the Doghouse, like Big Wallow, did not yet exist), wearing a frame pack and lugging a used Winchester 30-30 lever-action carbine. And on both mornings both years I killed a fat spike.

In wapiti terminology a spike is a yearling male—eighteen months old on average, born in May or June two springs before. This nickname arises from the adolescent's trademark tall, forkless, thus spikelike antlers. On the hoof, the average spike weighs about five hundred pounds, the same as the average mature cow, at three years or older. Spike meat is tender and delicious—almost as good as calf, and there's more than twice as much of it. But for the past several years here, spikes have been forbidden to hunters in an effort by state wildlife managers to produce more mature bulls and more big antlers. This is good for the trophy boys but a loss for meatheads like me. At least we were able to enjoy devouring a couple of spikes before the law changed. And having shot both of those youngsters at under thirty yards, I felt I'd paid my dues and could confidently hang up the rifle and unpack my stick bow, an elegantly simple tool with which I'd grown up hunting whitetails.

For dedicated hunters who don't mind working extra long and hard—those of us who view hunting as a worthwhile end in itself, no matter the outcome—the advantages to hunting with a bow are many. Best of all for me, by sneaking around in the woods alone, camouflaged or at least dressed to blend in, quiet and cautious as a lynx, I invariably see more wildlife in more natural circumstances—close-up, unaware, going about their normal lives—than anyone else I know. Thanks to such "accidental" encounters, every bowhunt is supremely successful, whether or not it ends with meat.

Among the blessings of my first years of bowhunting for elk was the discovery of Hillside Spring, to which I was lured by a bugling bull. After sneaking in as close as I dared, I determined that the bugler was accompanied by a milling mob of cows and calves. It's almost impossible to get within bow range of such a herd, with all those searching eyes, radar ears, and bloodhound noses on the job (I have managed it, getting in and back out again undetected, only twice), so I retreated and walked home in the dark. The next morning I returned and found the spring. After that I took to hiding nearby each evening, and I eventually killed a tough old cow. Given her age, size, and position at the front of the long single-file line of wapiti that trotted from the woods just at dusk, headed for the spring, she was obviously the matriarch, the one who guides and directs the herd in its movements to and from feeding grounds, water, and resting areas each day, as well as on its seasonal migrations.

No matter that she was old and her flesh as chewy as harness leather; I was thankful, and before converting animal to meat I made sure to tell her so. One expression of that gratitude was to pack the hide and every scrap of meat out on my back, necessitating five brutal round-trips spread over two days. Though far from prime, it still was elk meat and delicious, and through trial and error Caroline found ways to give our jaws a break—grilled steaks tenderized with marinades; thin-cut slabs of rump meat pounded and breaded as country-fried steaks; shoulder meat ground coarse (we have an antique hand-crank grinder passed down from Caroline's mother) for burgers, chili, spaghetti sauce, meat loaf—and we ate all two hundred pounds.

On subsequent scouting hikes I discovered the other springs along the shallow aquifer chain and have killed elk at one or another most Septembers since. But maybe not this year, thanks to the heat and drought, which has sent a majority of the elk to the timberline and will hold them up there—where water is more abundant, the bugs not quite so buggy, the forage richly diverse, and the hunters relatively few—until the first big snow.

When Otis and I arrive at Hillside, the spring is flowing and the pool is almost full, yet there isn't an elk track in sight, the overflow seep is slow, and Big Wallow is cracked-earth dry. A quick search of the area reinforces the bad news: no elk nowhere.

One hope down, two hopes left to hope for.

Before we move along, confident it won't disturb the wildlife that isn't here, I signal Otis with a gesture that it's okay to splash in, lie down (as dogs are wont to do), and drink his drooling fill, leaving the pool a muddy mess . . . as if a bear had just bathed there, which delightful sight I have witnessed twice from hunting hides nearby, or as if a whole herd of elk had recently come, jousted for position, serially drank, and gone, which I've seen here countless times. Before morning, the silt will have settled and the pool will be clear again.

We move on, my mud-caked mutt and I.

· 37 ·

While engrossed in scouting the Hillside environs, with the sky largely shrouded from view by the lush forest overstory, I hadn't noticed the changing weather. So it comes as a bit of a shock now, on our way up and over a low rise toward the second pool, to see that the sky has gone dark as a bruise and the temperature has tumbled what feels on the thermometer of my bare arms and legs like twenty degrees. Before we get where we're going, the rising wind and lowering clouds are joined by lightning arcing in the distance. I shiver and mutter a curse, disgusted with myself for not having packed a jacket, or at least a long-sleeved shirt.

But passion is a potent drug, and my meteorological concerns are all but forgotten the moment we reach Killing Spring, formerly Wapiti Spring, renamed in pagan honor of its consistent productiveness. Its knee-deep pool, clear as polished glass when undisturbed, today is turgid with churned-up silt. From years of paying attention I know that this pool needs only about four hours to clear, so the action is recent, as verified by the abundance of cloven prints everywhere. Big, green-black mounds of summer-soft droppings litter the ground as well. The barnyard smell of elk is bold and intoxicating.

So, my beloved wapiti haven't deserted us after all, but are merely—

Zzzzzt . . .

Ka-BLAM!

A jag of lightning sizzles down so close by that the gray hairs on my neck stand erect—I distinctly feel them stiffen. I am perfectly stunned. An instant later, as my head clears and I note that the air smells like a burning match, comes an explosion so violent that I slap my hands to my ears and drop to my knees at the concussion. Otis too hits the ground and bays out a horrified howl. Not only the sky but the very air around us has turned an acid green, and hailstones like mothballs come rattling down. We sprint for the nearest shelter—a big Douglas fir whose dense lower boughs droop almost to the ground. I dive in feetfirst and kick frantically at several small dead branches projecting from the lower trunk to clear a little space, then snuggle up close to the tree. Filthy Otis crowds hard against me, trembling.

Cowering thus, gratefully protected from the worst of the pelting ice, I rummage through my fanny pack for the big plastic garbage bag I rolled up and stuck in months ago. And there it is, welcome as a Christmas bonus. With my Swiss Army knife I cut a slit in the center of the bottom, through which to poke my head. I slash armholes in both bottom corners and work the flimsy garment carefully down over my torso, like a full-body prophylactic. While the impromptu poncho reaches to below my waist, it leaves head, neck, and extremities unprotected—if you can call a thin plastic bag "protection," which I now realize it is not.

Ironically, if I were hunting rather than just scouting today, I'd be handsomely equipped with a waterproof backpack stuffed with everything necessary not only for hunting and caring for game meat but for minor medical emergencies and surviving an overnight stay in the woods in relative comfort no matter the weather, including several hundred calories' worth of snack foods, fire-making essentials, and a *real* rain suit. But who'd expect to need foul-weather gear when stepping out on a bright summer afternoon for a few leisurely hours of snooping through a familiar patch of woods just a couple of miles from home, under a midday sky so midnight blue you're surprised the stars aren't out. I am not well known as an optimist. Yet today I've let complacency get the best of me. And now, having bought the ticket, I must take the ride.

Coldly, I reflect that things needn't have come to this.

For a long time, my fanny pack contained a military nylon poncho. While impractical for bowhunting, these big flat sheets with a hole in the middle for your head, an attached hood with a drawstring, and snaps up both sides, offer good insurance against wet-weather misery. They're cheap enough and roll into compact packages. And in a pinch—by cinching up the head hole, staking one edge to the ground, and tying off the opposite corners to a tree or cut poles a few feet above the ground—a poncho can be rigged as a lean-to against wind, rain, and snow, and warmed by a small trench fire along the open front. But I rarely used the thing (that, of course, is the nature of emergency gear) and it weighed a pound or two, so one halcyon day last spring, in a fit of fair-weather streamlining, I tossed out the poncho and substituted this worthless body bag.

Serves me right.

After we've spent a boisterous quarter hour beneath the dripping tree, the wind settles some and the hail softens to a cold, slushy rain. I ask Otis, "Should we stay put or run for it?"

Silence, portending no opinion.

Late-summer mountain thunderstorms like this can blow

through in minutes or continue for hours, pulsing in intensity. My bare arms and legs are the biggest worry, giving away body warmth fast enough to already have reduced me to bone-rattling shakes—not good. Ironically, being physically fit can sometimes work against a body. I am essentially fatless, enjoy low blood pressure, and consequently am heart-attack proof. But I have little resistance to cold. If I don't get moving soon, I could find myself unable to move at all. Unlike freezing to death, hypothermia involves a gradual cooling of the body's core temperature to the point where normal metabolism ceases and key organs shut down. Neither freezing of flesh nor deep cold is required. In fact, with the swamp-cooler effect of wind and rain, precisely as I'm experiencing now, death by hypothermia often occurs at fifty degrees or warmer. Thanks to its insidious nature, hypothermia is the Darwinian culler of the smugly unprepared, the overly opti-mistic, and—as in my case, since I do know better—the just too dumb to live. Unless a person knows and heeds the earliest warn-ing signs—chills soon worsening to spasmodic trembling accom-panied by radical gooseflesh—by the time you realize you're in trouble, you're *really* in trouble: your mind is dull, your body exhausted, your shakes debilitating, your extremities clublike and uncooperative, your judgment fatally impaired. And because men, on average, pack less body fat than women, we make better candidates. Bearing out the truth of this, Caroline has suffered frost nip, or light frostbite—the superficial freezing of flesh, in her case the toes of both feet—but never hypothermia. I have never been frostbitten but have too-often played Russian roulette with hypothermia.

Lacking shelter and a source of introduced heat—fire, hot liq-uids to drink, warm water to soak in, a warm naked body lying next to your cold naked body in a dry sleeping bag—your only option is to exercise vigorously enough to generate internal body heat. But unless you have plenty of high-energy food on hand and athletic endurance, you can't exercise long under hypothermic stress before collapsing . . . and there you are. For that reason the trick is to move, while you can, with thoughtful direction—in my case, directly home.

With no further debate I make my break, crawling from beneath the shelter tree and wobbling to my feet. Otis is right behind, and we start off at a trot. But perhaps I've waited too long already. As we speed through dripping brush with the wind quartering in stiff and cold from the west and icy rain pounding down, I grow increasingly clumsy. Exhaustion and fear of falling and injuring myself force me to slow to a brisk walk. While I should probably be scared witless, I'm simply too numb to sweat it. Besides, confidence is essential to triumph, even if you have to fake it. *Stay on your feet, keep moving, watch every step, and you'll be home before you know it,* I chant as we go, a mantra for survival.

In point of fact, and barring complications, we should make the downhill distance home in an hour or less, hardly "before I know it" but easily beating darkness, with its radical temperature drop, increased navigation problems, and sentence of near-certain death. Threats to the success of this plan, which I ponder as we go, include spraining an ankle or twisting a knee, breaking a leg or jamming a broken tree limb deep into belly or groin while thrashing half blind through the wet woods. Although my pride hates to admit it, I could become disoriented in the thickening gloom, as happened one bad night some years ago in a far gentler rain than this but abetted by ground fog. Just before midnight, after walking in circles for hours, I finally stumbled onto the county road, two miles upriver from home. A family of vacationing Texans happened by and gave me a lift in the open back of their big diesel pickup, possibly saving my life. That unsettling memory reminds me in turn of several recklessly adventurous scouting trips and day hikes undertaken in my early years here, when I regularly probed alone miles into confusingly crenulated and wholly unknown terrain, dangerously unprepared. I moan aloud now to think what might have happened on any of those occasions had Big Weather come swooping in with killer claws extended, hiding landmarks, soaking my thin cotton clothing (worse than worthless when wet), chilling me beyond thoughtful function. It is said that freezing to death is fast and peaceful, once you sink beyond the pain. Hypothermia, by contrast, is a slow and miserable exit.

As we slog on, I envy Otis his ability to shake off accumulated water whenever he wants, before it can reach his skin to chill him—exactly as I've seen elk, deer, bears, moose, and caribou do. My arms and legs have gone purple and are bleeding from pricks and slashes. My discount-store shoes squish like sponges with every step. My "rain suit," like my naked flesh, has been shredded by tree limbs and grabby brush. Hypothermia is winning this race and only fast, careful walking separates me from eternity. I'm exhausted. A brief sit-down would be heaven.

But you do what you must when you have no other choice, and so I keep moving, one stiff blue leg at a time.

Almost home.

When we finally reach the cabin I am shaking so violently I can hardly stand. Unable even to remove my clothing or wait for Caroline to strip me, I stumble into the shower fully dressed. Resisting the urge to excess, I turn the water on lukewarm at first, gradually cranking it hotter, then slump down in a corner of the little stall. Life is restored.

Rain continues throughout the night, but I do not hear it.

· 38 ·

Come morning, celebrating my survival with a feast of coffee, wheat toast with Flo Shepard's homemade strawberry-rhubarb jam, scrambled eggs with cheese (from organically fed, free-ranging chickens and cows, since we try not to support the caged-animal industry), and other good hot things, I thank Caroline for not panicking and going out to search for me in the storm. No matter that she knows this mountain as well as I do and parts of it better. Had I gotten home and found her gone, the extra stress might have put me over the edge. To lessen her worry, what I don't tell my wife is that only now, in the clarity of hindsight, do I fully comprehend just how dicey the deal had gotten along toward the end. One bad fall, resulting in even a minor injury, would likely have rendered me immobile, inviting final disaster. How embarrassing it would be to die so ignobly, and for reasons so brilliantly dumb.

While last night's soaking rain fell far short of ending the summer's drought, it broke the back of the August heat and replenished the springs and our well. For a while, anyway. Caroline's wildflower garden is grateful, as are my aspens and elk.

In the warmth of the cabin, I daydream about elk . . . elk season . . . bugling and chuckling and wallowing and stinking . . . sneaking and peeking and watching and waiting . . . blood and guts and painful hard work and, finally, fresh elk tenderloin, basted with garlic butter, grilled hot-pink and served with sautéed morels and a chilled garden salad . . . the best time of year is almost here.

· 39 ·

Summer's heat is gone at last. Angel the elder dog clearly feels the difference, as evidenced by her uncharacteristic spunkiness this morning, making it known that she was ready for a real walk, beyond the bounds of the yard. Since she hasn't ventured out of sight of the cabin in months, Caroline decided to create an adventure for her, aware that it might be her last.

While I was working, C and the dogs drove to the Vallecito Creek trailhead, our closest gateway into the Weminuche Wilderness. (The creek's name is Spanish for "little valley" and is correctly pronounced *Vi-ya-SEE-tow*. If you pronounce it *Vally-see-tuh*, locals will brand you a Texan.) For the first mile or so the trail is nearly level, following a clear, shallow brook where dogs can drink, wade, and swim, thus providing a wonderful easy adventure for a terminally arthritic pooch. But adventures tend to plan themselves, and my gang hadn't been walking long at all when a naked brown porcupine appeared on the trail just ahead. While it's hard to imagine how a porky could lose every last one of its countless quills, this one somehow had. Without its needle armor, it looked comically slender and small, like a burned-up weasel or cat. Caroline told the dogs to stay, and Otis, who has never been quilled or skunked, sat obediently beside her. But Angel, suddenly a puppy again, went for the little beastie and chased it up a tree. Fortified by that small victory, she tried to climb up after but could barely manage to hoist her front feet up against the trunk. The porky stopped just a few feet above her, sensing it was safe. For a while the two adversaries traded stares, with Angel growling from deep in her chest. So intent was she to get at the defenseless animal that my ninety-six-pound wife had to wrestle the 110-pound dog off the tree and lead her away on a leash.

Angel came to us with a puncture-scarred muzzle, and we've always wondered if those old wounds were the legacy of dogfights or porky encounters. Now I think we know. In doggy memory, as in my own, old wounds are never forgotten. Alas, when the gang got home, Angel went straight to her corner and hasn't come out since, utterly exhausted and clearly content.

· 40 ·

After a long, dull day indoors, staring at a computer screen, contemplating my novel, I'm outside again at last, relaxing with physical chores. As the sun sags low in the autumn sky, an eerie wail comes floating across the valley, its high, shrill notes lent cadence by the beat of my wood-splitting maul. I recognize the singer at once, and cannot help but smile. Leaning my fat-headed axe against the slow-growing pile of aspen splits, I wipe the grit from eyes, ears, and face, then turn toward the fading sound, hoping to hear more.

After a while, sure enough, the wailing comes again—a low, throat-clearing tremolo wavering upward to soprano vibrato and sustaining there briefly, then trailing off rapidly in pitch and volume, like a cry blown away on the wind; the finale is a staccato triad of sharp coughs. There is no mistaking that voice.

The wapiti's most passionate time of year, and my own, is here again at last. Beginning now and continuing for the next several weeks, bugling elk and my sneaking attempts to see, hear, smell, and, sooner or later, bring one home for dinner will color my dreams, replenish my soul, harden my body, and consume more of my thoughts, energy, and time than I can logically justify to anyone who doesn't already know. The elk, as a friend once allowed, is my personal spirit animal. I take that as a compliment and don't deny its truth, but frankly, were I into zoomorphic transmutation I'd rather be a bear. Nothing new age there; it's just that bears seem already at least half human to me. And the other half, as I've noted, looks to me like dog. The friend who linked me spiritually with the wapiti was merely acknowledging the fact that for me, elk hunting is no mere diversion, no petty recreation, no contest of man against nature, no paltry "sport," no grocery transaction. For wild-man

Dave, simple elk hunting is life at its fullest, religion at its most personally meaningful . . . and practice for old friend death.

All who have heard it agree that the shrill, brassy blast of a bull elk's bugle is vocal magic, one of the most thrillingly mysterious sounds in nature, to my ears equaled only by the chilling nocturnal chorus of a wild timber wolf or the lonely wails of loons on a moon-mirrored north-country lake. Loons are not native to this region, and sadly, we have no wolves here in the southern Rockies. (Wolves were exterminated statewide by 1947, though the Colorado Division of Wildlife is currently predicting their spontaneous return.) Consequently, the wapiti's bugle is the music that defines the best of what's left of wildness in this place, sung from an aching, troubled heart. If you were to hear a wapiti scream in the night, having never heard the sound before and thus without a clue, you'd think it was some tortured soul from hell, howling in anguish and pain. And then you would run away.

An eerie cry it is. But to those who know it well, the bull elk's bugle is an anthem of freedom and dignity. To me it is transformative, like a werewolf's full-moon fate. When the wapiti calls, I *must* respond.

Typically throughout this surreal month, evening after evening (and a few early mornings as well) I dress to blend in, take up my bow and a heavy day pack, shoot a few practice arrows at a target in my yard, then creep up the mountain and into the woods. I hunt from the moment I leave home, trying to make my movements and mood flow like time. Now, more than any other season, my senses are alive: eyes prying into shadows, searching for anomalies in contrast and color or the slightest flick of movement; ears noting every rustle of leaf, every nuance of squirrel and birdcall; nose testing the pine-scented breeze for the funky barnyard stench that says a rutting bull elk is or recently was nearby.

During the early autumn rut, the bull elk is the horniest critter I know, rivaling even young college studs and old-fart satyrs like me. So overwhelming is the wapiti's lust that passion bloodies his eyes and swells his black-maned neck. So agitated is his mood that merely to round up a harem of as many as thirty cows, mating with each female repeatedly during her one-day estrus, is simply not enough. The lust-drugged bull requires additional outlets for his surging libido—such innocent diversions as horning (antler rubbing) brush and saplings to toothpicks, wallowing often, and bugling incessantly.

Throughout all this macho excitement, the cows remain for the most part aloof, feigning disinterest. When not being actively tended by a bull, cow elk in rut go about their herbivorous business as usual: grazing morning, evening, and night; relaxing in the shade (elk are intolerant of heat and direct sunlight) to chew their cud like a mandibular mantra; doing their best to ignore those wild and crazy guys swirling around them and fussing for attention. It's rather like the affected aloofness of bikini-clad beauties profiling at the beach. How I feel for the bulls!

Ironically, the herd bulls—the biggest, strongest, and wisest—often fall victim to their own breeding triumphs. All those weeks of round-the-clock bugling, sparring, and herding, defending and mating a harem of cows, take their brutal toll. And so it is that many a rut-spent bull enters winter malnourished, exhausted, and battle-scarred—liabilities that can conspire to prove fatal should the season prove harsh. And even before winter comes, tired, distracted bulls are targets of choice for many large predators—not only bears, wolves, and mountain lions, but human hunters as well.

Of this last contingent, I am a passionate, if somewhat peculiar, one. As Caroline is wont to say of my approach to hunting in recent years, echoing the transmutation myth, "David doesn't want to *kill* an elk nearly so much as he wants to *be* one."

Nice sentiment. But I'm already the animal I want to be: a natural-born predatory omnivore, a flat-faced bear with a romantic flair.

And so, once again and at last, the autumn hunt is on.

· 41 ·

It begins gently, softly. Just one small sound in the silent woods. While the brittle crack of limb is neither loud nor close, it clearly stands out against the background stillness, like one star gleaming in a cloudy sky.

To most people idling in the woods, such a minor disturbance would likely go unnoticed, or prompt just a flicker of curiosity. After all, a living forest is never quiet for long. But every sound holds meaning to the focused hunter—Spanish philosopher José Ortega y Gasset's "alert man" (or woman, in the case of my hunting buddy Erica and a growing number of others, about 1.5 million in the United States alone). In dense forest, the ears can always see farther than the eyes, and soon you learn that it pays to heed them—not just listening but thoughtfully weighing each sound: Was that a squirrel tossing itself from branch to branch in the trees, a red-shafted flicker tapping on bark, a wild turkey scratching in leaf litter, a grouse or other ground-foraging bird, a falling spruce cone? Or something heavier, thus bigger?

The small sound I'm weighing just now triggers keen excitement. Though its volume was muted by distance, the limb crack was heavy and hard, investing the evening with hope, like a wink from a lovely stranger.

Snapping to full alert, I pull up my camouflage face mask,

which, when not in play, I wear like a bandanna around my neck; my face is always painted. My bow, lying at the ready beside me, comes naturally to hand, an arrow ready on the string. Soon I'm encouraged by another sharp snap, followed by a brief, brittle clatter, like hoof kicking rocks, then a flurry of earthy thuds and one weird, muted vocalization. All from the same direction, each sound an enticing bit closer and louder than the one before.

An intense silence ensues as I sit entranced, utterly focused, hardly daring to breathe, never more alive than now, a reckoning near at hand.

As if picking this moment to dramatize his role, an unseen bull bugles, farther away than my approaching noisemaker but not really far, warming up for the night. Both the low, spooky growl that precedes the wail and the throaty chuckle after are loud and clear: the singer is confident, and he is near, just beyond Big Gully, a hundred yards to the west. A nearby loud crack of limb tells me that the closer and approaching animal has also heard the bugle and taken note. In my mind's eye I see the nearer elk suddenly stop and stiffen, planting its front hooves firmly, ears erect, listening.

Moments later yet another bugler sings, this one directly opposite the first and about the same distance away. Equally cocky, he is answering the challenge, even raising the ante a bit. Should they decide to come together, with me here in the middle, things could get exciting.

But the first bugler fails to respond to the second, and the woods go quiet again. No more noise from nearby, either. The approaching animal, apparently, has either stopped or snuck away.

Several more minutes creep by and I'm starting to relax again when a huge dark head appears above a copse of oak brush thirty yards out, on the far side of Killing Spring, swiveling and scanning like an antlered periscope, surveying the scene all around. Not a sound did he make on his final approach, moving as quietly as a cloud ghost. And clearly, even by naturally nervous cervid standards, this bull is edgy: neck craned high, dark eyes bulging, ears out stiff and facing forward, nostrils wide as funnels. This is not one of the two cocky buglers, but a shy youngster of two or three years.

And nervous he should be, for a predator lurks nearby. (In point of fact, I'm not really lurking but sitting sidesaddle on a log, with a fir tree as a backrest and a screen of cut boughs arranged behind me to further confuse my camouflaged human form.) This isn't the trophy calf I had hoped to kill this year—toward which end, over the past two weeks, I've ignored close shots at three young bulls and two prime cows, patiently awaiting a 250-pound package of the most tender meat in these mountains. ("Spoon meat," one friend calls it.) It's also the most ecologically sound choice of meat, the one that harms the herd's health the least. Four years ago I first set out to kill a calf, having switched my priority from antlers and good meat to biological concern and the best meat. And all four years I have failed, run out of time, and been forced to settle for a young bull or cow. Thus the tongue-in-cheek trophy status I've come to grant to calves. Even so, the archery season is winding down and neglected work is stacking up and that antsy young bull over yonder would be a most welcome guest at our table this winter. If I fail to kill an elk myself, I'll be left to cruise local highways hunting roadkill, just like in our first years here.

Priorities shift. The trophy calf can wait another year. A commitment is made. Adrenaline starts to pump.

And from where I now sit, barring some cosmic practical joke, it appears that my chances are better than good. Most important in that regard, I'm confident that it's not me this hyperalert young fellow senses and so obviously fears. I am, after all, invisible.

As always when approaching an ambush site, I slipped in from the downhill side during late afternoon, waiting for the day to cool, the air to grow heavy, and the breeze, obeying the demands of thermal dynamics, to begin its cooling downhill slide. From the moment I left the cabin I touched nothing with my clean-gloved hands. My aging body, freshly scrubbed with scentless soap, is cloaked head to toe in clothing laundered in that same scentless soap and hung out to dry in the sun and pine-scented air. My feet are shod in rubber-soled (thus scentproof) boots, and my handsome gray-bearded face hides behind a mask of camo mesh. To defeat glare or shine, my bow and hickory arrows are finished dark and dull. Finally, the umbrella-boughed tree I'm sitting beneath floods me in a blue-black pool of shade.

What more can a body do?

One important thing: two decades of devoted wapiti watching and hundreds of thrilling hours spent close to elk, deer, bears, and turkeys have convinced me that all evolved prey species are sensitive to front-set predatory eyes and can *feel* a carnivorous stare. It's a major element, I believe, of the mysterious "sixth sense" hunters superstitiously grant to their prey and speak of with awe and frustration. Accordingly, as the nervous bull inches closer, I squint my eyes to slits and look slightly away, avoiding direct visual contact, tracking my prey peripherally. From time to time his roving gaze falls directly on me, but it never lingers long. I *am* invisible. So long, at least, as he stays upwind. While an elk might overlook your stepping on a limb, mistaking you for another elk, and while it might even give you the visual benefit of the doubt—countless times I've frozen while elk, deer, or bear stared long and hard only, eventually, to relax and return to the business at hand—a wild animal will never, ever hang around to contemplate the human smell. In such instances, lowly instinct easily outshines thoughtful intellect, catapulting the potential victim instantly out of potential harm's way.

No, it isn't me this fretful fellow is sweating but the two deep-throated big boys who have started singing again, turn on turn, still on opposite sides of us, right where they were before. Perhaps this lanky lad has recently had his ample butt kicked by one of those bad boys out there—or else he simply knows enough to know he doesn't want to let that happen. And so he refrains from revealing himself through bugling and is keeping a wary eye out for trouble as he approaches the spring to drink. Yet the day has been warm and parchingly dry. The rut is raging, and—I speak from personal experience—testosterone poisoning gives a guy a big thirst. The scent of water beckons, so near.

When my partner in this ancient dance finally reaches the small, clear pool that is Killing Spring, he takes one last, long look around and wades in knee-deep. A moment later his head dips down, disappearing behind the low earth embankment surrounding the sunken pool. He can't see me at all when his head is down, and I can't see his eyes. Yet his body above the knees remains in full view. Glancing at his antlers, I count five thin, polished tines on the right main beam, four on the left. A three-year-old. The ribby, roan-colored chest, wholly exposed, looks big as a billboard. Willing myself to relax, to wait for all to be perfect, I suck in a long, slow breath and confirm that the arrow sits securely on its narrow shelf above my hand and that the bowstring rests deep in the arrow's notch. Thus reassured, I slowly raise the bow from my lap and bring it up to vertical, then on to one o'clock. My left hand encircles the slim handle grip. Three fingers of my right hand hold snugly the string, one above and two below the arrow. I'm ready as can be, awaiting the predictable "pronghorn caper."

Sure enough, having been down only moments, up snaps the clever head, looking to surprise any approaching threat: mountain lion, bigger bull, bear, or bowman.

I've heard the opinion that ambushing a water hole is an unfair way to hunt, since "animals have to drink." From the outside looking in, I understand that viewpoint, and in the case of isolated stock tanks (cow ponds) in arid country, I agree and will not do it. Yet this mountain is dotted with springs and bordered on one side by a creek, the other by a river. Elk have many choices and I can be but one place at a time, which most often is the wrong place. More significantly, human hunters are hardly the only predators who ambush water holes. Since before the time of saber-toothed cats, dire wolves, and Neanderthal man, predators have ambushed prey at water. Consequently, prey animals have a strong and deeply ingrained instinctive edginess when visiting such places, especially when alone, as reflected in their creeping approach, greatly heightened watchfulness, and sense of urgency to drink fast and get out.

They also have other defensive tricks, like what I call the pronghorn caper. In this case, had I tried to make my move— draw, aim, and shoot—when the bull first dipped its head to drink, the animal would have caught me in the act and I'd now be hearing the heart-sinking thunder of hooves pounding away. To confuse matters more, unlike pronghorn antelope, elk don't always play this "Gotcha!" head-bobbing game before drinking. But this evening, this nervous fellow clearly wants to. So again, and yet again, we do the head-bob peekaboo. The fourth time down, the head stays down, and I hear the loud, sucking sound of water being vacuumed in, horselike, through clenched teeth. The up and down of the bull's Adam's apple confirms that he is seriously drinking.

After weeks of work and waiting, this is it. Leaning forward to free my back from the backrest tree, I draw, anchor deep (right thumb behind right jawbone), and aim without aiming (that's why it's called instinctive shooting; rather like tossing a football). There is no thought or feeling now, no past and no tomorrow, no right or wrong, elation, intellectualization, or hesitation. Just this long frozen slice of two lives twining, pure as glacial ice. Acting in unison, three fingers relax and arrow flashes away . . . and there is no turning back.

Water erupts. Mud flies. Hooves pound. Deadfall cracks like pistol shots. Heartbeats (mine) boom like howitzers as the bushwhacked bull storms away.

Amid all this dizzying, deafening, supercharged confusion of sound and visual fury, I fail to note where my arrow struck, so instantly and completely does the shaft disappear into flesh, and so chaotically does that flesh depart.

Either that or I missed.

But I barely have time to register this moment of doubt, this prelude to despair, before the running bull slams headlong into a tree. From my catbird's seat I see the big pine shudder, absorbing the quarter-ton blow, accompanied by a mysterious clatter, like shattering glass. Following a moment's suspended animation, the short-stopped bull rocks backward and drops—not onto one side or the other, as gravity would seem to dictate, but upright on his belly, as if he were sitting down: knees folded under, legs slightly astraddle, chin resting on the ground, antlers pointing straight up. You'd almost think he was napping.

Five seconds, thirty yards—that's all it took, as far as he got.

With the fallen beast reposing in full view and motionless, and with a second arrow on the string (just in case), I cautiously approach. Only now do I note that the top third of his left antler—the foot-deep terminal fork and a foot of main beam below—lies scattered on the ground in cigar-sized shards. This explains the sound of shattering glass.

This—a near-instant kill—is what every ethical hunter wants. If he matures, it is what he comes to *demand* of himself, ensuring a humane and honorable closure to a wild and dignified life. We all should die so well.

After thanking the fallen bull—not some empty, showy, new agey "noble savage" superciliousness but a simple, heartfelt expression of empathy, unity, respect, and gratitude—I collect the scattered antler pieces (to take home and puzzle together with glue), then wrestle the big, warm body onto its right side, hone my little knife (the bigger the blade, the less experienced the skinner), and set to making meat. As noted earlier, the average adult elk weighs five hundred to six hundred pounds. Reduced to edible boneless meat, the yield averages two hundred pounds, which tomorrow I'll haul out on a pack frame in three knee-crushing loads. (Although Erica always volunteers to do pack-mule duty, she's not around right now.) This evening's chore is to convert animal to meat and to bag that meat for the night.

But first, to indulge a certain—how best to describe it?—curiosity.

"Give us a wilderness whose glance no civilization can endure," urged Thoreau, "as if we lived on the marrow of koodoos devoured raw." In his youth, odd Henry hunted and fished for food and praised the experience highly. As an adult at Walden Pond, he turned sour on hunting but continued to fish for dinner, his fare augmented by gardening and mooching meals from neighbors.

In any event, this is no koodoo. Moreover, in these tragic days of chronic wasting disease (the cervid version of mad cow disease), it's reckless to devour, raw *or* cooked, the marrow of any North American wild ungulate, given that such nervous-system tissues as marrow and brains are packed with protein prions, the primary carriers of CWD. Even so, none such has been found in the wild here in the San Juan biosystem, so far. Nor is there any proof that CWD can be transmitted to humans, so far. And there's something I've been wanting, needing, hungering to do for a very long time, so with no hesitation I force the pointed tip of my skinning knife straight down through the thick hide, slightly to one side of the surrogate koodoo's spine and just behind the shoulder. With a circular motion I detach a cone-shaped plug of warm red flesh, about a teaspoonful. After trimming off the hide, I pop the meat into my mouth, close my eyes, and chew. The chewing is easy, the flesh moist and tender, the flavor mild and pleasant, if not so delicious as grilled. Meat gets no fresher than this, no more organic or "free ranging," and the give-and-take of life and death on Earth, the sacred metabolic transfer of energy and spirit, has never felt more real or personal. I swallow easily and say aloud once again, "Thank you, elk."

· **42** ·

How, my nonhunting friends have asked—and a fair question it is—can I claim to love and respect the same animals I work so hard, with such obvious enthusiasm, to kill?

What so many do not understand is that the enthusiasm of hunting properly belongs to the *hunt*. The kill, once it is certain, is anticlimactic and carried out with mere resolve.

"Slaughter doesn't necessarily preclude respect," writes *New York Times Magazine* contributor Michael Pollan, suggesting how a moral livestock industry should operate but does not because it is not.

In hunting, the humane killing of fairly and honorably out-witted prey is precisely the opposite of slaughter—a word that implies that the victim has no chance of escape, as in domesticated species. Consequently, rather than *precluding* respect on the part of the honorable hunter, the final act enhances it. And this dying respect, to those who understand, amounts to no less than love.

Does the wolf not love the caribou? And does she not, even so, undertake her daily hunts with enthusiasm and joy?

· **43** ·

Throughout the focused minutes before and after the killing, and now as I work to make meat, mesmerized by the rhythmic sweep

of knife blade shearing hide from muscle—*snick-snick, snick*—
I've been only peripherally aware of the two bugling bulls, who by
now have worked each other into a screaming and grunting
frenzy punctuated here and there by a conspicuous thrashing of
limbs. A typical late-evening performance at this advanced stage
of the rut. Obviously, they remain entirely innocent of the near-
silent drama that's just played out midway between them, down
here in the little vale that keeps my scent from rising to them. But
as I slice and tug and strain at hide, meat, and bone, their bugling
and brush bashing, their ground stomping and grunting grow
incrementally louder, inching closer, getting harder to ignore.

Suddenly, a herd of twenty or so cows and their long-legged
babes (my trophy calf!) come chirping out of the shadowy woods
and into the twilight open, directly downwind of me, picking up
speed as they move within sight and scent of the spring, all wanting to get there first and drink before the water gets muddied.
Almost immediately the wise old lead cow catches the terrifying
odor of man, the iron-sweet scent of blood, locks her front legs,
and barks a startled alarm. As one body and without hesitation—
instinct in action again—the entire herd explodes in noisy retreat,
back to the sheltering woods. Safely out of sight and feeling secure,
one cow, most likely the leader, lingers as the others crash off, barking her thirsty annoyance—sounding just ike Otis, only shriller.

"Sorry, elk," I say aloud. "I'll be gone as soon as I can. Meanwhile, there's another spring just over the hill, and another
beyond that . . . you know."

No more bugling is heard. The boys have gotten the word.

My only companions now are the brittle autumn aspens, a
shimmering mosaic of yellow-green leaves buzzing drily in the
evening breeze; this warm, naked body in my arms; and four
low-circling wings that arrived with the elk and did not leave.
Tilting steeply in their effortless, buoyant turns, the obsidian
shields of their raven-black backs shimmer and gleam beneath

the low-angle sun. Outspokenly excited, the big birds celebrate our mutual good luck with a gurgling of impatient chatter. Tonight, roosted nearby, they'll dream of guts and glory. And tomorrow they will feast.

In past hunts on this mountain, the persistent calls of ravens—sometimes a single, usually a pair—have either guided me to elk or forewarned of their path of movement and pending approach, granting me time to prepare. This happens often, in fact, though only during the rut, when elk congregate in boisterous herds. And only in the evening, never in the morning, at least in my experience. From what I've observed over the years, I'm satisfied that what attracts ravens to rutting elk is the frenzied activity and cacophony of vocalizing that erupts when a herd rises in late afternoon from their day beds. For half an hour or so the elk will stretch and yawn and otherwise make ready to move out for another night of feeding and breeding—the adults milling around anxiously, the calves cavorting, all of them chirping and mewing excitedly, the herd bull limbering his voice for another night of singing. Then suddenly, on some signal invisible to me, the lead cow heads out at a trot and the rest of the herd falls in line behind her. It's all this frenetic movement and noisy activity that attracts ravens and prompts them to follow the moving band, absorbing the excitement and joining the party with their own cadenced calls.

Others who have witnessed this remarkable behavior surmise that ravens are consciously helping human hunters find game—just as they are known to team with wolves—working for the generous wages of scrap meat, gut piles, eyeballs, and fat. At times, this may have been the way with me and my local birds. But more often, the fliers have no idea I even exist, nixing the possibility of teamwork. More likely, in sum, they are simply playing.

In any event, these two ravens, who've done nothing to earn a feast, having provided no help to me whatsoever this time around, have found us. And like Thoreau at the Emersons' table, they aren't inclined to leave.

Thanks to the favorable conditions I've been blessed with on this gentle autumn eve—twilight rather than flashlight; relatively open and level ground rather than steep, rocky slope or brush-choked gully bottom; no rain or snow; and I'm equipped for once with a small bone saw (whereas I usually pack only a knife)—I set a personal record of just over ninety minutes from whole animal to four big bags of bone-in meat. A single huge hindquarter fills each of the first two bags. The third bag gets both shoulders. The fourth bag is reserved for the twenty to thirty pounds of backstraps and tenderloins. The former are two long, thick tubes of prime meat that lie along either side of the spine on the outside of the rib cage. Cut across the grain into steaks, elk backstraps produce the equivalent of the larger side of T-bones or pork chops. The tenderloins are even better, the kindest of all cuts in fact, like the smaller, melt-in-your-mouth side of a T-bone or chop. They lie opposite the backstraps along the inside of the spine, behind the diaphragm and above the innards. Since we don't eat organs, C and I, and considering my outside-in method of field dressing, if it weren't for the necessity to spill the paunch in order to reach in (up to my shoulder) and cut free the tenderloins, I would have no need to gut an animal at all. As it is, by leaving the evisceration for last, I minimize the risk of tainting the meat by contact with spilled urine, feces, or bile.

Since the light is running low, I'll leave the final step until morning. When I return then I'll press one of the big linen meat bags into service as a ground cloth, remove the leg bones from each of the four quarters, and rebag the meat before packing it out, considerably lightening my loads. Until then, three of the four bags will cool overnight leaned upright against the trunks of spruce trees, whose low-limbed boughs will provide good shade, should the sun beat me here in the morning. By dragging the bags a good ways upwind of the gut pile, I can hope that any scavenger who follows its nose to the feast will stop right there to eat its fill of liver and heart, leaving my meat alone. The fourth and lightest bag, containing the precious tenderloins and backstraps, I'll sling over my shoulder and lug out tonight, awkward as it is, to make certain that some industrious and selective bruin or coyote doesn't get the best of it. Basted with garlic butter and grilled hot and fast, back-strap and tenderloin of elk are sublime.

With my family's winter store of meat quite literally in the bag (the dogs get only table scraps and trimmings cooked rare), my penultimate task is to extract the matched pair of ivories. Like tiny rounded tusks, these vestigial upper canines, when mounted simply in silver, will make two lovely earrings for two lovely ears (neither of them my own).

Finally, I hoist the disembodied head, with its one whole and one shattered antler, as high as I can into the brushy mass of a fir tree and lash it to the trunk with parachute cord.

And that is that, for now.

Come Thanksgiving Day, two months away—when the birds and bugs have done their work and the skull is exposed, if not entirely clean—I'll return, on snowshoes, I hope (we need the snow *so* badly), bringing with me the mended antler top, some epoxy glue, and a length of baling wire. After reassembling the busted antler I'll relocate the crudely rendered skull-mount to a prominent aspen overlooking Killing Spring, securing it high and tight to the naked white trunk. During future visits to this personally sacred place (where I hope to have my own carcass planted, preferably and conveniently after croaking here), this artful totem, this reminder of so many memorable hunts, will mean more to me out here—*in situ, in medias res*—than it ever could back home, in or on the cabin, lost there among the crowd.

Very well.

The bloody deed is done. Only the packing, cutting, wrapping, and freezing remain. Good work, start to finish.

· 44 ·

Earlier this evening, while I was out hunting elk with Erica (she's a gunner and her season is October), Caroline was working in her garden when a coyote came trotting down the drive, saw her, and stopped . . . then, while looking right at C from thirty yards away, started yipping and howling. Otis and Angel, both inside the Doghouse, came to the screen door and snuffled and whined, but neither chose to bark. We don't often get coyotes here, at least not vocal coyotes in broad daylight; they seem to stay up higher, where there's more to eat and no dogs to harass them. Here in the yard, bears are far more common. What was that coyote thinking? After a minute or so it trotted away, to be heard no more.

Our howler has returned. Shortly after we went to bed last night a coyote started singing from down by Caroline's garden and the fire ring, thirty yards from our bed. To say the sounds were startlingly loud and marvelously weird is insufficient praise. Was it the same dog Caroline saw and heard here just last week? This time—or this one, as the case may be—the visitor yodeled and yapped enthusiastically for a good ten minutes. Then, as before, it quietly disappeared. We wonder if the animal is trying to tell us something, and what that something might be.

· 45 ·

On what I fear may be my last long hike alone before snow comes to shroud and shrink our mountain world, I'm loafing along the ragged edge of a Colorado mountain meadow adjacent to the South San Juan Wilderness, sixty miles east-southeast of home, in recently former grizzly country. I'm two hours from the truck and paralleling the Continental Divide when the blue sky goes suddenly black. Once again, just like back in August, what began as a carefree day hike threatens to get drowned out.

Sure enough, within minutes I'm under assault from lightning, thunder, rain like a car wash, and swirling fog—a typical "surprise" thunderstorm of the sort that's rarely a surprise at all here in the southern Rockies from mid-July through late August. But this lovely fall morning I was once again a foolish optimist, and my high-tech rain gear is back in the truck, where it won't get wet. When hard, heavy hail joins the attack, I flee like a panicked animal for the iffy shelter of a nearby finger of forest.

As I slog into the dripping woods, something huge and the color of shadow materializes a few yards ahead, then dissolves into the gloom. This is dead center the only place in Colorado that might still hide a last few grizzlies, and my pulse quickens at the possibility, no matter how remote. But the accompanying thud of hooves cancels my paranoia.

I go to where the creature had been, and there, at the leeward base of an old-growth Douglas fir, I find a bathtub-sized oval of cushy duff scraped clean of limbs, rocks, and other lumpy ground litter. And dry as Noah's socks. A pungent barnyard stench confirms it: wapiti bull. The familiar smell is reassuring, as if I were at home. With that thought, I promptly claim the abandoned nest for my own, settling in to wait out the storm. It's hardly the lap of luxury, but the alternative is another miserable race with hypothermia and death. Happens all the time in these fickle old mountains to Pollyanna day-trippers, which today I have proven to be. But here I sit, dry and safe and almost comfy, thanks to a wise wapiti.

It's amazing, a wild animal's skill in locating such superlative natural shelter as this, albeit the workings of mere mindless instinct—like a dog circling before it lies down—an innate inclination hardwired into the beastly cerebral circuits through countless millennia of Darwinian pick and choose. Or, perhaps, the elk's knack of finding bedding sites that will remain sheltered and dry in almost any weather is a skill at least partially learned, passed down from cow to calf, generation upon generation, practiced and refined.

Whatever it is, the wapiti haven't yet informed me.

· 46 ·

Certainly, many wild animals know more than we do about basic creature comforts, celestial navigation, all-season survival, and other essentials of what once was hailed, in human terms, as woodsmanship. (Nowadays, to avoid the charge of sexism, the preferred word—its earlier meaning resurrected—is *woodcraft*.) Consider the ptarmigan, an alpine grouse that escapes killing blizzards by diving into powdery snow, where it finds shelter from screaming winter winds and insulation against the subzero cold. Moreover, its pure-white winter phase (like a feathered ermine) helps it blend in, hiding it from such toothy appetites as the arctic fox—which also blends with and shelters beneath snow, as do arctic and varying hares. Thus did each of these species independently invent not only seasonal camouflage but the emergency snow cave as well.

At the opposite extreme, desert animals have learned to conduct most of their business at night and along the cool, dusky edges of day, then siesta in relatively cool hidey-holes during the frying hours. In this way they defeat dehydration, heat prostration, sunburn, cataracts, cancer, and scorched feet while demonstrating a basic survival intelligence that's rare, often fatally so, among human desert rats.

And almost all wild beings know enough to relax and enjoy life, each in its peculiar way. For example, one late summer a friend and I were sitting quietly in the shade just a few miles from here, eating lunch while watching a mess of mallards fool around in a beaver pond a few yards in front of us. Suddenly a cow elk appeared from the woods behind us and leapt explosively into the little pond, sending the ducks into quacking flight and waves sloshing everywhere. For the next fifteen minutes we watched in captive silence as the big deer splashed, blew bubbles, kicked at the water with her right front hoof, and stared, mesmerized, as the wave circles she intentionally made expanded concentrically outward, like well-lived lives.

This, quite clearly, was play for play's sake.

Yet what do such behaviors as these, impressive though they are to witness, really tell us about whether or not animals possess conscious intellect—the ability to think, reason, plan, and act from self-directed choice? Or to learn from experience, projecting lessons acquired in the past to future possibilities? Not much, says traditional biology, arguing that even such seemingly spontaneous behaviors as play should be chalked up to "innate tendencies" rather than conscious intent, much less "mood," which would suggest that nonhuman animals possess humanlike emotions.

Only in the twentieth century did there finally arise a school of serious scientific investigation into animal intelligence. Its name is behaviorism, and its founder was the psychologist B. F. Skinner. Intrigued by the work of the infamous Russian dog trainer, Skinner furthered Pavlov's discoveries by tormenting lab rats and other animals with mazes, surgically implanted electrodes, food deprivation, drugs, and similar joys in hopes of demonstrating that for every stimulus (say, cramming more and more rats into the same small cage), there follows a predictable response (radically increased frustration, aggression, murder, rape, incest, depression, angst, and other ills commonly found in urban settings). It worked, and "Skinnerian behaviorism" came to dominate the academic study of animal intelligence so thoroughly that for several decades researchers with conflicting data were reluctant to publish their findings or otherwise come out of their academic closets for fear of professional ridicule.

Only recently has fundamentalist behaviorism begun to give way to a kinder and gentler school of inquiry, dubbed cognitive ethology. *Cognition* is a fancy word for conscious thought. Ethology is the study of animal behavior under more or less natural, as opposed to coldly clinical, conditions. Nor is it really new. As early as the fifth century B.C., a Greek slave writing under the pen name Aesop dabbled in cognitive ethology when he observed and recorded in a fable the striking intelligence of a thirsty raven he'd seen dropping pebbles into a narrow-necked jug filled halfway with water, gradually and—dare we say?—with *premeditation* raising the level of the liquid until the bird could reach it and drink. Since then, researchers have repeatedly reported observing similarly clever behavior among birdbrained ravens.

What are we to make of such anecdotal reports? Is the physical concept of displacement of volume instinctive knowledge among ravens? Or are these birds intelligent enough in human terms—that is, calculating—to figure it out on their own, individually, time and again?

Experiments conducted by the University of Vermont's world-renowned cognitive ethologist Bernd Heinrich suggest the latter, largely validating the raven's far-flung historical reputation for ingenuity. After suspending a bit of food on a long string below a perch pole, Heinrich photographed one of his birds solving the problem by lifting a length of string with its beak, then anchoring the coil to the perch with a foot, doing this over and over again until it had effectively reeled in the bait. A second Heinrich raven, watching the first, didn't merely learn from—that is, ape—what it saw but made an apparent intuitive leap to one-up its clever neighbor by grasping the string loosely in its beak and walking the length of the perch pole to draw it up, rather like a pulley, bringing home the bacon both faster and with far less effort. Crows, in Heinrich's experiments, never got past trying to snatch the suspended morsel on the fly, only to have it jerked rudely and repeatedly from their beaks.

Cultural anthropologist, writer, and subsistence hunter Richard Nelson reports that ravens are believed by the Koyukon natives of interior Alaska to lead human hunters to game. Having repeatedly witnessed and personally benefited from a local variation of this fascinating behavior myself, I too have come to view the raven as a hunter's helper. At least on fortuitous occasions.

But then, as any behaviorist worth his Skinner box will argue, innate behavior patterns are known to provide animals with an impressively broad choice of responses to apparently unique stimuli, often leaving observers with the false impression that true thinking has taken place or humanlike emotion has been expressed when, "in fact," it has not.

Certainly, such *can* be the case. But, I wonder, does it *have* to be—always? I find it easier to believe that the occasional Einstein of a raven has smarts enough to purposely join forces with predators than to accept that natural selection would go to all the trouble to imprint such complex, individualized, and exotic behaviors in instinct.

Like humans who earn their meat in the marketplace jungle, some animals are not above deceiving and overtly harming other animals in ruthless competition for personal gain. Among the best-documented of animal "liars" is the female piping plover, which deftly decoys predators away from her ground nest by employing such inventive deceits as flopping around with a faked wing injury or squeaking like a rodent from behind a screen of foliage; the style of her pretense is apparently tailored to fit the nature of the threat. Similarly, Caroline and I and many other outdoor folk have had female grouse and nighthawks, mule deer does, and elk cows try to decoy us away from their hidden young when we've stumbled a bit too close. Yet such deceits as these are "honorable" lies, told not for greedy Enron ends but to protect home, family, and species posterity. More self-serving and thus more humanlike are the screeching hawk imitations frequently uttered by Steller's jays at our backyard feeder, effectively if only temporarily clearing the area of chickadees, nuthatches, juncos, and even other jays. Do "selfish" acts such as this not suggest a thoughtful, even creative intelligence and premeditation?

Deceit aside, consider this report from Tom Beck. Your standard bear live trap, like the one warden Cary Carron used to catch a goat-killing bruin a few years ago, consists of a section of large-diameter steel culvert pipe with one end capped and the other fitted with a heavy guillotine-type door that slides up between parallel tracks and is held open with a big metal pin. The pin, in turn, is connected via a cable to a pedal trigger attached to the floor near the back of the trap. The bait is placed on or behind the pedal. When a bear enters the barrel and steps on the trigger, the pin is pulled and the heavy door slams down to trap the bruin within.

Says Beck: "I've watched bears who've never seen a culvert trap walk up to one, check it out from various angles, then stand up, grab the raised door projecting from the top of the culvert, and with a powerful twisting motion wrench it sideways to bind it open . . . then step inside, take the bait, and walk away."

Tom also reports seeing bears toss rocks or sticks onto the triggers of spring-activated leg snares to disarm them before going for the goodies. "Bears," this sober expert will tell you, "appear to be capable of reasoning, planning, and spontaneous problem solving."

But bears are notoriously smart. Late last summer, while my personal physician and bow-building guru, Doc Dave Sigurslid, and I were scouting for a place to hunt elk on nearby public land, we found where an underground seep emerged near the bottom of a steep incline, muddying a large area of dirt. To convert that unusable mud to drinkable water in a drought summer, an elk had carved out a bowl with a hoof, using the mud scraped from the excavation to form a dam below. This makeshift reservoir— about one foot in diameter and nearly that deep—contained a gallon or more of water, which, due to the constant flow-through of the seep, was perfectly clear and delightfully drinkable. Elk tracks surrounded the makeshift pool at a neck's-stretch distance, as if the animals were making a conscious effort not to break the dam or muddy the water with their hooves.

Doc Dave, who spent ten years as a wildlife biologist before entering medical school, seemed as shocked and impressed as I was.

"That's not instinct," I quipped.

"No sir, it sure isn't," my doctor agreed, confirming my diagnosis.

Even so—all such feats of apparent animal imagination, forethought, and conscious reasoning notwithstanding—it remains likely that without true language with which to share, record, and expand whatever smarts and thoughts they may possess, animals are doomed (or blessed) never to enjoy (or endure) the complex abstract mental athletics that define the human mind.

· 47 ·

Beyond the invisible walls of my limb-thatched shelter the tempest rages on. The lightning and thunder are moving on to torment other unprepared hikers. The hail has petered out. But the wind still howls and rain pours down with vigor. Yet here I squat, dry and warm, carefree as any Caliban—all thanks to an elk.

Only as dusk approaches does the wind finally flag and the rain fizzle out. The marathon hike I had planned, alas, is a brilliant bust. Yet thanks to the practical intellect of the cud-chewing ungulate that selected and improved this remarkably well-sheltered nest I'm squatting in, I've ridden out a life-threatening storm sitting pretty—pretty dry, pretty warm, pretty comfortable . . . and very grateful. Intelligence, it seems to me, is what works best to satisfy a particular creature's needs in the particular circumstance it must adapt to.

It has been suggested that even if we could find some Dr. Dolittlish way to talk with the animals, what they have to say would be foreign to us, and vice versa, so different are our perceptions of life. If this is true (and I suspect it is), why do we persist in ranking animal intelligence based on a human model?

Yet if we simply shift the question from what the animals *know* to what they *feel*, the human-animal comparison becomes vital. No matter a creature's "IQ," if it experiences emotions more similar to our own than we've heretofore believed or acknowledged, we are morally obliged to forge new ways to interact with that fellow being. One of the most observable indicators of human-like emotion in animals is play, insofar as play implies joy. Traditional biology attributes play in young animals to their need to develop muscles and build essential skills, which no doubt is true. Yet this fails to go far enough. I have witnessed a variety of spontaneous, amazingly clever games among animals of every age and social status, groups and singles, as you may have too.

For instance, to what instinct or "utility" can we attribute a dozen cow elk and calves and a mature bull running a tail chase in a tight circle, jumping in and out of a small spring pool (Killing Spring, in fact), one after another, as they play ring-around-the-rosy, leaping and kicking and chirping and bugling excitedly? To date, I've witnessed such wapiti waterplay three different times, always during the rut—though that may be simply because that's when I'm out among them most often. And what of the adult black bear that sledded down a steep snowbank on its butt, spinning like a fat, furry top, then sprinted back up to do it again, and again? And how to explain as "instinctive" or "utilitarian" an adult grizzly sow and an alpha she-wolf playing tag on a June snowfield in Montana, *taking turns* chasing and being chased, back and forth, the wolf leaping and bouncing and wagging its tail as all dogs do in play, with absolutely no sign of aggression from either party?

How can any open-eyed, open-minded person, scientist or not, witness such events as these—each of which I have personally observed, often in the company of others—yet deny that animals, adults as well as young, play simply for the fun, for the flaming *joy* of it?

By logical extension, any animal that can experience joy must be capable of opposite feelings as well, such as depression and grief. For without the one extreme, the other has no grounding, no relativity, no meaning.

And what of love? Few people who've been charged by a bear sow protecting her cubs, or boldly challenged by a barking, hoof-stamping elk or moose cow whose hidden calf they have happened too near, or watched how lovingly most mammal mothers nurse and groom their young would deny the existence of apparent affection in animal parents (at least the females). Yet the scientific tendency has been to credit parental devotion among animals not to love as we know it but to short-term, hormone-controlled procreative instinct—the I-word again. Yet if we interpret love, in any of its many forms (romantic, platonic, sibling, parental, patriotic, religious) as being evidenced by observable affection and self-sacrificing loyalty among individuals—whether of the same species or different—and if we grant that few, if any, instincts in any animal species, including humans, are stronger than that for personal survival, then something a lot like love is evident among many vertebrates.

Personally—as an omnivore by evolution and a semisubsistence hunter and animal lover by inclination—I embrace the concept of rich emotional lives in animals. Not on a par with those of humans, insofar as animals don't likely share with us the ability to philosophically ponder the meanings of love or grief. Yet sufficiently rich to be *felt by the animal,* and thus of moral merit. Consequently, I sicken at the thought of the myriad ways our socially sanctioned agricultural, pet, outdoor-recreation, and medical-industrial-research industries continue to embody cruelty for profit.

Still, having considered all of this and more at painful length, I remain loyal to the biological imperative of species-specific roles and the bottom-line truth that life feeds on death. It's hard, but it works. Elk evolved as prey. Humans evolved as opportunistic predatory omnivores (upright bears). For each of us, elk and human, to express our full personal and evolutionary (genetic) potential, our biological roles must be acted out. Or, as in the case of modern "sport" hunting, at least earnestly played at.

But acted out and played at—here's the really tricky bit—according to whose rules?

Indirectly, the great American naturalist, hunter, ecologist, and biophilosopher Aldo Leopold had that one figured out more than half a century ago when he declared his famous land ethic: "A thing is right when it tends to preserve the integrity, stability, and beauty of the biotic community. It is wrong when it does otherwise."

It is a tragic and unarguable fact that—no matter if the weapon of destruction is bow and arrow, rifle, commercial fishing fleet, farmer's combine, logging truck, nuclear test site, backhoe, or ATV—human predation that fails to respect the unity of the global biotic community is a major and growing problem everywhere today. The richer and more technologically advanced a nation or culture, the bigger and more hurtful the problem. A solution—workable, if not very likely—would be to employ Leopold's land ethic as a model for establishing a biologically and morally healthy human-animal relationship.

Looking from the inside out, as it were, I see no way, and no need, to deny that wild animals suffer emotional as well as physical pain at the hands of hunters—including, of course, myself— just as they suffer from disease and parasites and natural (i.e., nonhuman) predators and weather and roads and subdivisions and fences and game farms and domestication and the pet industry and heavy-handed research biologists and well-meaning animal rightists and nominally "conservative" motorheads ripping around the boonies on screaming, stinking machines (*vox machinae*) and distracted soccer moms speeding around in gas-gulping oversized SUVs. But the wisest moral and biological option, I'm convinced, is not to deny or abandon humanity's evolved predator-prey relationship with wild animals, which would be to allow an ideology to overrule biology. Rather, our moral imperative as humane humans, hunters and non, is to view and treat our fellow creatures far more carefully and caringly than we presently do or historically ever have, never stealing their lives or their freedom or subjecting them to injury or pain—emotional or physical—for trivial or purely profit-driven reasons or in a humancentric or care-less manner. No matter that we *must* kill in order to live, our duty as the "thinking animal" is to respect and love them all—these, our partners in the sacred, ancient dance of death begetting life.

In the end, people are humans and elk are deer, and never the twain shall meet, at least not on intellectually level ground. Nor should we. Yet our intellectual differences are likely not so vast as we prefer to think, and they certainly don't give us moral license to declare technological war on wildlife in the name of recreation, profit, or even scientific advancement, or to willfully or carelessly cause, ignore, or deny suffering among that glori-ous (in Melville's words) "plurality of other mortals with whom we are inextricably connected," body and soul, like Siamese twins, on this wild, strange trip out of the darkness, through the light, into the great unknown.

With the storm moved on and darkness moving in, I stand and stumble out through the dripping twilight woods and back to the open meadow, where it all began. Between the evening gloom and the lingering fog, all landmarks are erased from this unfa-miliar place, shifting my mood from philosophic to paranoid: Where the hell *am* I? And which way back to the truck?

From somewhere out in the soggy void, and not too far away, rises an eerie fluted wail. My displaced wapiti host, no doubt, enjoying the last horse laugh. The bull elk's bugle, I reflect, is a language imbued with more mystery, magic, passion, and down-to-Earth wisdom than we soulful humans will ever comprehend.

That beast out there is already home, while I have yet to find my way.

· 48 ·

While Caroline was walking up Bigbutt Trail one recent morning, accompanied by Otis and his temporary pal Willy the Bad Dog, whom we were reluctantly puppy-sitting for a friend in need, a bobcat trotted insouciantly across in front of them and into the recently leafless snowberry brush on the other side—where the kitty sat down and turned to face the startled trio.

"It was almost as if it *wanted* us to know it was there," Caroline would tell me later.

Otis came immediately to heel, as he is trained to do without command when surprised by wildlife on walks, but Willy started creeping toward the cat as if stalking it. The bob's reaction was to back a couple of feet deeper into the brush, then sit again and wait. Since the cat was bigger than the dog and acting so bold, Caroline suspected that it might be luring Willy into an ambush, so she and Otis moved toward the two of them. At that turn of events the wildcat bounded away and Willy the Bad Dog, being good for once, calmly watched it go, perhaps somewhat relieved.

Just another walk in the woods, an antidote to mortal angst.

This very morning, the girl and her handsome black bodyguard were outbound on a typical up-mountain stroll, still climbing, when a somewhat early and very sudden ground blizzard—a heavy snowfall driven horizontally by a blasting wind—came screaming in from the west and was upon them in an instant, a meteorological ambush. These arctic events generally are restricted in area and predictably blow out as quickly as they blow in, but they are ferocious and dangerous while they last. Even here in the sturdy comfort of the Outhouse, this morning's squall was impressive. The visibility outside was slammed to zero; we went from daylight to twilight in mere moments. The wind roared so viciously that I worried that the fork-topped old-growth ponderosa leaning from the hillside over this little wooden box might snap like a wishbone and drop several hundred pounds of death right smack on my head.

They're not called widow-makers for nothing.

But mostly I worried about my family.

And there was naught to be done till the squall had passed.

In such a maelstrom of snow and wind, bootprints refill instantly, leaving no trail to follow. The loudest shout is absorbed by the din and reduced to a silent scream. And C, spontaneous and independent, never volunteers where she's headed or by what route, even if she herself happens to know before she goes. When I ask, her standard reply is "Oh, up the mountain, some-where." That's a damn big somewhere, and so it was this fierce November morn that she and Otis were on their own to find what windbreak they could and tough out the storm. Predictably, instinctively, she would shelter on the leeward side of some big tree, hunkering there as low as possible with Otis hugged close until they could see to walk again. Or, should this not be a squall after all but a true, if early, winter blizzard, I would find their frozen corpses emerging from the snow come spring, like a pair of avalanched chickadees.

Happily, it didn't come to that.

"From the moment the squall caught us," Caroline told me when she returned—still bundled in her winter walking garb and zapped on adrenaline, trembling from the cold and fright, talk-ing fast while hugging the woodstove—"I was snow-blind, could barely see Otis just a few steps ahead of me. I yelled for him to take us home, but he was blinded too. The wind was blowing so hard it moaned, like a foghorn or one of those throaty train-whistle teakettles. The snowflakes were huge and dry and stung like sleet on my face. I ducked behind the nearest Doug fir and Otis had just tucked in beside me when I saw a gray-orange leaf come whipping down at an angle just inches from my face and go skittering across the snow from right to left, then flutter briefly back into the air, only to get knocked back down again and disappear. By the time I realized it wasn't a leaf at all but a bird—a junco, I think—it was gone, buried alive. I felt around in the snow until my hands went numb but just couldn't find it. It was heartbreaking that there was nothing I could do."

Heartbreaking, of course. All death and suffering is. Yet in the terrible beauty of nature, at least there is a plan.

· **49** ·

Death, nature, and us—that ancient troubling trio, the essential conundrum of sentient life.

Right now I'm troubled about death, nature, and *myself* because rabbit season is here, and while I suppose I'll go out some snowy morning soon, my heart just isn't in it. That's what I find troubling, and the heart of the trouble is named Yard Bunny; in the process of taming herself, Yard Bunny has apparently tamed me as well. She—we're assuming the feminine gender because of her calm and trusting nature, her modest size, and her inherent "sweetness"—showed up early last spring, just as the dandelions were blooming. And right from the start she ignored us. Not really ignored; in fact, she would sit and stare for minutes on end, seemingly fascinated with our sudden comings and goings. Apparently, she was unafraid. That's why, at first, I called her Dumb Bunny, referring to her reckless abandonment of the wild and flighty instincts by which rabbits struggle to stay alive in a realm where everything wants to eat them, including Caroline and me. But that name struck C as unfairly demeaning, so we switched to Yard Bunny. While we've had dozens of rabbits and hares come and go here over the years, Yard Bunny was unique in her domesticity . . . and doomed, I fear, because of it.

But then, all wild bunnies, rabbits and hares alike, are "doomed" to a brief existence and what in human terms would be a terrifying one. Happily for them, however, they are not human, so they don't let it get them down.

Rabbit. Hare.

What's the difference, and who really cares?

Few folks know *or* care, judging from the widespread confusion in common and regional usage of the two terms. In point of biological fact, the jack "rabbit" is a hare, while the Belgian "hare" is a rabbit and the snowshoe "rabbit" is a (varying) hare. Historically, the most famous misnomer of all applies to the infamous Easter Bunny, who actually began his mythical career as a European hare of Celtic vintage, in a time and place where there were no cottontails.

Nomenclature aside, both rabbits and hares belong to the order Lagomorpha (literally, "hare-shaped"). While lagomorphs likely first appeared in Asia (along with elk and grizzly bears), they've been resident in North America for the past fifty million years or so. The order Lagomorpha includes two families: the alpine-dwelling Ochotonidae, whose members are better known as pikas or conies; and the Leporidae, rabbits and hares. All lagomorphs have cleft upper lips (giving rise to the unfortunate expression *harelip*) and long, rodentlike incisors that grow constantly to compensate for wear. But contrary to popular misconception, lagomorphs aren't rodents.

Most hares are larger than most rabbits and have bigger ears in proportion to their bodies. Additionally, most hares have black-tipped ears, while most rabbits do not. Rabbit kittens (though seldom used, that's the proper term) are born helpless in nursery nests, often shallow ground dens constructed especially for the occasion by the expectant doe. Hare kits, meanwhile, are birthed in the open, wherever the parturient doe happens to be at the time, and enter the world with vision, a warm coat of fur, and, within a few minutes of birth, the ability to run like . . . rabbits. In a final distinction of some importance to some of us, rabbits are generally more tender and tasty than hares, though hares make dandy table fare; and both forms of this "other white meat" are essentially fatless. (It's actually possible to die of fat deprivation with your belly full of bunny.)

The familiar American cottontail, genus *Sylvilagus*, numbers an incredible fourteen species, including eastern, western, New England, mountain, marsh, and desert varieties. As its regional names suggest, the cottontail is common all across the Americas, ranging from East Coast to West, and from southern Canada as far south as Argentina and Paraguay. Most widespread and plentiful of the fourteen species is the eastern variety, present in all the contiguous states and beyond.

When you consider that virtually every North American predator—from the tiny least weasel to the great grizzly bear, plus most winged hunters and millions of earthy humans—considers the cottontail to be one of the most delectable items on nature's menu, the abundance and tenacious prosperity of the little mammal is downright amazing. While rabbits are adept at running (up to twenty miles per hour), dodging, and hiding from those who would invite them to dinner, the real secret of the cottontail's long-term success is its *own* voracious appetite—for sex. Not only has evolution blessed cottontails with a libido rivaling that of humans but bunnies attain sexual maturity remarkably early; in some species, does can be ready to breed just eighty days after birth. Meanwhile, a gestation period of less than a month allows for the production of from two to six litters during the annual half-year breeding season (roughly February through August in the Northern Hemisphere, peaking in May).

The cottontail's litter size is generous, with three to six kittens common and up to eight not unusual. Moreover, cottontail does can become reimpregnated immediately after giving birth, and some species, in a remarkable survival adaptation called super-fetation, can begin a new litter even before off-loading the old, achieving overlapping pregnancies.

In sum, a single cottontail doe has the potential to produce as many as fifty young per year—more than even Otis could eat.

To further ensure the genus's survival, cottontails can live up to ten years. But few animals die of old age in the wild, and pre-dation (including hunting), disease, and harsh weather combine to reduce the average life span to just fifteen months. Amid all this bunny destruction, in healthy cottontail populations, hunt-ing is believed to have minimal impact—which is to say, a high percentage of bunnies are doomed to die each year, one way or another. As in all wild species, by far the heaviest mortality in rabbits is among the young, with only about 10 percent reaching maturity.

And little wonder death is so common for young bunnies. They begin life weighing only an ounce or two and sounding (*squeak-squeak*) like mice—the perfect predator call. But after just a week of being suckled on their mother's nutritious milk, cottontail infants are well furred, bright-eyed, and actively squirming about in the nest. Another week and they'll have tripled their birth weight and be ready to venture out on short treks. Within a month of birth, young bunnies are weaned and on their own to have sex and other fun while they can.

Adult cottontails are eating machines, devouring a salad bar of wild greens, plus nuts, berries, seeds, and Caroline's garden goodies. They will even eat insects. And to get the most from all of it, they eat everything twice. In a phenomenon known as refection, most of what is swallowed by lagomorphs is recycled—defecated as soft pellets, swallowed again, and run through the digestive system a second time; it's rather like a backward form of chewing cud. This unusual survival strategy is particularly important in winter, since cottontails neither hibernate nor hoard food for the hard months and so must make the most of what they can find.

Growing up where abandoned farms and cottontails were plentiful and the culture roundly endorsed hunting and eating them, both practices got early into my blood. As a teen, I'd hunt cottontails with and without hounds (beagles are born to the bunny chase), alone and with friends. Occasionally, several school chums and their dads (though never my own) would congregate on a frosty Saturday morning along some particularly bunny-rich, briar-tangled cottonwood river bottom, where we'd spread out in a line and walk slowly forward. With inbred beagles to help flush the hiders and a platoon of practiced shotgunners, it wasn't unusual for us to bag two dozen rabbits in a morning's hunt and still leave plenty more "for seed." The following afternoon we'd all gather at Kenny Fultz's house—mothers, wives, and sisters included—for a redneck rabbit fry.

Yum!

Thus is cottontail hunting and feasting embedded deep in my personal history. Here in Colorado, we have plenty of cottontails, though not so plentiful as in Oklahoma back in the 1950s and '60s. With elk as our mainstay here—our substitute for beef—I hunt bunnies only to provide a bit of carnivorous culinary variety and for an excuse to get out and go wild in winter. Rarely do I kill more than one or two per hunt or half a dozen per winter. And I never hunt them near home. Rather, I drive alone or with friends to a nearby mesa that's dominated by sage, piñon pines, junipers, sprinklings of oak brush, and widely scattered ponderosa pines. Generally, a long morning of walking and kicking at brush piles yields only a rabbit or two. And those dry-land bunnies, enjoying as they do less hiding cover and more predation, tend to jump and run before you even see them. But I usually manage to kill one or two. Afterward, emulating my childhood heritage, we enjoy our own, if notably smaller, community rabbit fries, often at Erica's house. While E is a deep-fry chef, C has a way of her own.

Caroline's Chicken-fried Poor Helpless Bunny

Cut one or more cottontails (younger bunnies are best) into logical pieces (four legs and the back saddle), leaving the bones in place. Soak the pieces for an hour in cold salted water, then rinse and blot dry.

Dust pieces in flour, seasoned with salt and pepper.

Dip dusted pieces in a whipped blend of one cup milk and one whole egg. (Egg white will suffice if it must.)

Roll pieces once again in flour.

Fry in a medium-hot skillet uncovered, using just enough olive oil—two tablespoons or so—to generously coat the bottom. When the pieces are golden brown on their bottom sides, gently (so as not to crumble the batter) turn and brown the other side. (Erica's less healthy but equally tasty alternative is to deep-fry in two inches of your favorite "grease," avoiding partially hydrogenated oils, which, of course, are poison.)

After removing the golden pieces from the pan, use the remaining oil, with its crunchy "fryings," to make country gravy. Serve with mashed potatoes, biscuits, or corn bread and your favorite green vegetables.

Hot damn and pass the bunny!

· 50 ·

While critics grimace and bristle at the "blood lust, violence, macho domination, and senseless cruelty" involved in hunting and killing one's own meat, how many of them, I wonder, have witnessed, smelled, heard the screams, or even considered the nightmarish horrors of the cage-raised pig and poultry factories?

There's little we can do to influence the sources of the restaurant meat we eat—although I make a point to complain to the management whenever I see venison or elk on the menu, knowing what I do about the cruelty and dangers of oxymoronic "game farming." Caroline and I eat in restaurants rarely and at home buy what little meat we purchase, and all of our eggs as well, from a local market that vends only organic, free-range animal products, including cheese, milk, and eggs.

But mostly, when it comes to meat, we eat elk, with the occasional addition of pronghorn, wild turkey, blue grouse, and rabbit. Since mule deer are currently suffering a population decline throughout the West due to the rampant subdivision of former agricultural land, I no longer hunt them. Elk tastes better, and a single wapiti life feeds us for a year, whereas two deer would be required for the same time period. Although we're rich in lakes and streams jumping with rainbow, brown, and cutthroat trout, we rarely eat fish these days, having subsisted on little more than trout (plus elk and a local rancher's eggs) through our first few lean years here. (The "roadkill, catch-and-cook period," I call it.) Consequently, we burned out on trout and I have never regained a taste for it. And because I don't care to "play with my food" via catch-and-release techniques, I've largely, for now, given up fishing. Not so with rabbit, which graces our meals only seasonally and so infrequently as to always be a treat.

But this year, thanks to Yard Bunny, I feel differently. And that troubles me a lot. I mean, have you ever had a wild rabbit—a creature you have not fed or otherwise encouraged to hang around but that seems determined to tame itself, for no apparent personal gain—follow you around and around the yard, sit patiently and watch from ten feet away as you split firewood, sit down right behind you in the dark while you're enjoying a blazing campfire, and, weirdest of all, yawn in your face? One afternoon last May, I was contemplating Yard Bunny through 6x binoculars from inside the Doghouse, door open, the bunny some twenty feet away. With such a view you can see ticks and tiny red mites crawling around the hairless insides of a rabbit's ears, which explains the head-shaking and scratching they constantly engage in. After I'd been watching her for a while, suddenly Yard Bunny turned and studied me, then stretched her front legs forward, humped her shoulders, and gave a huge yawn, so that I was looking right down her little pink throat.

And here's another bit of lagomorph individuality that Yard Bunny shared with us: she always bit off vegetation near the base, then raised her head and ate it bottoms up. With grass and clover this is merely curious; with flowering dandelions I always wished I had a camera ready (and why the heck didn't I?) to snap a portrait at just the point where the big yellow flower was all that was left showing, projecting from the little pink mouth as if it were sprouting from her nose.

Caroline suggests that this stem-first eating habit is due to the fact that the basal portions of plants are the moistest, sweetest, and most nutritious. Perhaps. But from my Darwinian perspective I am led to view the cottontail's "dip, bite, raise head, and nibble" feeding pattern as an effective and necessary survival instinct. If a rabbit were to graze plants from the top down, as do larger herbivores, it would necessitate the head staying down for prolonged periods. By ducking the head, nipping off a stem near the bottom, then raising the head up while masticating the mouth-ful, a rabbit minimizes the time it spends effectively blinded, while maximizing the time it spends with its head up, watching for approaching danger.

Elk and other wild ungulates have evolved a variation on this theme by grazing fast for relatively short periods of time. Typi-cally they feed at first and last light, not really chewing but just nipping and gulping. Then, with their rumens full, they retreat to the comfort of some shady hide to regurgitate and masticate the cud in relative safety from predation.

All of which is to say that I learned a lot about rabbits in general from Yard Bunny in particular. And part of what I learned is that with familiarity comes emotional attachment. Thus are rural residents, especially newcomers, wont to adopt, domesticate, and "protect" wild animals, having come to view rabbits, to continue the example, as wee little folk in cute bunny suits. Thinking along this line, I'm reminded of a cover story on the hunting-versus-antihunting controversy that ran in *Time* maga-zine a few years ago. Speaking for the anti side was Heidi Prescott, then (and still) national director of the strident animal-rights group the Fund for Animals. Beneath a photo of Prescott scratch-ing the chin of a scraggly-looking white-tailed doe, the caption challenged, "Shoot this?" Well no, of course not; hunters don't hunt in petting zoos. But out in the woods, out in the wilds, it's a whole different world, the *real* world—and a whole different ani-mal. Which brings us back to my Yard Bunny fix.

As a naturalist and an outspoken animal welfarist—embracing a view distinct from and infinitely more pragmatic than an ani-mal rightist's—nothing makes my skin crawl like seeing some self-proclaimed "nonconsumptive" vegan animal-rights zealot feeding or petting some poor helpless would-be wild creature that has fallen victim to human "protection." Only through hundreds and thousands of generations of being constantly hounded and hunted by hungry predators did the deer, elk, rabbit, and wild turkey evolve the gracefully athletic forms, high-tech senses, and high-strung natures that make them the magnificent self-defense organisms we know and love today. And only through continued predatory pressure will they remain as they are meant to be: truly wild.

To tame a wild creature is to murder its soul.

You've likely seen human-habituated deer and maybe even bears eating vanilla wafers from the soft hands of clueless tourists in park settings; or magnificent wapiti lying around in pastures near roaring highways and tract homes in winter (because those homes and highways have displaced the elk's essential low-lying winter habitat, forcing them to compromise or starve); or turkeys that readily relinquish their hair-trigger aloofness to hang out near people in exchange for cracked corn; or geese, deer, and elk that have become addicted to the nitrogen-fertilized grass of lawns and golf courses. I find it all revolting. From an evolutionary perspective—that is, from the long-term survival and prosperity point of view—a thousand petting-zoo Bambis have less genetic value than one truly wild deer, which, being truly wild, if cornered and forced to a choice, would rather kick your face in and run for its life, win or lose, than accept humiliating alms from condescending human hands.

"Shoot this?" On second thought, maybe I would. Just to get the pitiful specimen out of a proud species' gene pool.

Thus do I feel guilty for not chasing Yard Bunny away, thereby helping to keep her wild, free, and possibly alive, and guiltier yet for allowing her to become a pet, in heart if not in hand, threatening my desire to hunt.

In any event, suddenly and sadly, Yard Bunny is no more. No more around here, at least. Simply disappeared. And whether she's dead or alive, it's for the better. Dogs belong in the yard. Wildlife belongs in the woods. For natural wildness to survive and prosper, there can be no other way.

And so it is, all things quite honestly considered: the next time it snows, I'm going rabbit hunting.

· 51 ·

December 21: Caroline's birthday, the winter solstice, and the day old Angel died. Of course, barring fatal accidents, companion animals these days rarely are left to suffer and die on their own. Angel was helped on her way by Paul Rumsey, her personal physician, who came all the slick way up here to the Doghouse on the shortest day of the year to spare Angel, and us, an unpleasant trip to town. After we phoned Paul I went outside and dug an Angel-sized hole near Lacey (Angel's predecessor in the old-dog corner) in the dog graveyard, beneath aspens that now stand naked but spring through fall provide shade and the restful music of fresh winds in their leaves. I will be lucky to enjoy such a restful resting place.

The deed was done as Angel lay calmly beside her open grave. With simple ceremony we buried an old friend, wrapped in her favorite blanket.

Not a dry eye to be found.

And why, I'm left to wonder with aging anger, aren't you and I allowed to die, when *we* are ready, with the same pain-free and economical dignity we grant to our pets?

The ugliest word in the English language is *censorship*.

In a sane and just world, Dr. Kevorkian would have been given a Nobel Prize and sainthood. In our contemporary, death-fearing Christian censorial culture, he was hauled away to prison.

Where there is moral censorship, democracy and freedom have failed. Except, of course, among outlaws, a predictable product of repression.

When *my* time comes, mark my words, I'll die as I damn well please.

This morning a friend phoned to invite me out hunting. I eagerly accepted Jamin's last-minute offer to join him on a midday stroll around the piñon-juniper and sagebrush farmstead where he grew up, so strong and so well, in the long evening shadow of a mountain called Sleeping Ute. Jamin and I had been hunting and fishing buddies since he was fifteen. Now he was grown and off to college, already well along in his own search for a natural, meaningful, self-directed life in this increasingly unnatural, meaningless, corporate-choreographed world.

In a couple of hours of walking and shooting, accompanied by a bitterly cold wind, bright sunshine, and a mated pair of bald eagles circling, grappling, and keening passionately above us, Jamin and I together bagged two cottontails and ten Gambel's quail. A very good hunt.

Quail are the rarest of gifts hereabouts. Back in Oklahoma when I was a kid, bobwhite quail were abundant. I grew up hunting them and cottontails under the guidance of my second cousin Harlis and the fathers of various friends. While my father never hunted and rarely fished, he encouraged both activities in me, facilitating an incremental rite of passage from childhood to self-reliance and nature love that too few young men experience today. So the quail came not only as a regional rarity but as feathered nostalgia as well.

Although quail are plentiful farther south, in New Mexico and Arizona, mountainous southwestern Colorado isn't good quail habitat, so we get only a transient few. In fact, these were the first quail I've ever killed here, and they may well be the last. Apropos, and as a day-late birthday gift for Caroline, for this evening I have planned, and shall myself prepare, a festive dinner, to wit:

Solstice Quail à la Caroline (For Two)

Kill, thank, clean, and pluck five fat wild quail.

Separate legs from breasts.

Soak for an hour in cool salted water.

Blot dry.

Baste with melted butter.

Grill on a low flame and not too long, being careful to keep the naturally light meat from drying and turning gray.

Serve with rice, a green vegetable (it's hard to beat fresh asparagus, if you can afford it), a half loaf of freshly baked bread, a chilled salad tossed with chilled ranch dressing and topped with croutons and salted sunflower seeds, and (the critical ingredient) a liter of Sauvignon Blanc.

"Heaven," says my birthday girl, "is a wild man in my kitchen."

· 52 ·

"Christmas Eve," uttered with a sigh.

Earlier this morning I stepped outside the cozy cabin and into a five-below winter world. With a camp saw in one leather-gloved hand I walked out through a fresh skiff of snow a short ways up the hill that rises to the north. There I cut a young white fir that Caroline selected yesterday. This bushy conifer, with limbs that sweep to the ground, is a problematic species hereabouts. Normally a minority, it has increased its numbers in recent decades until now it threatens to take over and diminish the diverse personality, beauty, and ecological fecundity of this aspen-defined ecology.

Under natural (that is, historical) conditions, the white fir population was kept in check and the forest ecology kept in balance by frequent small fires, most set by lightning but some by clever natives who had observed that a great many species of wild animals and birds are attracted by postfire regrowth. Since its low-slung needles are rich in turpentine, fir burns much more readily than tough-barked, high-crowned ponderosa pine or aspen, with which it tends to associate. But since the coming of Europen settlers and our obsessions with fire suppression and selective high-grade logging, the invaders have proliferated. (White fir is essentially worthless as lumber and makes piss-poor firewood as well, so is generally left standing; meanwhile, mature Douglas fir and ponderosa pine are selectively cut and hauled away.)

It's an old story. Much the same thing happens when rangeland is overgrazed by cattle: after years of selective cropping, all that's left to sprout and grow each spring—all that's left for wildlife and livestock alike—are the ugly culls. ("A thing is right when it tends to preserve the integrity, stability, and beauty of the biotic community. It is wrong when it tends otherwise." Who said that? And why do our public-land management agencies continue steadfastly to ignore or try to bullshit their way around this immutable land ethic? We all know why, and so do they. Yet nothing ever changes for the better.)

As mentioned earlier, fir seedlings need aspens to shade them through their sun-sensitive infancy. By way of thanks, those saplings eventually mature to shade out, crowd out, and insidiously replace their mentoring aspen groves, replacing at the same time an ecologically rich and diverse aspen understory comprising hundreds of species of nutritious grasses, sedges, forbs, and brush—prime wildlife food and habitat—with a carpet of oily needles that stifle understory growth and love to catch fire.

So it is that my killing of a sacrificial fir to bring indoors for Christmas is, in this instance, an ecological plus. It's also a lot more fun and satisfying than buying a plantation tree from a commercial lot, as is most everything we take the time to do for ourselves. Caroline and I greatly enjoy embodying the American holiday greeting-card tradition by walking into the woods, selecting a seven-foot fir, sawing it down by hand, and dragging it through the snow back to the shack, then trimming with Caroline's homemade ornaments.

From Christmas to New Year's every winter here, a local living tree (it takes conifers weeks to know they are dead) brightens our little cabin and lends it the clean, fresh smell of warm grapefruit. Beneath the tree lie few if any presents, which is our chosen way as well as a quiet statement against our market culture's commandment to "buy and spend on schedule, according to designated commercial holidays." Caroline and I long ago agreed not to exchange gifts on "mandatory" gifting occasions—Christmas, birthdays, even our wedding anniversary—beyond perhaps a special dinner at home or, very rarely, in town. For us, the tree itself and the warming ritual of simplicity and good work it represents—and, most important, the fact that I can step out the door to cut one, no permission, permits, or money required—are gifts plenty enough.

In the passage between daylight and dark, Otis and I take a walk.

· 53 ·

More so even than New Year's, the prolonged Christmas hoopla and hype tend to provoke a pensive, blue-toned mood, at least among those of us who tend toward pensive blue-toned moodiness. With each such chronological marker we are reminded of people and places—and, in the fullness of time, our own youthful years—all irrevocably gone. Consequently, the brightest spots in the holiday season for C and me are the dinner parties hosted by George and Nancy at their sagging, century-old cabin on the banks of the loveliest stretch of our loveliest local river, a mile or so upstream from here. For all involved, these are more than dinner parties. They are antidotes to cabin fever and lifestyle choices confirmed.

We are reluctant socialites, Caroline and I, and these midwinter orgies of good food, abundant drink, spirited conversation, and healing laughter are generally the only real parties we attend all year. We not only love and feel absolutely at home with George and Nancy—they are family, the hub of our social clan here—but we also know everyone in attendance, and thus there are no unpleasant surprises. Predictably, it's a colorfully motley crew of career bachelors, every one a character. In the old days, half a dozen or more showed up; these days, only two or three, as the others have moved away, drifted away, gotten married, or otherwise left the local fold. Rarely, one or another graying bachelor will bring a new girlfriend (with never, so far, a repeat). And it's just as well, since our conversation, increasingly lubricated as the evening progresses, grows shockingly raw and uncensored.

It's Nancy's thing, these bachelor holiday parties—one of her things at least, in addition to painting and leatherworking and dog mothering and George mothering and cross-country skiing. Without Nancy's massive feasts, prepared for eccentric social outcasts on family holiday occasions, all of us would be alone and blue. Other than the hosts, Caroline and I are the only regular couple. The newest and youngest member of the clan is bachelorette Erica—my hunting buddy, George's fly-fishing pal, Nancy and Caroline's mutual friend, and the life of any party.

So that's the plan for tonight and sweetly anticipated. For that brief while we will forget all woes, real and imagined, and come together to celebrate and confirm life in the *here* and *now*.

· 54 ·

By following my own sage advice to "be here *now*" (absorbed thirty years or so ago from Baba Ram Dass's best-selling spiritual self-helper by the same name, which is about as much of it as I could understand), I truly enjoy life most of the time. I am a happy camper, most of the time. And like the Talking Heads' desperado "Psycho Killer," I hate people when they're not polite. But, yet, still—Caroline is likely right when she accuses me at times of "thinking too much." What she means, and I agree, is that thoughtfulness, in this warped and thoughtless world, too often leads to disappointment, discontent, anger, rage, and even psychosis. And all such problems are most pronounced in those of us who take life, perhaps, a bit too seriously. I mean—you don't see the village idiot lamenting the fate of his immortal soul. And the holidays are an acutely thoughtful time.

Right now, as Otis and I shuffle and snuffle up the mountain, my thoughts run back to our sweet dead Angel, still warm in her cold dark grave.

And from there I think of Caroline's cancer, some five years clean now and gone forever, we boldly dare to hope.

Given my low and unreliable income and our resultant inability to afford (and refusal to pay the immorally inflated price of) medical insurance, one of the more questionable methods Caroline had adopted for saving money was to avoid seeing doctors.

So when I noticed one day that a mole on her back—near the spine between the shoulder blades—which had been removed two years previously, had sprouted anew and had a dark, nasty look about it, she made little of it. But the mole kept growing bigger and uglier. I finally nagged her into getting it looked at. When she finally did, the news hit us like a shotgun blast, filling our world with holes. Though I'd loved and lived with this lady for twenty grateful years, only then did I fully realize how utterly I'd invested all of my emotional eggs in one basket, and that basket's name was Caroline.

Caroline had malignant melanoma, among the dead-last cancers you ever want to get and the last disease you may ever have, given how fast it can kill. Like a terrorist in disguise, it bores vertically into and through your skin, eventually reaching the fascia, that cellophane-like membrane that sheathes the muscles. Once there, the horror spreads laterally to invade the lymph system, which, in turn, transports the killer to lungs and liver. And all of this, just like prostate and breast cancer, proceeds with no obvious early warning signs. Seeing the lab reports—which, according to C's dermatologist, were "off the scale"—doctor after doctor braced us for the worst: no doubt already metastasized beyond the point of repair; maybe only months to live.

Months, that is, of oncologists, dermatologists, bloody laboratory tests, surgery, chemo, and, in spite of it all, oblivion.

And where would I find the money?

Suddenly, violently, and for the first time ever, my prideful life of elective semipoverty and arrogant independence struck me as stupid and selfish. Choosing to elect doom rather than debt for myself if diagnosed with a terminal disease was one thing, but what right did I have to condemn my wife to an early grave because I couldn't afford possibly life saving medical help? I was angry at America as well as at myself, the richest country in the history of the universe yet the only advanced industrial nation on

Earth with no health-care safety net for its citizens. And why the hell not? Three clear reasons: greed, greed, and greed. I'd never felt less patriotic.

Caroline's first oncologist, a local physician, was an odd but likable fellow whose appearance, dress, and demeanor reminded us of the actor Robin Williams—or even more so, with his big baggy trousers and remnants of lunch dried on his lips, Charlie Chaplin's little tramp. After opening our visit with an overly honest confession—"I have to tell you that melanoma can lead to rapid death"—Dr. Charlie went on to offer guarded hope. Having seen the same lab results the dermatologist had interpreted so negatively, now amplified by detailed blood work and chest X-rays, he suggested that Caroline's cancer "miraculously, may not have metastasized to the lymph system yet." Should that be the happy case, immediate surgery might just save the day. And if it worked, if they "got it all," Dr. Charlie ventured that Caroline would have "an eighty percent chance of survival over the next ten years."

Great!

Yet . . . what did that mean, exactly? Ten years maximum to live? Ten years and we'd be home free? I probed, Charlie dodged.

In any event and for the nonce we were both in the clouds—after all, it could have been yet another fatal opinion, yet another nail in her premature coffin.

After asking around to determine the best melanoma surgeon in the region, we made an appointment with a plastic surgeon who specialized in removing killer skin cancers, right here in Durango. Surgery was scheduled for the following week. Likely, said Dr. Ritz, he would need to remove a patch of skin from Caroline's thigh to plug the huge hole in her back the excavation would leave. While cosmetics was the least of our worries just then, we both expressed a preference for scarring on her back over scarring on a thigh and the much higher cost of a graft. He said he'd do the best he could.

And that he surely did, carving out a circle of flesh the diameter of a DVD—essentially, shoulder blade to shoulder blade—and all the way down to the fascia. It was "a challenge," he later confessed, but he'd been able to pull things together without the skin graft, leaving C with a long vertical scar down her spine.

Even more of a challenge was C's requirement to go six weeks without raising her arms above her waist.

Best of all—all that really matters—subsequent laboratory tests showed that the surgery had "gotten it all." Not only did Ron Ritz save my wife's life, he did so without putting us in the poorhouse.

The above report is a time compression of several weeks spent waiting for test results and worrying like I'd never worried before. Intensifying the problem, under such dire stress I found it almost impossible to work. But work I must, harder and faster and better and more profitably than ever before. Alternative possibilities: Borrow from friends. Borrow commercially. Rob a bank.

The first two I found morally abhorrent.

There was, at least, one happy leaf in this tree full of sorrow and angst. A wonderful tenderness blessed our days and nights. Under the weight of possible permanent separation—the end, in effect, of both of our lives—we found ourselves touching constantly, kissing more frequently and more passionately, and neither could stand to be away from the other for more than a few empty minutes. Although we'd lived together virtually around the clock since 1978, every moment now became incalculably precious.

I recall thinking that sooner or later I'd cry myself dry—big, tough ex-Marine mountain man, me—but there seemed no bottom to my tearful well, brimful with sorrow and worry.

For her part, Caroline was externally stoic. No apparent disbelief, anger, or panic. No "Why me?" self-pity. So far as I could see, she was essentially unaffected. But of course, I could not see. Later, she would admit that at first, while still under the initial death sentence, "I was in a daze and couldn't concentrate. It's like having an alien inside you; it's *always there,* no matter how hard you try to push it aside. You can't read or even watch a movie without it intruding. No concentration whatsoever. While you worked through *your* worries about me by sharing them with everyone, I really didn't want to talk about it with anyone. In that way I was lucky, since very few people know anything about melanoma. 'Skin cancer?' they think, dismissing it as minor. Which was fine by me. If they don't know about it, I don't have to talk about it. And I craved to be alone. That was when I doubled and tripled my walking to several hours a day, which helped right from the start. And for a while, you know, I took up painting and singing, activities that require full concentration and helped to relax. And always there was you."

"What do you mean?" I asked.

"I thought constantly about how much I loved and would miss you and family and friends. I thought about how lucky I was to have had you all, and how I needed to work harder to let you know how I felt, while I still could. And I worried about practical things like who would take care of you when I was gone. Who could you find to love you as much as I do?"

Good questions.

Today, halfway through those ten years and counting, Caroline is holding her own, and then some. Ask her how she's doing and she'll come right back with "Great!" And thanks to her marathon walking, she's stronger, lovelier, and more self-confident than ever. Yet once you're caught in cancer's web your life is forever changed. And there always are reminders. Until recently we made annual visits to an oncologist in New Mexico. We continue with the regimen of annual chest X-rays and wide-spectrum blood tests, plus regular at-home skin inspections and frequent trips to the dermatologist, where even modestly suspicious moles are removed and sent to a lab in New York for the best melanoma biopsies anyone's money can buy. Some are benign. More are not, leading us both to silently moan, *Here we go again.* And so on, round and round and up and down, until the end of time.

· 55 ·

Caroline's return to good health, this happy state, ironically opens emotional space for me to fret over another worrisome concern when I get to thinking too much. I'm thinking too much now of the crushing reality that this place in which we've invested our past and planned our future is being so rapidly and horribly disfigured. While we could never desert Spring Mountain, the mountain is deserting us—or, more precisely, it is being torn away from us, excoriated and dismembered by external forces euphemized as progress, prosperity, and private property rights.

Manifest destiny at terminal velocity, approaching our terminal days.

The population of Durango and the surrounding areas doubled during the 1990s. Although mobs of moral nonentities—land speculators, land developers, and real estate whores—have driven house and land prices beyond the reach of most middle-class families and gas wells pock the landscape like pimples on a pubescent face, La Plata County, Colorado, continues to bloat and swell like the festering cash cow it has chosen to become, forecasting yet another redoubling of people in the current decade. And everywhere human numbers rise, wild and human natures suffer. A single example among too many:

Up on College Hill, across from the oldest of our several local golf courses, lies a lovely linear meadow. Or used to. Until recently, this scenic grassy expanse provided a summer playground for children, hikers, bikers, and dogs, and essential winter habitat for elk. What a thrill, what a blessing it was to drive by there and see those stoic creatures, sometimes a hundred or more, grazing peacefully where a tongue of wildness penetrated the city limits. Now that refuge is no more, the tongue macerated, the wildness driven out. What was the meadow is now fronted by a gouged-out goose pond, a gas station and convenience store, and, behind those insults, row-house condos so dense, uniform, and numerous as to be beyond counting. Those condos house, in turn, thousands of heavily mortgaged humans, most of them freshly escaped from urban or suburban bastions of growth and progress gone insane. Fine and friendly folk, most of them, but that is not the point. The point is that by bringing their old values with them here, they are importing and promoting the selfsame congestive heart failure they had hoped to escape.

But there is no escaping ourselves.

Where will the elk find a replacement for this essential piece of winter habitat, and all the others so recently consumed by progress? Where will we humans find a replacement for the wapiti's blessing of natural wildness among us? What effect does such as this have, insidiously and collectively, on the human spirit? On our children and theirs?

Thanks also to growth and progress, traffic in Durango has become obnoxious year-round and a downright dangerous, lung-polluting, ear-splitting hell in summer; it's a microcosm of metro madness everywhere. Parking is increasingly hard to find, meter prices are high, and every meter seems to have its own maid.

Worse yet, worst of all, the very personality of the place, the town and surrounding rural areas, has been twisted and transmogrified by ill-planned growth. What once was a middle-class paradise of small-town friendliness and wraparound nature has been reduced to just another rich person's playground of choppity-chop subdivisions and fenced-in ranchettes littered with a nauseating profundity of tacky trailer houses at one extreme, ostentatious and obscenely wasteful trophy homes at the other. The latter frequently sport a couple of rarely ridden hobby horses housed in tiny, trampled piss-mud pastures. The vehicles of choice are noisy, poisonous, oversized macho diesel trucks for the men ("The bigger the truck," the cowgirls say, "the smaller the penis") and equally piggish SUVs for the moms. And thanks to an annual "Iron Horse" motorcycle rally, we are doubly cursed by the fatuous fad of graying potbellied Harley "outlaws" seeking individuality through store-bought conformity. Since most are apparently deaf, they see no need for mufflers. From miles up any mountain you can hear their popcorn drone, and very little else.

"Times change," I'm smugly advised by those with a financial stake in the ongoing destruction of nature and natural lives. And by those who just don't give a damn about much of anything beyond paycheck, TV, personal comfort, and conspicuous consumption.

And so it has come to pass that we who are dubbed the "old hippie mentality" are left to nod in silence.

Closer to home, thus more painful yet, our tacky old mountain subdivision, only lightly and mostly seasonally inhabited until recent years, has become a cacophonous and increasingly dysfunctional "community" of year-round households, crammed an acre each along and above a once scenic creek valley, the creek itself now polluted by septic fields. Visually and acoustically, as it has filled with more houses, cars, and motorized toys, our valley has gone from delight to blight. In winter, when the deciduous leaves are off, we now can see the bright metal roofs of several homes across the valley, no few of them newly constructed and all of them within hearing when playful children or angry adults come outside and scream, neglected dogs bark, or filth-spewing cowboy Cadillacs go rumbling and rattling along the network of interior roads (all blessedly still dirt). More and more people, with mountain bikes, snowmobiles, and goddamned ATVs, giving not a hoot about the emotional and physical value, much less the intrinsic sacredness of peace and quiet, personal privacy, mutual respect, and natural wildness, work relentlessly to overrun the mountain that for so long belonged, de facto, to the aspens, the elk, and us.

Selfish and self-centered, aren't I?

Perhaps. Yet we are left increasingly often feeling like a couple of Hans Brinker Petersens, C and me, our fingers too few and weak to plug all the leaks in this fast-crumbling dike of a formerly heavenly place.

"When I thought about it," quipped our old friend Edward Abbey, "it hurt too much. So I quit thinking about it."

Caroline, Ed, and the village idiots all have it right, I guess: I too must quit thinking so much.

Eventually, as our walk winds down and darkness approaches, Otis and I come to a juncture of choice. Life, it occurs, is nothing but a series of junctures. We are the products of our decisions, minute by minute. In some things we have no choice. But in more ways than many will admit, we make our own ways in the world, our own heavens and hells. Through our ongoing choices we climb our own mountains and dig our own graves.

In the choice at foot right now, both paths lead homeward. One way climbs a short, steep pitch over a north-south ridge—a little lung- and leg-burner—then drops steeply down, through shadowy woods, over rock-strewn ground to home; it's a shortcut that comes at a steep price. The other way is longer, more circuitous, incorporating a stretch of subdivision road that even now, in the white grip of winter, poses the threat of encountering cars and people "walking" their dogs behind ATVs. Yet it's downhill to level and pie-easy every step of the way.

"Will you tell me please," I ask Mr. Otis, "which way we should go from here?"

· **56** ·

This *is* the question, for everyone alive or looking to come alive, across every moment of life: Which way from here?

In my case, more and more of late, I'm compelled to ask, Have I made the right choices? Is our life out here on the edge—as my father and others have often suggested, with culture cheering them on—an anachronistic romantic fantasy doomed to someday fail? Is that gloomy someday about to arrive? Are the various fights for survival and sanity that increasingly force themselves on us worth the emotional blood? Is it time at long last, as my father would say, to "give in to common sense" and rejoin the rodent race? Assuming that such is even still possible for us today, here in our middle ages.

From where I now stand, boot-deep in snow and dead broke as always, here amid my "peak earning years" with more tax deductions than income, increasingly distressed by external loss and internal aging . . . where to from here?

Even by ignoring the choices, we are making choices.

In my ongoing dialogue with the nagging question *What does it mean to be human?* I've come time and again to a troublesome triad of spin-off queries—quandaries that five thousand years of messianic religion and civilized philosophy have utterly failed to answer and often don't even ask. As summed up by Paul Gauguin (that politically incorrect, edge-dwelling lover and painter of bare-skinned Tahitian beauties):

Where do we come from?
What are we?
Where are we going?

And those three questions, in their turn, evoke in me a trio of tertiary concerns:

On what authority should we base our morality?
How should we conduct our lives, including our deaths?
How can we be truly happy?

That latter, of course, simply by its asking, implies that we as a species, or at least we as a culture, are not. Happy, that is.
What to do?
Which way to go from here?

· 57 ·

If there is a universal human desire, it is to live well. Even the gauntest psychotic ascetic, supine in ecstatic agony on a bed of rusty nails, is striving in his own deluded way to live well. Likewise, the coke-sniffing narcissist; the land-grabbing, profit-grubbing, nature-raping, soulless land developer; the slave-making global entrepreneur; the oil baron and professional politico; the terrorist and religious martyr; the holy pope in Rome; the career criminal; you; and certainly me. While not everyone wants to live eternally, we all want to make life work while we have it. No sane person wishes otherwise.

The factor that fractures universal agreement in our universal desire for personal weal is the infinity of ways we define, or allow ourselves to accept someone else's definition of, "living well." For most people living in the postagricultural world throughout recorded history, living well has been perceived as hitched tight to material wealth and the power, comfort, pleasures, respect, leisure, and escape from fear, worry, and harassment we are conditioned to believe money will buy—and which, it must be admitted, on a spiritually and intellectually shallow level, it often can.

For others, far fewer, living well is less material and more ethereal, predicated on an unblinking embrace of devout spirituality—though the concepts of devoutness and spirituality, like "living well" itself, remain prey to far-flung interpretation.

For fewer yet, perhaps fewest of all, a well-lived life means striving for personal, moral, and physical autonomy: self-direction, intellectual and spiritual independence, self-control, self-responsibility—in sum, self-realization through self-determination. As a dues-paying member of this unintentionally masochistic minority, I can testify that the price of personal freedom and soulful individuality today—the cost of living a self-determined life—is often social, material, physical, and even geographical marginalization, all of which can act themselves out in a big city as well as a small town or a rural homestead and must be construed as culture's punishment for being different. Or perhaps, as some will say, such are the just deserts of freaks and other sinners. Humankind, said Henry, through its own inventions and lust for comfort, is invariably driven to desperation. Misery loves company, and the dominant culture, jealous of those who evade desperate angst, is never happy with mavericks, those of us who, even in the most liberal social realms, are barely tolerated.

And so, if so, why even bother to swim upstream? Why not just go with the easy flow?

Good questions—to which gonzo journalist and political pundit Hunter S. Thompson supplies answer enough when he proclaims, "This is the real point: that we are not really freaks at all. . . . [Rather,] the twisted realities of the world we are trying to live in have somehow combined to make us feel like freaks. We argue, we protest, we petition—but nothing changes."

And so again, if so . . . why bother?

I'm reminded of an old Earth First! bumper sticker. In this one-frame cartoon an eagle (symbolic of what?)—talons extended, eyes flashing red as fresh-let blood, a triumphant smile on its beak—is descending for the kill toward a tiny defenseless mouse . . . defenseless, yet extending an arm and thrusting a proud middle finger in the face of its approaching death. The caption reads, "One last brave act of defiance."

And why not. Why the hell not?

"You have to quit thinking so much."

· 58 ·

Otis, lucky dog, never thinks too much (if he ever thinks at all). Never worries, though he sometimes seems to fret. At the moment, having instinctively decided the best way to go from here, he is demonstrating his choice by feigning in that direction— running ahead and circling back, urging me to follow, eager to begin the climb. Sensing that my attention has shrunken inward again, he grabs a fallen limb the size of a pool stick and comes running straight for me, wagging the bait, teasing, tempting me to try and grab it, to follow him and play. Predictably, when I reach for the carrot he whips around and runs ahead, snatching it away—then stops and waits and wags, luring me on, coaxing me out of my self-defeating self and into the challenge ahead.

"Okay, pal. I'm coming."

"Christmas Eve," I sigh again, taking a good, deep hit of cold, clean air. Putting one boot in front of the other, I launch into the homeward stretch. There's a party to attend tonight, I remind myself. Food, wine, women, and song to be enjoyed. And when it's all over I'll be bringing my favorite gal home—my own little hippie chick. I've always had a thing for hippie chicks, and I hope I always will.

Life is good, and let us not forget it.

· **59** ·

Many among my boomer generation proudly claim to be "stuck in the sixties." I too nurse a throbbing nostalgia for the patchouli-scented neo-Renaissance purple-haze decade of the late 1960s and early '70s—in large part, no doubt, because I was young then and as strong and free as a young man can be, with miles yet to travel. The music, mescaline, sex, sand, and sun added up to a personal heaven. Even so, today my greatest nostalgia and longing remains firmly rooted in the Pleistocene—that icy 1.6 million–year Pale-olithic stage upon which the sacred game of becoming human was slowly acted out. By my reckoning, *those* were the truly good old days. Everything since—since trading spears, berry baskets, and tribal egalitarianism for harness, hoe, Humvee, and hierarchical havoc—amounts to little more than a floundering attempt to regain some of what we lost when the big bad deal went down. As Pulitzer Prize–winning anthropologist Jared Diamond says of our climate- and population-forced transition from an excitingly unpredictable, satisfyingly simple, seminomadic life of foraging to

the unimaginative drudgery of sedentary agriculture and the con-
flicts and complexities of trade, it was, quite simply, "the worst mistake in the history of the human race."

And once that mistake was made, there was no turning back.
The forbidden fruit had been bitten; the Garden was clear-cut
and plowed.

"When the Pleiades and the wind in the grass are no longer a
part of the human spirit, a part of very flesh and bone," warns
Henry Beston in his Cape Cod classic, *The Outermost House*,
"man becomes, as it were, a kind of cosmic outlaw, having neither
the completeness and integrity of the animal nor the birthright
of a true humanity."

Have we come to that?

· 60 ·

Breathing hard, in-out, and feeling better again. Struggling to
keep up with my dog.

Elective exercise that leaves a body panting and too tired to
think has a wonderful way of normalizing an off-kilter mood,
herding our wandering attention back to the here and now, back
to the palpable, immediate, and *real* . . . suck another breath of
life, *anima*; exhale the poison exhaust, suck another breath . . .
and give thanks for every last one, as every one might be.

As we top the ridge, suddenly the southwestern horizon appears
spread below, capped by a sinking red sun. I stop and stare and
pant and gradually regain my breath and composure, and damned
if I don't start thinking again.

Oh well. No magic always works. And nothing works forever.

At this stage in life my bed is irrevocably made. No matter
that lately the mattress is sagging, the sheets have become a bit

wrinkled, and quills poke out through the pillows; I'll continue sleeping where I fall.

· 61 ·

Otis, still trotting out ahead, suddenly comes to a midstep stop, assuming what passes in his untrained state for a pointing-dog pose: left front paw caught off the ground and locked there by instinct, neck low, frozen in concentration, ears erect, tail straight out and rigid. At this signal I stop too. When my old pup turns his head to look at me, I point with a finger at the ground: doggy talk for "sit down and stay put." Which my buddy smartly does. I creep forward until I can see down the slope and into the shadowy timber, searching for what my dog has seen. A ways beyond those woods and a bit below our line of sight awaits our humble home, warm and welcoming as always; in my mind's eye I see Caroline's lighted Christmas tree, winking from the windows. But that can wait a little longer, since now there's mystery afoot. By shading my eyes from the sun with a hand, I see at last what Otis saw first: half a dozen elk. Three sleek cows, three fat calves. Perhaps it's the same three pair, then accompanied by a six-point bull, who delighted me last September by splashing and cavorting in Pond Spring while I squatted, breathless with awe and delight, mere yards away. Necks dark brown, almost black. Bodies dull in evening shadows. Big beige butts reflecting the softness of winter twilight.

Perfect.

Alternating his attention between the wapiti and me, Otis holds steady as I creep slowly past him, maneuvering for a closer look without disturbing the winter-stressed animals, who remain, so far, unawares. The snow is unseasonably shallow, as it is throughout the San Juans. For elk, this means that the scant winter browse, victim of the summer's heat and drought, is easy to get at; the industrious animals' heavy front hooves kick backward, flailing away the snow to reveal freeze-dried sprigs of still-green carex, a hardy sedge.

As always when I watch elk, I am reassured by the tranquillity of the scene. And watching them now, I am reminded what a fool I am to worry over the downer side of life. *My life.* As if it were something permanent or special! Our problems—personal and global, human and nature—are real, mounting, and must be dealt with. But to focus and obsess on the negative, emulating the nightly news, is a sinful waste of our demigod intellect and heretical to the blessing of life itself.

Unspeakably grateful for this unexpected gift of good example, Otis and I enjoy a nice long look at the wildly peaceful scene, then back away quietly, leaving the elk to their own time-tested version of a Christmas celebration. A modest detour down and around will get us home all in good time, unknown to the wapiti. No need to be rude. Home, like the sheltering grave, will be there when we arrive. Life is as good as we make it.

Thank you, elk.

Let's go, Otis. Almost home.

acknowledgments

On the Wild Edge represents more than twenty years of living and three years of scribbling. In the living, I've been blessed with enough friends, guides, teachers, and critics that to properly acknowledge each of them I would need another book. Here I can only say, and truly mean it, thanks for the memories—and the new ones yet to come.

Regarding the book in hand: its conception, construction, and final direction are due in large part to the patient and demanding guidance of John Macrae III, my editor at Henry Holt and Company in New York (who was also Edward Abbey's editor, which makes me proud as punch). Thank you, Jack. Additional indispensable literary cohorts include Supurna Banerjee, Carl Brandt, Margaret Macumber, John Nichols, Caroline Petersen, Bonnie Thompson, Mark Richards, Kenn Russell, and Florence Rose Shepard.

Concerning the years chronicled and compressed into the foregoing pages, my acknowledgments must be even more restricted, given the extensive list of friends we love and owe beyond payback. Always and always are Clarke and Flossie. Additionally, our edgy lifestyle has been invaluably facilitated by Edward Abbey, Matt and Janet Kenna, Ken and Cookie Hodges, Darren Woodson and Margie Alvarez, Dave Sigurslid and Brenda Huffman, George Hassan, Nancy Portera, and Tom Beck.

And a special thanks to Mr. Otis, easily the most stoic and steadfast character in our motley crew of players. It broke our hearts when

Otis died on "good" Friday, even as this book, in so many ways *his* book, was suffering the pains of pending birth. At only eleven years, Otis's life was far too short—but ah, it was a *good* life, wasn't it pal? Even in death, Otis continues to teach us, in this instance reinforcing my lifelong preference for quality over quantity. As the Oatster reminds us now, while we have little control over personal longevity, we have huge control over what we think, say, and do while here, and thus how much we enjoy it. And how much others enjoy us.

Otis's passing from cancer (the way most old dogs die) was eased start to finish by Darren and Margie, his personal physicians and our cherished friends. Just as the sun was setting, Caroline and I planted the big black brute out beneath the aspens, between his two blond predecessors, Lacey and Angel. (Our first dog, Amigo, remains aloof in his private digs down by the campfire ring.) After the shoveling was done, I converted a meaningless and bulky copper-and-granite award plaque I was given long ago into a dandy headstone, then strung a chain of prayer flags above the cluster of graves. Only after several months, when those once-bright flags had faded and disintegrated, their remnants scattered by the autumn winds, did we adopt another dog.

Welcome aboard, Clara, golden retriever girl. You've got some mighty big pawprints to fill.

about the author

David Petersen lives with a permanent wife, Caroline, and a series of dogs in a little cabin on a big mountain in the American Southwest. Prior to "fading out of the real world" to become a self-described "semisubsistence elk hunter and underemployed writer of best-nonsellers," David was an officer and a pilot ("but never a gentle-man") in the Marines, a managing editor of a national motorcycle magazine ("I detested the damn things even then, though the job was a lot of fun"), a two-time college graduate and one-time law school dropout, a mailman, a beach bum, the western editor for *Mother Earth News,* a college teacher, a firewood cutter, and a road-kill collector. *On the Wild Edge* is David's "lucky thirteenth" book.